Ethnographies of Grey Zones in Eastern Europe

Ethnographies of Grey Zones in Eastern Europe

Relations, Borders and Invisibilities

Edited by Ida Harboe Knudsen
and
Martin Demant Frederiksen

ANTHEM PRESS

Anthem Press
An imprint of Wimbledon Publishing Company
www.anthempress.com

This edition first published in UK and USA 2015
by ANTHEM PRESS
75–76 Blackfriars Road, London SE1 8HA, UK
or PO Box 9779, London SW19 7ZG, UK
and
244 Madison Ave #116, New York, NY 10016, USA

British Library Cataloguing-in-Publication Data
A catalogue record for this book is available from the British Library.

Library of Congress Cataloging-in-Publication Data
Exploring the Grey Zones : Governance, Conflict and (In)security in Eastern Europe
(Conference) (2013 Denmark)
Ethnographies of grey zones in Eastern Europe : relations, borders and invisibilities /
edited by Ida Harboe Knudsen and Martin Demant Frederiksen.
pages cm. – (Anthem series on Russian, East European and Eurasian studies)
"The volume is based on the international conference "Exploring the Grey Zones:
Governance, Conflict and (In)security in Eastern Europe", which was held at Aarhus
University in Denmark on 1-2 November 2013."
Includes bibliographical references and index.
ISBN 978-1-78308-412-8 (hard back : alk. paper) – ISBN 978-1-78308-413-5
(paper back : alk. paper) – ISBN978-1-78308-414-2 (pdf ebook) –
ISBN 978-1-78308-435-7 (epub ebook)
1. Post-communism–Europe, Eastern. 2. Informal sector (Economics)–Europe,
Eastern. 3. Europe, Eastern–Economic conditions–1989- 4. Europe, Eastern–Social
conditions–1989- 5. Europe, Eastern–Politics and government–1989- I. Knudsen,
Ida Harboe. II. Frederiksen, Martin Demant, 1981- III. Title.
HN380.7.A8E97 2013
306.09437'09049–dc23
2015003721

ISBN-13: 978 1 78308 412 8 (Hbk)
ISBN-10: 1 78308 412 X (Hbk)

ISBN-13: 978 1 78308 413 5 (Pbk)
ISBN-10: 1 78308 413 8 (Pbk)

Cover photo © 2015 Martin Demant Frederiksen

This title is also available as an ebook.

CONTENTS

Chapter 1

INTRODUCTION: WHAT IS A GREY ZONE AND WHY IS EASTERN EUROPE ONE?

Martin Demant Frederiksen and Ida Harboe Knudsen

The concept of grey zones, which is the unifying concept of this volume, is probably most well known from Primo Levi's account of his experiences in a Nazi concentration camp during World War II. In *The Drowned and the Saved* (1988) he describes the confusion and ambiguity experienced by those arriving at a concentration camp. Contrary to the expectations of the newcomers, such places were not split into neatly decipherable blocs of victims and perpetrators. This was due to the existence of a hybrid class of 'prisoner-functionaries': fellow inmates who, in order to secure their own survival, assisted SS officers in both mundane and brutal ways. Levi describes how 'the "we" lost its limits, the contenders were not two, one could not discern a single frontier but rather many confused, perhaps innumerable frontiers, which stretched out before us' (1988, 37). For those who experienced the atrocities of the camps, this disrupted the common tendency to separate good from evil, and as Levi notes, those who have since sought to understand and describe the camps have encountered the same difficulty. The *Lager*, as Levi calls the concentration camp, is a grey zone in which 'the two camps of masters and servants both diverge and converge. This grey zone possesses an incredibly complicated internal structure and contains within itself enough to confuse our need to judge' (Levi 1988, 42; see also Petropoulos and Roth 2005).

As Javier Auyero has argued in relation to Levi's writings, the 'grey zone' stands forth as a zone of ambiguity that severely challenges pervasive polarities such as we/they, friend/enemy and good/evil – what Levi refers to as the 'Manichean tendency, which shuns half-tints and complexities […] prone to reduce the river of human occurrences to conflicts, and the conflicts to duels – we and they' (Levi, quoted in Auyero 2007, 32). For Primo Levi, Auyero asserts, the grey zone is an actual physical space, the concentration camp, but also just as much a conceptual tool that warns us against rigid or even misleading dichotomies. The grey zone here is 'both an empirical object and an analytical lens that draws our attention toward a murky area where normative boundaries dissolve' (Auyero 2007, 32). It is this conceptualisation of the grey zone that forms the premise of the present volume. The chapters that follow depict grey zones that are much more quotidian than the zones of terror described by Primo Levi. Yet, when read together these chapters are united in approaching the grey zone as something that can be both a concrete geographical space or object and also an analytical approach to understanding a given area or situation marked by ambiguity or porous boundaries. The chapters illuminate the ways in which grey zones have come to define, disrupt or create various forms of borders, relations and invisibilities in contemporary Eastern Europe. The volume consists of ethnographic explorations of grey zones in Lithuania, Poland, Belarus, Bosnia and Herzegovina, Moldova, Greece, Albania, Turkey and Georgia, along with chapters that assess the region at large, and a final chapter that considers the notion of grey zones – as it is developed throughout the book – beyond Eastern Europe.

The volume is based on the international conference 'Exploring the Grey Zones: Governance, Conflict and (In)security in Eastern Europe', which was held at Aarhus University in Denmark on 1–2 November 2013. For this conference we made an open call for participants to submit papers dealing with ethnographic depictions of various forms of uncertainty, ambiguity and turbidity in present-day Eastern Europe. We proposed that sociopolitical changes in the region within the last two decades have been so plentiful that they in themselves have become a permanent stage of being with no end point in sight. Transition has become its own goal; to this extent the idea of transition has lost its entire meaning along the way. Our attempt with this conference was to overcome the problematic fact that, despite criticisms from the field of social science, such unsettled situations are still often seen as but a phase in a larger transition from a Soviet socialist past to a presumed capitalist society.

As an alternative vantage point, the concept of grey zones encapsulates the intriguing and confusing developments that have taken place in the region of Eastern Europe. We have witnessed attempts to establish liberal democracies, reorientations from planned to market economies, and a political desire to create 'new states' and internationally minded 'new citizens'. While parts of the populations of Eastern Europe have benefitted from these developments, other parts have instead experienced increased poverty, unemployment and social insecurity. Today we see that people in such vulnerable positions are often increasingly relying on normative coping and semiautonomous strategies, sometimes even crime and violence, to obtain the security and social guarantees they feel deprived of in their present-day societies. Such processes testify to a paradoxical situation between political attempts to create well-functioning, modern civil societies on the one hand, and reliance on normative laws at the margins of society on the other. In what follows, we view these situations not merely as legacies of socialism but as things in and of themselves; that is, as areas, phenomena or situations that can no longer be seen as transitory but which have instead become embedded in Eastern Europe. We thus seek to present a deeper understanding of contemporary sociopolitical circumstances in the region by deploying the notion that grey zones are both empirical objects and an analytical lens. We do so in order to find new ways of approaching and conceptualising current situations in Eastern Europe, ways that are not necessarily preconfigured in the terms of (what are by now) classical analytical lenses such as 'postsocialism' or 'transition'. Hence, as in Primo Levi's conceptualisation, we make use of the notion of grey zones to break away from misleading dichotomies, such as, in this case, 'West vs. East' or 'Soviet vs. post-Soviet'. In this introduction we carve out further defining features of the notion of grey zones and relate them to these dichotomies and to the notion of postsocialism. Following this, we consider grey zones specifically in relation to three broad themes that emerge from the chapters of the volume: relations, borders and invisibilities.

The Grey Zone as Object and Lens

In recent years 'grey' has undoubtedly had its most prominent exposure through the title of E. L. James's bestselling novel *Fifty Shades of Grey* (2012). Although this novel inevitably will connote eroticism among most who know it, the title also suggests an important feature of the colour grey – namely that it can be and mean many different things. Although grey is an achromatic colour – that is, a colour without colour – it is also a blend of all colours, a mix of white (created by blending all colours in the light spectrum) and black (created by mixing all pigments). Although it is easy to see, it contains differences within it.

It may well seem a stereotype to call Eastern Europe 'grey' (see Fehérváry 2013), and indeed, as we will discuss later, the grey zone is far from being a condition that applies only to this region. We apply it here not merely to signify the dullness of concrete, but equally the exact opposite: the combination of all colours in one place. Indeed, when we look into the features and interpretations of the colour grey it appears that one of its main characteristics is ambiguity. A grey zone can thus be seen as an object or situation that confounds ordinary distinctions, such as those made between 'public' and 'private' worlds or experiences of trust and betrayal (Roy 2008). It speaks also to the lines between faith and uncertainty, resulting in doubt (Pelkmans 2013), or to the often blurry lines between truth and conspiracy (West and Sanders 2003), legality and illegality (Robertson 2006a; Loren and Metelmann 2014), justice and injustice (Sanford 2003), and even democracy and dictatorship (Carothers 2002; Ledeneva 2006). Such blurring of boundaries has been explored in a series of recent social science studies.

Jirina Siklova has written about the vast number of citizens in Czechoslovakia in the late 1980s who were neither proponents of the communist system nor dissidents. Despite the fact that people in this group largely agreed with the views of dissidents, and although they might have been hesitant and reluctant to cooperate with the establishment, they still accepted benefits in exchange for their relative conformity (Siklova 1990, 351). The remarkable thing, Siklova notes, is that this group was surprisingly big and existed within 'every social, professional or interest group' (1990, 353). Another form of collusion is present in Donna Goldstein's ethnographic study focusing on 'police-bandits' operating in a shantytown in Rio de Janeiro. Here it is state actors (the police) and local gang members that collude (Goldstein 2003). Javier Auyero's ethnographic study on lootings in Argentina reveals how the boundaries between institutionalised and non-institutionalised politics are fluid, fuzzy and permeable. When looking into the networks and meanings that make up looting dynamics, he writes, 'we begin to detect the existence of a grey zone where analytical distinctions (among government agents, repressive forces, challengers, polity members, etc.) that the literature on collective action takes for granted collapse' (Auyero 2007, 19). Jane Schneider and Peter Schneider have depicted a similar situation in their ethnographic work on organised crime in Palermo, Italy. Here, relations between the local mafia and state authorities blur lines between legality and illegality, rendering it difficult, if not outright impossible, to determine where one ends and the other begins (Schneider and Schneider 2003). The notion of grey zones has also been applied by Michel Anteby in his study on workplace regulations in a French organisation. He shows how workers constantly breach regulations despite the fact that they are well aware of this being both immoral and potentially illegal. However, such grey zones, he asserts, entail a productive element in that they both contribute to fashioning workers' identities while also allowing management to maintain their control (Anteby 2008). A. F. Robertson, writing about corruption and bureaucracy, similarly notes that 'every office drudge knows that it's the "grey area", not the rules, which actually makes bureaucracy work, for better or for worse' (Robertson 2006b, 9).

Despite the variation in settings, we see in all the above-mentioned cases traces of the prisoner-functionaries described by Primo Levi, and likewise ambiguity of boundaries that we tend to take for granted as being clear cut. Moreover, what is revealing in these cases is that the emergence of such forms of suspicion, doubt, uncertainty and ambiguity may gain a sense of *ordinariness*. In her study focusing on India, Veena Das has shown how violence, rather than being an interruption of life, may enter into the recesses of the ordinary (2006). In this volume we adopt a similar perspective with grey zones. The authors show situations where politics comes to be seen as inherently opaque, where groups of citizens turn invisible, where borders become arbitrary and where ambiguity becomes the ordinary. Such processes can be read in relation to studies of how instability comes to mark everyday lives in the midst of political and social transformation (Warren 2002). Yet, the societal frameworks the authors in this volume describe are not ones in which taken-for-granted realities are being altered by radical transformation (cf. Greenhouse 2002; Benda-Beckmann and Benda-Beckmann 2007); rather, they are frameworks within which transformations have created a taken-for-granted reality of ambiguity. Hence, rather than emerging solely as temporary outcomes of crises or sociopolitical changes, these grey zones gain a sense of permanence and thus may even become backdrops from which something new emerges – whether on an empirical or an analytical level. In this book we therefore conceptualise grey zones as: 1) an analytical approach to understanding a given area or situation marked by ambiguity or porous boundaries; 2) concrete geographical spaces or objects – a grey zone can be both a larger space like Eastern Europe, or a much smaller physical space forming a specific grey zone within the larger overall grey zone; and 3) being consistently present throughout different time periods, all marked by their particular set-up of contradictions and uncertainties. Based on this definition our contributors have developed their takes on the concept with regard to their specific research areas and analyses, thus all using grey zones as an analytical tool in their works.

In the following parts of the introduction we will lay out our regional perspective and discuss the idea of grey zones as an analytical alternative to the concepts of postsocialism and Europeanisation.

Is Eastern Europe Still 'the East'?

In 1984 Milan Kundera published an essay in which he argued that Czechoslovakia, Poland and Hungary should not be seen as the eastern border of the West. Rather, he argued, these countries should be understood geographically, culturally, historically and in spirit as the western border of the East. Thus, centrally located, they were a natural part of Europe. According to Kundera, the East started with Russia, which he viewed as a civilisation in itself (1984). As critically argued by the historians Bideleux and Jeffries, Kundera's division of Europe, with the inclusion of Czechoslovakia, Hungary and Poland in Europe's middle, might itself be a Eurocentric violation of the European map, excluding the importance and 'Europeanness' of a range of other countries and citizens. 'Does Kundera's "Central Europe" include the millions of former Ukrainian, Belorussian and Lithuanian inhabitants of inter-war Poland, Hungary and Czechoslovakia?' Bideleux and Jeffries ask (1998, 11). And as they further postulate in relation to Kundera's heartfelt argumentation for restoring the European map: 'It can indeed be argued that "Europeanness" was most highly prized, not by those who took it for granted, but by those who lived in greatest fear of losing it' (Bideleux and Jeffries 1998, 10). Indeed, Lithuania's previous president Valdas Adamkus emphasised during his presidency that it was the obligation of people in the previously socialist countries to teach citizens in Europe's western parts a lesson about Europeanness – they had felt and lived it to such a greater degree because they had had to fight so much harder to (re)achieve it (Klumbytė 2006). The strong emotions arising from this debate about respective countries' locations show us that 'East' and 'West' are not solely indicative of a geographical location on a drawn map; rather, they are embedded in what James Wesley Scott (2012) calls 'the everyday construction of borders' through political discourses, institutions and media representations. With the end of the Cold War and the rise of the EU, internal European borders have to a large extent been dissolved through the promotion of free mobility of EU citizens. But while the physical border has ceased to exist in its previous capacity, the symbolic border separating East from West continues to exist (Vonderau 2008). With the events surrounding Russia's takeover of Crimea in 2014, including the increasing tensions between the EU and Russia, we have likewise witnessed how borders between the EU and the further east are sought to be strengthened. Yet, East and West in a European context still prove to be resistant categories, with the former embracing both eastern EU countries and countries located outside of the EU's borders.

How do we as scholars then defend publishing yet another volume on 'Eastern Europe' while seemingly ignoring the political tensions and discussions that have emerged from such labelling? Is this not an imperial 'Orientalisation' of Eastern Europe in a Western discourse – much in line with the Occidental representations of the Orient (Said 1995 [1978])? Or, posed in a different manner, do we not keep dividing Europe, stressing differences rather than similarities? Our answer is that, rather than an Occidental representation of 'the East', what we are arguing against is a much more colonial discourse, namely that 'we' need to teach 'them' how to become like 'us' by providing them with the right incentives and the right democratic ideals, served within an overarching capitalistic and neoliberalistic framework. It is this discourse, we hold, rather than our labelling of an Eastern Europe, that is driven by an ethnocentric point of view: the idea that 'the West' indeed holds the answers to whatever problems it might face in Europe's eastern parts. The lesson we have learned from Said's critique of Occidental presentations is the crucial importance of stressing particularities and differences in order to overcome flattening generalisations. Our point is precisely to overcome such flattening and generalising expressions of power inequality. We do so by analysing each of the countries in question in its own right and own socioeconomic context. The contributors to this volume (both 'Eastern' and 'Western' scholars) have conducted in-depth fieldwork with the exact aim of understanding, comprehending and analysing various aspects of everyday grey zones based on our informants' comprehensions and on their reflections about circumstances, past, present and future. Thus, the main objective of the volume is to focus on local negotiations of political and cultural boundaries (see Kramsch 2010) and people's everyday strategies when subjected to constant insecurity and ambiguity.

When furthering the discussion of power imbalances and scholarly representations of Europe's eastern parts, it is crucial to stay aware that the West does not necessarily symbolise something better or more advanced to our informants. While political and economic powers have worked on transforming Eastern European capitals and major cities into modern European metropoles, with businesses, shops, tourist attractions and diverse nightlives, large parts of Eastern European populations are critically negotiating the impact of these powers at the local level. As Frederiksen has shown in his study of urban reconstructions in Georgia, scepticism, doubt and estrangement may easily be the local outcomes of political incentives, reforms and projects aimed at creating Western-like cityscapes (see Frederiksen 2013). Consumer trends is another angle that offers insight into how people in Eastern Europe critically reflect upon and react to Western imports. An article by the anthropologist Neringa Klumbytė (2009) examines consumers' opinions about and consumption of two different sausage brands in Lithuania. One is the 'Soviet' sausage produced by the Samsonas company, and the other is the 'Euro' sausage produced by Biovela. The preference of the consumers was clear: Samsonas's profits skyrocketed after it began to produce Soviet sausages (Klumbytė 2009, 130). The Soviet sausage was perceived by Klumbytė's informants as being familiar and part of the traditional Lithuanian cuisine, while the Euro sausage, which fulfilled EU criteria, never gained the same kind of popularity. Klumbytė views this re-establishment of an imagined Soviet consumer identity as a response to the relative political dislocation experienced by the new EU member states, as they view themselves as being 'Europe's provinces' due to the unequal distribution of wealth and power in the EU (2009). Likewise, Harboe Knudsen (2010, 2015) shows how both producers and consumers view imported food products from the West as being of *lower* quality than what are perceived to be traditional Lithuanian products. Frances Pine demonstrates the political echoes of consumption, with her work on consumerism in Poland analysing how the understanding of goods imported from the West has changed during the past decades. From having been a status symbol in opposition to state power during the socialist regime, the disappointments following the breakup of the Soviet Union transformed Western products into a symbol of betrayed hopes and promises (Pine 2001a). The result was a turnaround in consumption, which gave Polish material culture and food products a comeback as a way of voicing disappointment with the West (Pine 2001a). In this way consumption inevitably bears political connotations as an approval, or rejection, of changes and ideologies. While these examples are taken from the realm of food and consumption, this volume follows the same line of critical analysis by drawing attention to understanding Eastern Europe in its own right and with an eye for our informants' critical relations with Western impacts when dealing with an uneven power balance. We do so through the prism of grey zones. What can we learn, we ask, about Eastern Europe if we consider it a 'grey zone' rather than a 'postsocialist space'? How may this provide us with a more succinct analytical vantage point from which to describe and understand contemporary social and political developments (or drawbacks) in the region?

From Postsocialism to Grey Zones

All colours have a colonial history, Michael Taussig (2009) has argued. If one were to choose a colour depicting the Soviet colonial history of large parts of Eastern Europe, grey might seem an obvious choice. As Sarah Green alludes to in her contribution to this volume, this may to a large extent be an external, stereotypical view, but it has likewise been a view from within. In a recent monograph on the politics of colour in Hungary, Krisztina Fehérváry recounts an article in a Hungarian interior decorating magazine that sought to 'rehabilitate' the colour grey (2013, 1). Rehabilitation was needed, it seemed, because grey locally had come to be seen as signifying 'life within a dark Iron Curtain, of enforced poverty and the fatigue of daily provisioning, of unsmiling salesclerks, scarce goods, and the lack of colourful advertising and commerce' (Fehérváry 2013, 1). Democracy and capitalism became the counterpart to this, signifying the colourful pleasure and possibilities of consumption. Indeed, colour became a powerful political tool for asserting the victory of capitalism over communism, as well as for the perceived legitimacy of this victory. A clear example of this is the use of colour as a symbol in the so-called 'colour revolutions' in the Balkans and in Ukraine and Georgia (see Manning 2007). Particularly at the political level, and in the view of external observers (whether academics or policymakers), the 'aesthetic regime' of grey became aligned with wider sociocultural values in ways that naturalised 'the relationship between state socialism and qualities of greyness, or capitalism with colour' (Fehérváry 2013, 8). As Fehérváry goes on to argue, this binary opposition between state socialism and bourgeois capitalism (and the colour code supporting it) has taken part in reinforcing a series of other binaries such as the private versus the public, the market versus the state and the individual versus the collective (2013, 14). Yet these politically (or even academically) drawn binaries have not always corresponded to the everyday lives of citizens in Eastern Europe, neither during nor after the collapse of state socialism. Alexei Yurchak has for instance convincingly described how youths in the late Soviet period lived their lives without paying much attention to political life or ideologically imposed binaries. Not only did they abide by political obligations with minimal effort, they also paid little attention to dissidence or resistance (Yurchak 2006). Despite such blurring of lines already taking place in the final years of the Soviet Union, there continues to be, Fehérváry holds, a problematic tendency among both journalists and scholars to simply reproduce the above-mentioned binaries (2013, 14). As she sums up, 'the metaphor of the Iron Curtain dividing East from West, or dark, colourless oppressive communism from bright, colourful, and democratic capitalism, has obscured the actual porousness of this boundary to the flow of commodities, images and aspirations' (Fehérváry 2013, 20).

The main framework within which these binaries have been approached over the last two decades has been that of postsocialism. The dramatic social and political changes taking place in Eastern Europe (and Eurasia at large) in the aftermath of the collapse of state socialism has been a key raison d'être for numerous researchers and departments throughout the world focusing on Russian and Eastern European studies. Not least within anthropology, scholars of postsocialism have contributed valuable discussions of socioeconomic change and have provided important critiques of the transition paradigm. The idea of a 'transition' from Soviet socialism to market capitalism (a 'pre-given future of capitalism'), it was argued from a variety of angles, was severely flawed. Not only did it rest on a neoevolutionist premise, it also overlooked the local-level uncertainties that accompanied the everyday management of changing social and economic landscapes (e.g. Burawoy and Verdery 1999; Creed 1995; Humphrey 2002a; Kaneff 2002; Lampland 2002; Lemon 1998; Lindquist 2005; Pine 2002; Ries 2002; Verdery 2003; see also Buyandelgeriyn 2008 for an overview). Another critique pointed to the implied ethnocentric element of the idea, as the terminology and models used to describe the so-called phase of transition emerged from a Western European model of textbook capitalism, and were adapted to the situation in the former Socialist countries without taking the influence of the previous system into close consideration (Hann 1994; Humphrey 2002b; Pine 1993, 1996).

The fact that anthropologists at large disagreed with transition theories did not mean that they internally agreed on how to conceptualise change. This can, for example, be seen in Verdery's (1991) attempt to theorise the postsocialist changes. Verdery pointed out five main results of the ongoing restructurings and changes: the emergence of civil society; increasing social pluralism; and as follows, alienation and the rise of ethnic conflicts; decentralisation of decision making; and the expectancy of mass unemployment (1991). This evoked a response from Chris Hann (1994), who argued that one cannot make a single theory neither for the socialist past nor for the outcome of transition (a concept he by and large was unhappy with). Since the Soviet Union had included such a large and diverse territory, ranging from Central and Eastern Europe to China, argued Hann, it would be difficult to predict a shared outcome (1994). This debate brings up some core issues and points to tensions between specific local conditions and conditions with general validity. Indeed, as Frances Pine (2001b) suggests in her mediation of the Verdery–Hann debate, despite the enormous regional and cultural differences that gave rise to highly diverse experiences of socialism and the following Soviet breakdown, some patterns of everyday life under a hegemonic ideology and an economic and social system like the Soviet Union remain.

Despite the variety of interpretations and angles of postsocialism, the concept has still lingered as an overarching model encompassing all which used to be, but no longer is, socialism. But at present, exactly what is the analytical value of postsocialism? Over a decade ago Steven Sampson (2002) noted that labels such as 'transition' and 'postsocialism' were no longer able to fully capture the situation faced by citizens in the former Soviet bloc. David Kideckel, in a contribution to the same volume, emphasised that it would be more adequate to view the systems in the previously socialist countries as *neocapitalist*, as capitalist principles had been altered through their implementation in this new context, thereby creating 'a social system that re-works basic capitalist principles in new, even more inegalitarian ways than the Western system from which it derives' (2002, 115). Dominic Boyer and Alexei Yurchak (2008) have argued that postsocialism is a vanishing object and has therefore lost its payoff as an analytical lens. There are several examples of debates about this question. One recent debate took place in the journal *Critique of Anthropology*, in which Tatjana Thelen (2011) argued in an article that postsocialism is a problematic analytical category because it is derived from economic grounds focusing almost only on property and labour, particularly in the now classical writings of anthropologists such as Elizabeth Dunn and Katherine Verdery. However, despite the fact that economic grounds have substantially changed, the focus on postsocialism has not. In contemporary studies of Eastern Europe and Central Asia, Thelen held, this results in dead ends, because these studies fail to reach beyond the region and the concept. Said differently, postsocialist studies (or researchers) are only capable of talking to themselves. Furthermore, there has been an inadequate degree of theoretical development deriving from postsocialist anthropology. Elizabeth Dunn and Katherine Verdery responded to Thelen in a subsequent article in which they stated that, although postsocialism as a concept should not be seen as the only possible vantage point for studying the region, postsocialist anthropology had in fact contributed significantly to a diverse range of theoretical debates, and that 'as the socialist experience recedes into the background and becomes less defining of the political, economic and social changes in the region, the diversity of theoretical approaches will continue to increase' (Dunn and Verdery 2012, 254). Thelen responded that she fully acknowledged the fact that there had been a diversification of theoretical perspectives emerging from postsocialist anthropology, but that it was the 'common ground' itself – postsocialism – that needed to diversify (2012).

Indeed, although there might be reasons to study the *afterlives* of postsocialism in particular empirical contexts (e.g. Frederiksen 2013), or remnants of 'actually existing postsocialism' (Berdahl 2009), or forms of ruination and the affective qualities of postsocialist landscapes (e.g. Schwenkel 2013; Szmagalska-Follis 2008), postsocialism might not prove the most relevant notion through which (or from which) to consider political changes or everyday lives in the region at large. For instance, in the introduction to a comparative ethnographic study on postrevolutionary Georgia, Elizabeth Dunn and Martin Demant Frederiksen (2014) propose that notions such as 'absence' and 'voids' might prove more relevant vantage points from which to study both repeated transformation and inertia. Our aim here, it should be noted, is not to attempt to discredit postsocialism and call for its complete dismissal. Indeed, as Yael Navaro-Yashin (2008) has argued in a different context, academics are often too eager to dismantle former concepts in the promotion of new ones. However, we do contend that scholars of Eastern Europe should be wary of whether or not postsocialism is in fact the right concept to use in a given empirical context and, further, whether postsocialism has lost its value as an overarching framework when considering the region as a whole.

It might be argued that with the absence of the previously dominant conceptual framework of postsocialism Eastern Europe as a region is at risk of becoming difficult to define. Yet, as this volume demonstrates, there is still good reason to study the region *as* a region because looking into what characterises the Eastern Europe of today reveals new vocabularies. As is clear in many of the contributions to the volume (see the chapters by Pine, Šliavaitė, Harboe Knudsen and Frederiksen), it may no longer be a matter of unmaking Soviet life (pace Humphrey 2002a), but of unmaking postsocialism/transition itself. Attention to this is also an analytical necessity, and the concept of grey zones allows us to work towards it. Many things or situations in life could be seen as being marked by a sense of being 'in between' (see Stoller 2009), but they may not necessarily be experienced as such by those who find themselves in the midst of such situations. Hence, being in between may in some cases be an analytical construct that renders it easier for onlookers to explain a given situation or context. This is exactly the tendency Primo Levi speaks of in his depiction of grey zones; that is, the tendency to look at that which is in between dichotomies in instances in which dichotomies have in fact dissolved. One such case in point is the role of informality in contemporary Eastern Europe which, as recently noted by Abel Polese and Jeremy Morris, has increasingly become an embedded phenomenon rather than a transitory one (2014, 1). Furthermore, as several chapters in this volume aptly illustrate, informality has increasingly blurred the lines between legality and illegality (see for instance the chapters by Joyce and Frederiksen).

Another issue that needs to be taken into consideration in studies of contemporary Eastern Europe is that while postsocialism has been a cover term for largely diverse and uneven processes, continuously pointing to influence from the former Soviet system, the region is currently embedded in new geopolitical border drawings, dividing it according to new connotations and connections. With the enlargements in 2004 and 2007, nine former socialist countries became formally encapsulated in the EU, although they had been subjected to its influence for nearly a decade prior to that. In the literature dealing with this enlargement and its consequences, the new overarching concept has been that of 'Europeanisation', which has often been used uncritically to create a new European reality in the east (Ågh 1993; Grabbe 2005; Schimmelfennig and Sedelmeyer 2005; Bafoil 2009). As the anthropologists John Borneman and Nick Fowler (1997) have rightly observed, Europeanisation has become a device where (old) Europe reorganises territory and peoplehood by exercising its power over colonial or previously socialist states. Furthermore, as Harboe Knudsen (2012) has argued in her contribution to the debate, the EU alters sizes that don't fit in order to squeeze them into a 'one-size-fits-all' model of Europeanness, at great regional and local cost. While we acknowledge the different developments in the region – the new drawing of borders and the emerging self-conceptualisations – we find new trends of glossing over highly different countries and livelihoods through Europeanisation to be as unfit a concept as postsocialism. After all, both concepts take for their starting point something that is not there presently. It has either been (postsocialism) or is about to become (Europeanisation), yet neither of the terms grasp the murky reality of the people of our studies.

Themes of the Volume: Relations, Borders and Invisibilities

Even when grappling with everyday complexities, this volume remains only a representation of Eastern Europe, based on choices of themes, as well as on the individual authors' choices of subjects and angles of analysis. As with all writing, it is imbued with certain simplifications so as to make the material accessible. As Levi contemplates as he struggles to lay out the complex life in the camp for his readers: 'What we commonly mean by "understand" coincides with "simplify": without profound simplification the world around us would be an infinite undefined tangle that would defy our ability to orient ourselves' (Levi 1988, 36). The following chapters are thus divided into three main themes that emerge from the notion of grey zones: relations, borders and invisibilities. The three shades of grey dealt with in this book capture different aspects of lives lived in uncertainty and ambiguity, while also sharing the main foundations of our informants' lives – insecurity and ever-changing circumstances.

Relations

As we have previously noted, grey zones can be seen as a collapse of distinctions between good and bad. They can thereby come to represent a peculiar kind of moral balance. This is not least so in relation to the moral ambiguities at play in intimate social relations, as the burgeoning literature on the anthropology of morality has shown (e.g. Newell 2006; Dalton 2007; Throop 2012). The chapters of this section highlight the role of greyness in relations of exchange, patronage and favours, and also in interethnic relations.

In the first chapter, Frances Pine draws on more than thirty years' experience of research in Poland to elaborate on the ever-present yet changing informal economy in Eastern Europe. Pine starts by considering the period of socialism, in which contradictions between the political set-up of the Soviet Union and 'actually lived socialism' created a grey zone of uncertainty and ambiguity in everyday life, which has lasted up to this very day. She continues by exploring what she calls the 'cowboy capitalism' of the 1990s: the forms of trading practised and the risks run as village people struggled to make money in a new phase of an all-too-well-known uncertainty. Finally, she takes us to the present day, exploring the divergence between EU programmes and their practical implementation as they are changed and straddled by people in their everyday lives. Through her discussion of the three periods, Pine explores how in Eastern European countries the grey and informal economy continues to parallel that of the state, and is even a constituent part of the so-called formal economy. Yet the everyday grey economic activities practised by ordinary people are perceived as different from those of the realms of crime and corruption, as they are embedded in a sphere of connections, trust and intimacy. While forms and situations may change, Pine convincingly shows that everyday uncertainty and ambiguity have followed people all along.

Jennifer R. Cash critically explores how household economy comes to form a distinct grey zone in what statistical measures have determined 'Europe's poorest country', Moldova. While official analyses portray a rural population on the brink of starvation, Cash notes that this not only contrasts with her own observations, but more importantly the way people in rural Moldova view themselves. The grey zone even emerges for these people themselves, as they do not recognise or recall the many informal elements that work together in constituting their economy. Taking us through a detailed analysis of the countryside economy and the importance of exchange and maintenance of good relations in the village, Cash provides a much more accurate picture of rural life than the shallow development reports on Moldova. Thereby she shows us how a rapidly changing global discourse on poverty obscures the actual living situation for the people in question, creating an apparent paradox between statistics and lived realities.

In the chapter by Čarna Brković we are taken to a town on the Bosnian–Serbian border. Brković explores how locals, when needing to access public welfare services, follow both institutional procedures and utilise personal relations known as *veze*, literally meaning 'relations' or 'connections'. From an analytical perspective, Brković notes, these are frustratingly confusing and ambiguous, as they are not quite bribes and not quite a question of patronage, and thereby blur the lines of the domain of the economy. Yet, as a strategy for survival, in both a physical and social sense they transform the exceptional into the rule and the indefinable into the norm. In this sense, while these relations are grey zones in economic terms, they are also that which transcends the blurriness of state–citizen relations. Brković convincingly shows how this grey zone of welfare arrangements should not be read as a remnant of stalled postsocialist transformation, but as a boundary between the Bosnian state and society.

Borders

The borderlands of Eastern Europe have changed dramatically throughout history and, as noted in relation to the EU, also within recent decades. Yet the clear-cut nature of political boundaries drawn on maps rarely corresponds to the fluid nature of boundaries and borders as people experience them in daily life (Green 2006). Qua the existence of phenomena such as border crossings or border trade, borders are often sites of ambiguity par excellence (see Flynn 1997; Pelkmans 2006) and they are in this respect often accompanied by colluding 'shades of grey' (Eilenberg 2012, 332). Indeed, the appearance of the colour grey is relative to that which it is next to: the lightness or darkness of its appearance depends on the colour it borders. A particular shade of grey will appear dark if placed next to white, whereas the same shade of grey will appear light if placed next to black. This quality of a grey zone, its ambiguity, its relativity and the collusion it brings forth, is illustrated in the three chapters that make up this section on borders.

Through a vivid ethnographic description, Aimee Joyce explores the stories and everyday practices of cross-border trading in a Polish village. The seemingly invisible border between Poland and Belarus turns into a contested space, where smuggling has become a feature running parallel to the state economy, both shaping it while being shaped by it. While the informal trading across borders expresses a grey zone of the economy, it entails in itself a further division between the ways of smuggling that are socially and morally acceptable and those that are not. In this way Joyce demonstrates how already murky and contested practices entail their own order and morality, which becomes defining for the grey zone of informal trading.

The chapter by Maja Halilovic-Pastuovic concerns Bosnian migrants who entered the Republic of Ireland in 1992 as refugees. They were placed into a lengthy reception and resettlement programme by the Irish authorities that was aimed at fully integrating them into Irish society. Yet even after two decades, the Bosnian migrants still do not feel at home in Ireland. During summer many of them visit Bosnia, only to experience that they have also ceased to feel at home in their old country. Halilovic-Pastuovic describes this as a case of post-refugee transnationalism and, drawing on the work of Agamben (1999), analyses it as a grey zone of potentiality. She shows how Bosnian migrants refuse to shape their existence in one state only, and instead carve out a zone in which notions of home and belonging are fluid and multifaceted – a space of possibility carved out as a response to being caught in between two nations.

In her chapter Kristina Šliavaitė focuses on the ethnically mixed Russian community living in the city of Visaginas in Lithuania. From being integrated citizens with high-prestige jobs at the Visaginas nuclear power plant during the Soviet period, they have, after the EU enlargement and the following closure of the plant, been moved to an unclear position of belonging. Caught in a situation where past affiliations are dismissed and new borders are drawn, people negotiate instability and belonging as features shaped by practical needs for security. Šliavaitė views her informants' relation to the Lithuanian state as ambiguous and situational – thus, as a grey zone where morality and feelings of belonging to a 'homeland' are constantly negotiated. Furthermore, the closure of the plant has made it a grey zone security-wise, as previously well-paid employees now find themselves living on minimal social welfare and incapable of finding new forms of employment.

Invisibilities

An oft-invoked feature of grey is its association with concealment. In a naturalistic sense this relates to grey clouds masking the blue sky or grey fog blurring the outlook. Grey, in this manner, comes to signify a lack of clarity, senses of opaqueness and secret shadows. It takes up a middle ground between the visible and the invisible and clouds otherwise transparent situations. It is perhaps not surprising that the concept of grey zones has been used to depict shadow politics (see Auyero 2007). In the seventeenth century the French friar and right-hand man to Cardinal Richelieu, François Leclerc du Tremblay, earned the nickname Éminence Grise (grey eminence). Although 'grey' originally referred to the colour of his robe, the notion has later, particularly after the publication of Aldous Huxley's *Grey Eminence* (1941), come to symbolise a person who exercises considerable political influence in the shadows. The chapters in this section examine that which is rendered invisible in political processes. They furthermore highlight how notions that are supposed to create clear lines in political documents (whether reforms or constitutions) may translate into ambiguity in both actual political practice and in everyday lives.

Based on fieldwork in the provincial town Gori in Georgia, Katrine Gotfredsen examines how large-scale politics in the wake of Georgia's Rose Revolution are perceived as inherently opaque by locals, and further how this trickles down and serves as a trope both explaining and reproducing opacity in more micropolitical contexts (such as in suspicion of neighbours, engagements with the municipality and obtaining favours). She shows how even supposedly clarifying stories about what people say and do (whether on a colloquial or political level), rather than eliminating doubt and uncertainty, are continuously left open to interpretation and speculation. What may be gained, she asks, from conceptualising such everyday ideas and practices as grey zones of fluctuating visibility and invisibility, clarity and opacity?

The chapter by Ida Harboe Knudsen takes us to an 'unemployment agency' located at the riverside in Lithuania's second largest city, Kaunas. Following a group of unemployed men that gather as day labourers outside the official system, Harboe Knudsen explores subaltern responses to recent developments, taking the grey zone to be both the actual physical location where the men gather and also the position they hold as poor day labourers in present-day Lithuanian society, placed in a situation where uncertainty and insecurity define their everyday lives. Incapable of accessing the system or being integrated as accepted members of society, the day labourers rely on normative strategies and counter-hegemonic symbols to create the sense of personhood and belonging they feel deprived of in present-day Lithuania.

Martin Demant Frederiksen's chapter follows a similar line of inquiry as Gotfredsen's by examining the introduction of 'transparency' in postrevolutionary reform processes in Georgia. The reforms depicted were introduced to eradicate the influence of organised crime in the country and oust or imprison the organised criminals that were seen to dominate socioeconomic life in the 1990s. The chapter recounts the story of a member of the Georgian mafia, an 'honest bandit' in his own understanding, as well as the political efforts that were undertaken to declare people such as him not only unequivocally dishonest but also a thing of the past. Frederiksen argues that rather than creating clarity, the political introduction of transparency embedded in these kinds of reforms created a societal grey zone in which illegality gained a spectral presence – both in relation to officially invisible or eradicated criminal figures, but also within politics itself. This chapter shows how the import of a concept, in this case transparency, does not necessarily create clarity in a before/after dichotomy, but merely feeds into, and possibly exacerbates, existing forms of ambiguity.

Broader perspectives

The volume concludes with contributions from Sarah Green and Nils Bubandt, who consider grey zones on the borders of the Eastern European region and beyond.

In relation to borders, Green examines grey zones as both literal and metaphysical locations marked by a sense of uncertainty about the difference between a 'here' and a 'somewhere else'. This contrasts with the ordinary intentions of a border, namely to banish such uncertainty. Drawing on a territorial dispute between the Greek and Turkish governments about two islets in the Aegean Sea, and on her work on the Greek–Albanian border, Green shows how different border regimes – such as national borders and the borders of the EU – can come to operate simultaneously in the same geographical space. Based on this she argues that some epistemologies valorise (and even deliberately generate) the idea of ambiguity and greyness in itself, something evident in the 'multiple posts' era, in which endless differences exist without any of these differences apparently making any difference.

In the final chapter, Nils Bubandt contributes an analysis of what he calls 'grey theory'. Through a critical examination of the contemporary fascination with uncertainty and ambiguity in anthropology, he seeks the analytical and methodological values that this might give us. He himself being a declared 'grey' anthropologist, Bubandt still struggles with an ambivalent relation to the concept, asking whether we can ever hope for grey to come out and declare its true colour. This (grey) ambivalence of his is taken into a wider geographical comparative perspective as he uses it to reflect upon contemporary Indonesia. By introducing various 'grey scenes' in Indonesia he both shows how the concept of grey zones is not tied to a single region, while putting it through a test by posing a range of critical questions: Is grey an experience or a condition? Is grey a local category and thus used by the people we study? Is the past grey – is it the future? And can grey really be contained in a zone?

Concluding Remarks

Our aim with this volume is not to state that the notion of grey zones should be taken as the only conceptual tool currently capable for depicting Eastern Europe, but that it is one possible angle for studying sociopolitical life in region more succinctly. What is more, though the issues that stand forth when grey zones are taken as an empirical object and analytical lens may have a particular or heightened salience in Eastern Europe, the themes that emerge from the chapters in this volume are likely to be found in many other regions of the world: places where postsocialism is not a historical context but where similar processes of normalising ambiguity are still at play. It is thus our hope that readers of the volume will not only gain a deeper understanding of contemporary Eastern Europe, but also find food for thought for exploring further how greyness and grey zones may potentially inflict upon, frame or alter social realities in other locales around the world where dissolved boundaries and dichotomies have become the ordinary.

Acknowledgements

The conference 'Exploring the Grey Zones', on which this volume is based, was supported by a grant from the Danish Council for Independent Research. We would like to thank all participants at this event. We would also like to thank the reviewers of this volume for their valuable input.

References

Agamben, G. 1999. *Potentialities: Collected Essays in Philosophy*. Stanford: Stanford University Press.

Ågh, A. 1993. 'Europeanization through privatization and pluralization in rural Hungary'. *Journal of Public Policy* 3(1): 1–35.

Anteby, M. 2008. *Moral Gray Zones: Side Productions, Identity, and Regulation in an Aeronautic Plant*. Princeton: Princeton University Press.

Auyero, J. 2007. *Routine Politics and Violence in Argentina: The Gray Zone of State Power*. Cambridge: Cambridge University Press.

Bafoil, F. 2009. *Central and Eastern Europe: Europeanization and Social Change*. New York: Palgrave Macmillan.

Benda-Beckmann, F. von and K. von Benda-Beckmann. 2007. 'Where structures merge: State and off-state involvement in rural social security on Ambon, Indonesia'. In F. von Benda-Beckmann and K. von Benda-Beckmann (eds), *Social Security between Past and Future: Ambonese Networks of Care and Supply*, 205–35. Münster: LIT Verlag.

Berdahl, D. 2009. *On the Social Life of Postsocialism: Memory, Consumption, Germany*. Bloomington: Indiana University Press.

Bideleux, R. and I. Jeffries. 1998. *A History of Eastern Europe: Crisis and Change*. London: Routledge.

Borneman, J. and N. Fowler. 1997. 'Europeanization'. *Annual Review of Anthropology* 26: 487–514.

Boyer, D. and A. Yurchak. 2008. 'Postsocialist studies, cultures of parody and American *stiob*'. *Anthropology News*, November.

Burawoy, M. and K. Verdery (eds). 1999. *Uncertain Transition: Ethnographies of Change in the Postsocialist World*. Lanham, MD: Rowman & Littlefield.

Buyandelgeriyn, M. 2008. 'Post-post-transition theories: Walking multiple paths'. *Annual Review of Anthropology* 37: 235–50.

Carothers, T. 2002. 'The end of the transition paradigm'. *Journal of Democracy* 13(1): 5–21.

Creed, G. W. 1995. 'An old song with a new voice: Decollectivization in Bulgaria'. In D. A. Kideckel (ed.), *East European Communities: The Struggle for Balance in Turbulent Times*, 25–46. Boulder: Westview Press.

Dalton, D. 2007. 'When is it moral to be a sorcerer?' In J. Barker (ed.), *The Anthropology of Morality in Melanesia and Beyond*, 39–59. Surrey: Ashgate.

Das, V. 2006. *Life and Words: Violence and the Descent into the Ordinary*. Berkeley: University of California Press.

Dunn, E. C. and M. D. Frederiksen. 2014. 'Introduction: Ethnographies of absence in contemporary Georgia'. *Slavic Review* 73(2): 241–45.

Dunn, E. C. and K. Verdery. 2012. 'Dead ends in the critique of (post)socialist anthropology: Reply to Thelen'. *Critique of Anthropology* 31(3): 251–55.

Eilenberg, M. 2012. *At the Edges of the State: Dynamics of State Formation in the Indonesian Borderlands*. Leiden: KITLV Press.

Fehérváry, K. 2013. *Politics in Color and Concrete: Socialist Materialities and the Middle Class in Hungary*. Bloomington and Indianapolis: Indiana University Press.

Flynn, D. 1997. '"We are the border": Identity, exchange, and the state along the Benin–Nigeria border". *American Ethnologist* 24(2): 311–30.

Frederiksen, M. D. 2013. *Young Men, Time and Boredom in the Republic of Georgia*. Philadelphia: Temple University Press.

Goldstein, D. 2003. *Laughter Out of Place: Race, Class, and Sexuality in a Rio Shantytown*. Berkeley: University of California Press.

Grabbe, H. 2005. *The EU's Transformative Power: Europeanization through Conditionality in Central and Eastern Europe*. New York: Palgrave Macmillan.

Green, S. F. 2006. *Notes from the Balkans: Locating Marginality and Ambiguity on the Greek–Albanian Border*. Princeton: Princeton University Press.

Greenhouse, C. J. 2002. 'Introduction: Altered states, altered lives'. In C. J. Greenhouse, E. Mertz and K. B. Warren (eds), *Ethnography in Unstable Places: Everyday Lives in Contexts of Dramatic Political Change*, 1–37. Durham, NC and London: Duke University Press.

Hann, C. M. 1994. 'After communism: Reflections on East European anthropology and the "transition"'. *Social Anthropology* 2(3): 229–49.

Harboe Knudsen, I. 2010. 'The insiders and the outsiders: Standardization and "failed" person-making in a Lithuanian market place'. *Journal of Legal Pluralism and Unofficial Law* 62: 71–94.

———. 2012. *New Lithuania in Old Hands: Effects and Outcomes of EUropeanizaton in Rural Lithuania*. London: Anthem Press.

———. 2015. 'The making of the consumer? Risk and consumption in EUropeanized Lithuania'. In D. Mincyte and U. Plath (eds), 'Food Culture in the Baltic Region', *Journal of Baltic Studies* (special issue).

Humphrey, C. 2002a. *The Unmaking Soviet Life: Everyday Economies after Socialism*. Ithaca, NY: Cornell University Press.

———. 2002b. 'Does the category postsocialist still make sense?' In C. M. Hann (ed.), *Postsocialism: Ideals, Ideologies and Practices in Eurasia*, 12–14. London: Routledge.

Huxley, A. 1941. *Grey Eminence*. New York: Harper & Brothers.

James, E. L. 2012. *Fifty Shades of Grey*. London: Vintage.

Kaneff, D. 2002. 'The shame and pride of market activity: Morality, identity and trading in postsocialist rural Bulgaria'. In R. Mandel and C. Humphrey (eds), *Markets and Moralities: Ethnographies of Postsocialism*, 33–52. Oxford: Berg.

Kideckel, D. A. 2002. 'The unmaking of an East-Central European working class'. In C. M. Hann (ed.), *Postsocialism: Ideals, Ideologies and Practices in Eurasia*, 114–33. London: Routledge.

Klumbytė, N. 2006. 'Biographic Citizenship: Memory, Subjectivity and Politics in Post-Soviet Lithuania'. PhD dissertation, University of Pittsburgh.

———. 2009. 'The geopolitics of taste: The "Euro" and Soviet sausage industries in Lithuania.' In M. Caldwell (ed.), *Food and Everyday Life in the Postsocialist World*, 130–53. Bloomington: Indiana University Press.

Kramsch, O. 2010. 'Regulating European borders: A cultural perspective'. In N. Veggeland (ed.), *Innovative Regulatory Approaches: Coping with Scandinavian and European Union Policies*, 71–84. New York: Nova Science Publishers.

Kundera, M. 1984. 'The tragedy of Central Europe'. *New York Review of Books*. Available at: http://www.uni-oldenburg.de/fileadmin/user_upload/materiellekultur/ag/migrationgender/download/zu_Annex_3_1_Kundera.pdf (accessed 28 September 2014).

Lampland, M. 2002. 'The advantages of being collectivized: Comparative farm managers in the postsocialist economy'. In C. M. Hann (ed.), *Postsocialism: Ideals, Ideologies and Practices in Eurasia*, 31–57. London and New York: Routledge.

Ledeneva, A. V. 2006. *How Russia Really Works: The Informal Practices that Shaped Post-Soviet Politics and Business*. Ithaca, NY and London: Cornell University Press.

Lemon, A. 1998. '"Your eyes are green like dollars": Counterfeit cash, national substance, and currency apartheid in 1990s Russia'. *Cultural Anthropology* 13(1): 22–55.

Levi, P. 1988. *The Drowned and the Saved*. New York: Simon & Schuster.

Lindquist, G. 2005. *Conjuring Hope: Healing and Magic in Contemporary Russia*. New York and Oxford: Berghahn Books.

Loren, S. and J. Metelmann. 2014. 'Rogue logics: Organization in the grey zone'. *Organizational Studies* 35(2): 233–53.

Manning, P. 2007. 'Rose-colored glasses? Color revolutions and cartoon chaos in postsocialist Georgia'. *Cultural Anthropology* 22(2): 171–213.

Morris, J. and A. Polese. 2014. 'Introduction: Informality – enduring practices, entwined livelihoods'. In J. Morris and A. Polese (eds), *The Informal Post-socialist Economy: Embedded Practices and Livelihoods*, 1–19. New York: Routledge.

Newell, S. 2006. 'Estranged belongings: A moral economy of theft in Abidjan, Côte d' Ivoire'. *Anthropological Theory* (6)2: 179–203.

Navaro-Yashin, Y. 2008. 'Affective spaces – melancholic objects: Ruination and the production of anthropological knowledge'. *Journal of the Royal Anthropological Institute* 15: 1–18.

Pelkmans, M. 2006. *Defending the Border: Identity, Religion, and Modernity in the Republic of Georgia*. Ithaca and London: Cornell University Press.

——— (ed.). 2013. *Ethnographies of Doubt: Faith and Uncertainty in Contemporary Societies*. London and New York: I.B. Tauris.

Petropoulos, J. and J. K. Roth. 2005. *Gray Zones: Ambiguity and Compromise in the Holocaust and its Aftermaths*. Berghahn Books.

Pine, F. 1993. '"The cows and pigs are his, the eggs are mine": Women's domestic economy and entrepreneurial activity in rural Poland."' In C. M. Hann (ed.), *Socialism: Ideals, Ideologies and Local Practice*, 227–42. London: Routledge.

———. 1996. 'Redefining women's work in rural Poland'. In R. Abrahams (ed.), *After Socialism: Land Reform and Social Change in Eastern Europe*, 133–56. New York and Oxford: Berghahn Books.

———. 2001a. 'From production to consumption in postsocialism?' In M. Buchowski (ed.), *Poland Beyond Communism: 'Transition' in Critical Perspective*, 209–24. Freiburg: Universitätsverlag.

———. 2001b 'Who better than your mother? Some problems with gender in rural Poland'. In H. Haukanes (ed.), *Women after Communism: Ideal Images and Real Lives*, 51–66. Bergen: University of Bergen.

———. 2002. 'Dealing with money: Zlotys, dollars and other currencies in the Polish highlands'. In R. Mandel and C. Humphrey (eds), *Markets and Moralities: Ethnographies of Postsocialism*, 75–97. Oxford: Berg.

Ries, N. 2002. '"Honest bandits" and "warped people": Russian narratives about money, corruption and moral decay'. In C. J. Greenhouse, E. Mertz and K. B. Warren (eds), *Ethnography in Unstable Places: Everyday Lives in Contexts of Dramatic Political Change*, 276–315. Durham, NC and London: Duke University Press.

Robertson, A. F. 2006a. 'The anthropology of grey zones'. *Ethnos* 71(4): 569–73.

———. 2006b. 'Misunderstanding corruption'. *Anthropology Today* 22(2): 8–11.

Roy, S. 2008. 'The grey zone: The "ordinary" violence of extraordinary times'. *Journal of the Royal Anthropological Institute* 14(2): 316–33.

Said, E. 1995 [1978]. *Orientalism: Western Conceptions of the Orient*. London: Penguin.

Sampson, S. L. 2002. 'Beyond transition: Rethinking elite configurations in the Balkans'. In C. M. Hann (ed.), *Postsocialism: Ideals, Ideologies and Practices in Eurasia*, 297–317. London: Routledge.

Sanford, V. 2003. 'The "grey zone" of justice: NGOs and rule of law in postwar Guatemala.' *Journal of Human Rights* 2(3): 393–405.

Schimmelfennig, F. and U. Sedelmeyer. 2005. 'Introduction: Conceptualizing the Europeanization of Central and Eastern Europe'. In F. Schimmelfennig and U. Sedelmeyer (eds), *The Europeanization of Central and Eastern Europe*, 1–29. Ithaca, NY: Cornell University Press.

Schneider, J. and P. Schneider 2003. *Reversible Destiny: Mafia, Antimafia, and the Struggle for Palermo*. Berkeley: University of California Press.

Schwenkel, C. 2013. 'Post/socialist affect: Ruination and reconstruction of the nation in urban Vietnam'. *Cultural Anthropology* 28(2): 252–77.

Scott, J. W. 2012. 'European politics of borders, border symbolism and cross-border cooperation'. In T. M. Wilson and H. Donnan (eds), *A Companion to Border Studies*, 83–100. Oxford: Wiley-Blackwell.

Siklova, J. 1990. 'The "gray zone" and the future of dissent in Czechoslovakia'. *Social Research* 57(2): 347–63.

Stoller, P. 2009. *The Power of the Between: An Anthropological Odyssey*. Chicago and London: University of Chicago Press.

Szmagalska-Follis, K. 2008. 'Repossession: Notes on restoration and redemption in Ukraine's western borderland'. *Cultural Anthropology* 23(2): 329–60.

Taussig, M. 2009. *What Color is the Sacred?* Chicago: University of Chicago Press.

Thelen, T. 2011. 'Shortage, fuzzy property and other dead ends in the anthropological analysis of (post)socialism'. *Critique of Anthropology* 31(1): 43–61.

_____. 2012. 'Economic concepts, common grounds and 'new' diversity in the anthropology of post-socialism: Reply to Dunn and Verdery'. *Critique of Anthropology* 3(1): 87–90.

Throop, J. 2012. 'Moral sentiments'. In D. Fassin (ed.), *A Companion to Moral Anthropology*, 150–68. Oxford: Wiley-Blackwell.

Verdery, K. 1991. 'Theorising socialism: A prologue to the transition'. *American Ethnologist* 18(3): 419–39.

_____. 2003. *The Vanishing Hectare: Property and Value in Postsocialist Transylvania*. Ithaca, NY: Cornell University Press.

Vonderau, A. 2008. 'Models of success in the free market: Transformations of the individual self-representation of the Lithuanian economic elite'. In I. W. Schröder and A. Vonderau (eds), *Changing Economies and Changing Identities in Postsocialist Eastern Europe*, 111–29. Münster: LIT Verlag.

Warren, K. B. 2002. 'Toward an anthropology of fragments, instabilities, and incomplete transitions'. In C. J. Greenhouse, E. Mertz and K. B. Warren (eds), *Ethnography in Unstable Places: Everyday Lives in Contexts of Dramatic Political Change*, 379–93. Durham, NC and London: Duke University Press.

West, H. G. and T. Sanders (eds). 2003. *Transparency and Conspiracy: Ethnographies of Suspicion in the New World Order*. Durham, NC: Duke University Press.

Yurchak, A. 2006. *Everything Was Forever, Until It Was No More: The Last Soviet Generation*. Princeton: Princeton University Press.

Part I
RELATIONS

Chapter 2

LIVING IN THE GREY ZONES: WHEN AMBIGUITY AND UNCERTAINTY ARE THE ORDINARY

Frances Pine

The gap between state socialism as a political and economic ideology and social plan, and socialism as it was 'actually lived' in the Soviet Union and the satellite states of Eastern Central Europe, created what might arguably be considered one of the most pervasive grey zones in history. The contradictions between ideology and lived lives, and the impossibility of matching the state plan to everyday economics, laid public social and economic spaces open to continual ambiguity and uncertainty. Uncertainty and ambiguity became ordinary, and created the conditions for social and economic practices that straddled the border between legal and illegal, acceptable and corrupt. Such practices were so widespread that they formed the common stuff of everyday lives.

In this chapter I address the question of the ordinariness of what is variously referred to as the second, informal or grey economy in Eastern Europe. Looking at ethnographic material I consider the vague and constantly shifting border that existed between the state and second economies during socialism, and the way that negotiating this border was very much part of everyday life and the ordinary. I then move on to compare the socialist period to the next two periods: the decade after socialism, marked by severe economic and political restructuring; and the period of EU accession, when a new economic authority and new rule of law were introduced. I show that in each of these periods the grey economy parallels that of the state, dominates many aspects of everyday life, and has its own kind of morality that links it to the family and household, relations of trust, and extended sociality. I suggest that this grey area of the ordinary and everyday is different from the realm of corruption and criminality because it is perceived as an area of trust, morality and intimacy.

Uncertainty, Ambiguity and Misrecognition

I first went to Poland in 1977. I arrived at Krakow airport on a cold September night, and it took me hours to get through customs. The inspector examined everything in my suitcase, opened and shook all of my books, took them away, consulted with other inspectors, and brought them back. He kept looking at me expectantly, but I had no idea what he was expecting. Finally, he waved me through with an irritated gesture, and I joined my Polish friends who had by then been waiting for over two hours. They asked why I had taken so long. I explained about the customs officer's diligence. They looked puzzled, and asked, hadn't I given him anything? They said they had given one of his colleagues a small amount of money to make sure I got through quickly, and that he had been looking for me, to hurry me through – but I was already at that point engaged with the second official. I realised I had totally failed to read any of the signs, not understanding either that I had to look for the official who was looking for me, to escort me out, or if that failed, that I had to make a further gift or payment to my own customs official. I was soon to realise that almost every action and transaction that took place in a public space in Poland had this shadowy, informal potential. Things could and did take place without mediation, without bribery – after all, I did eventually manage to move out of the airport buffer zone into the Krakow arrival hall. But I also became aware, from that moment on, that things worked more smoothly, and usually far more quickly, with some kind of incentive or mediation.

For an outsider, however, someone not raised in that particular social field and therefore well outside their own habitus or comfort zone, the rules there were and are often very hard to fathom. Even after years of working in Poland I have never really mastered the art of routine bribery. I know that at least in everyday terms it has to be very subtle, and not insulting to either the giver or the taker. It has to be ordinary. It is primarily the etiquette and performance of bribery that puzzles me, though; I find it hard to recognise the moment when a gift should be handed over, or to understand the form the prestation should take. Should it be money in the hand, or more discretely in an envelope? If in an envelope, should it be handed directly to the person, left on a table or desk, or tucked into a pocket? Different people tell me different things, explaining how they themselves leave an envelope on the table for the doctor, slip a few notes into the bus driver's hand or pocket, or leave a large denomination note folded up with their driver's licence or car papers. It is clear to me, however, that these kind of payments, to people with whom there is no prior relationship, or at least no intimate one, are very different from the kinds of favours and exchanges that take place between kin, neighbours and friends. I have over the years become very at home with networks of favours and connections, those added mediations that make life possible, which are sometimes legal, sometimes not, often unclear, but all a form of social capital.

Local knowledge of these practices, of how they should be conducted, what the embodiment and code of conduct of them are, of where the limits of the acceptable lie, is all knowledge that is utterly ordinary to the insider – a part of the habitus – but which involves understanding and practices from which outsiders are very often excluded. It is a language of the inside, of implicit meanings and judgements, or recognition, that often lies counter to the outsider's intuition, resulting in misrecognition. It is this internal familiarity and acceptance that makes these mediations part of everyday life, rather than a series of unusual events and questionable practices which stand out against the norm.

This ordinariness of the grey or informal economy in Poland intrigues me. I suspect that it is common to much of the rest of Eastern Central Europe as well. It seems to me that both during socialism and since, we have been able to look at grey economies and grey zones from various different angles. In this chapter I want to look at the span or spectrum of grey or shadow economies and practices, now and in the past, in certain postsocialist contexts, and also at the different moral spaces they occupied in the socialist past, and occupy now. I argue that there is considerable coherence and continuity in the way that different moralities attach to different spaces and types of practice, but that in some areas different moral assessments are now being made. I link the changes to wider shifts in political economy, notions of civil society, identification with the state and aspirations to (post)modernity. I argue that during socialism nearly everyone was to some extent implicated in the informal or grey economy, and that it was rarely seen as anything other than the ordinary, what was necessary for survival and for getting by. Corruption was associated with power and inappropriate, immoral or possibly amoral benefit to oneself – so it was linked to and sited in those with visible and usually explicit (formal) power and privilege: state and church leaders and officials; local politicians; sometimes teachers, doctors and other professionals who provided services; and party apparatchiks and nomenklatura. For ordinary villagers, and ordinary urban workers, corruption was located *elsewhere*. Their own grey areas, their grey activities, were seen as necessary for survival, linked to kinship, family and neighbourhood or workplace relations, and were comfortably contained within the moralities governing those private or domestic worlds. Corruption I would argue was firmly located in the immoral or amoral public world. It was also ordinary, but not in a positive sense. It was omnipresent and rarely shocking, but it belonged in a different social space and to a different moral order.

So, in the vignette of airport negotiation with which I began this section, my friends saw themselves as acting properly to help me, their friend and visitor. They saw the airport officials as corrupt, because they used their official position for gain. What I think is critical here is the fact that the officials and my friends had no personal relationship. Had they been connected, the transaction would have been represented differently – those asking the favour would have slipped their friend or connection a little something 'for the road', and the friend or connection's action in return would have been understood as helpful, not as corrupt and immoral. So, I would argue that in popular discourse and understanding it is very largely the context that creates the distinction between grey zones and grey activities, which are incorporated within a general moral framework, on the one hand, and sites and acts of corruption, which stand outside such a framework, on the other.

Defining Grey Zones

I am using the term grey zones to describe spaces of ambiguity – spaces where, for instance, statuses may be unclear. Examples that come to mind are border regions where people communicate between countries, legally and illegally, on a regular or sporadic basis; in-between places such as asylum or migrant detention centres where people are between countries and often living a 'bare existence' (Agamben 1998); and informal economic spaces, like the unlicensed market spaces in Lithuania that Harboe Knudsen (2012) describes, outside the formal, licensed marketplace – which I also saw in Lublin. All of these relate directly to what I call the grey economy – those equally ambiguous economic practices that are not necessarily illegal, but which may be shrouded in informality: for instance, marketing goods without a licence; selling goods from a train in transit between countries; or working in care, agriculture or construction, either within Poland or other postsocialist countries, or abroad in the 'West', without being registered. In other words, such practices that involve doing things which are often not in themselves illegal – they *may* involve stealing, or more rarely violent crime, or types of financial crime, but usually do not – but which are taking place/carried out below the radar of the state.

These grey spaces, and the associated grey economies, are not unique to the postsocialist world, nor to the less-developed or underdeveloped world. They exist in North America and throughout Western Europe – indeed I would argue that they are rife in the UK – but they are perhaps less ubiquitous there than they were in the socialist states. There seem to me to have been many reasons for their prevalence under socialism: the failure of the centralised distribution system described by Kornai (1980), Verdery (1996) and others, which generated nonofficial circuits of exchange that had to be based to some extent on face-to-face relations and trust; the *lack* of trust most people had for the state, and the cynicism with which state organisations and officials were viewed, which has been described by Kotkin (1995), Yurchak (1997) and others; the creation, against the dominant ideology of the public and the impersonal collective as the source of value, of a counter-ideology of private or domestic domains as sites of not only intimacy, but also of security and provision; and linked to this, the widespread sense of alienation from the public domain. I think all of these things were particularly acute in Poland, but I believe they were generally prevalent through the socialist bloc.

The other point about the grey economy, and the ambiguity surrounding activities within it, is that, as Ledeneva has shown in her work on *blat*, it is relatively easy to sanitise illegal and semilegal activities and transform them into domestic favours, good and kind acts to benefit one's friends and family (Ledeneva 1998). *Blat*, or corruption, or dishonest dealing, as I have said already, takes place elsewhere, in the lives of others. The ambiguity about legalities, and the slippage between activities seen as private or intimate and those seen as public, and indeed between the public and private domains themselves, creates highly layered or textured spaces that are always open to different kinds of interpretation, which is in part what allows different moral regimes to coexist side by side.

In Poland during socialism, if you wanted to buy anything from vodka to meat to a radio or a car, or to arrange anything from a quick exit at the airport to a place at university for your child, you arranged it through a connection. So, if you were hoping to buy a radio, your first question would be not where is a good radio shop, but do I know someone who works in a radio shop or factory, or who has close connections to someone who does?

What this meant was that economic fields were incredibly personalised and strangely intimate – markets facilitated the exchange and circulation of goods, commodities and services, but those exchanges were also relational to a very extreme degree, and very often were external to, and outside of, the kinds of public roles and relations regulated by the state.

People moved regularly between regulated and unregulated spaces – for example, they might work in a factory, but smuggle goods from the factory outside and sell or gift them on; they justified theft by claims of entitlement, fuelled both by state ownership (which meant these things belonged to 'the people') and by poor pay and work conditions (see for example Firlit and Chlopecki 1992). For instance, during my first piece of fieldwork in the late 1970s and the 1980s, villagers I knew regularly brought home goods from the factories and shops they worked in – wool from the state weaving cooperative, shoes from the shoe factory, meat or cheese from the butchers or dairy,[1] scarce school supplies from the central distribution warehouse. These were then used domestically, or incorporated into complex cycles of exchanges of goods and services among kin and neighbours, primarily within the village or immediate vicinity. I never heard these objects referred to as stolen goods, nor their procurement as theft. Rather, they were presented as things to which certain people had access, rather as they might have access to berries or mushrooms in a public forest. Of course, on a different discursive level everyone knew this was in fact illegal. People went to great pains to hide the goods they smuggled out of the workplace, and police and informants were equally feared as agents of surveillance and, consequently, punishment. Transactions involving clandestine goods were surrounded often by an air of slight mystery – I was fascinated when I first lived in the mountain village where I did my doctoral research by the leather hold-alls that everyone, even small children, seemed to carry with them from house to house, which would sometimes be left behind in someone's kitchen, or at other times emerge obviously much fuller and heavier than before. It looked to me as if everyone was involved in something rather dodgy. I realised fairly soon that that was an accurate observation, and it was not too long before I was carrying bags, or hiding items of dubious provenance (often, for instance, goods produced for private sale – such as sheepskin garments – without a licence) in my clothes trunk or my closet when there was a rumour that the police might arrive and search houses. So on that level, people, even the smallest children, clearly recognised the formal illegality of a variety of their practices, and went to some lengths to conceal them from outsiders and officials of the state. However, no one I knew saw any moral ambiguity in what they were doing or participating in; rather, what were judged negatively were the laws limiting private production and distribution, the state and the police, and, even worse, people who were suspected of being police informers.

I would argue that during socialism, particularly in rather marginal and excluded areas like the mountains where I worked, there was an immense ideological gap perceived between, the one hand, corrupt acts and practices of the state and those considered its officials (including professionals, managers, etc.), and on the other, ambiguous grey acts of 'ordinary people'. In a way this formed a kind of folk parallel to the classic definition of corruption as an act by someone using his or her public position for his or her private advantage. The immoral or unambiguously illegal behaviours that were judged negatively were those associated with public persons and institutions, while behaviours within private domains, relations and spaces were linked with levels of connectedness and intimacy. Also involved here, I would suggest, are questions of degree or scale. If Jasiek used the ambulance he drove for his job at the town hospital on his days off, to deliver coal to a neighbour, or to transport another villager to another town to buy scarce sausage, this was not seen as wrong. If on the other hand he had run a fleet of ambulances out of the hospital, for private errands, that would have been seen as wrong, dangerous or dishonest. Small amounts of wool smuggled out from the weaving cooperative could constitute an entitlement, but organised rings of workers regularly diverting shipments to their private addresses would be wrong. To be encompassed by the positive morality of a domestic ethos, the scale of the activity had to be compatible with intimacy, and had to be accommodated at the level of a personal, face-to-face social field.

Here I think the moralities in question were being determined by the cynicism and distrust with which people viewed the state, as well as by their disenchantment with the existing economic system and processes of distribution. The general rationale for activities in the grey zone – grey activities, things *na lewo* (on the left) or *na czarno* (on the black) – was that they were *necessary* for survival. They were imbued with a sense of inevitability. People did what they had to do. If the state had been doing its job, these grey, ambiguous activities and practices would not have been necessary. This is a kind of reasoning that finds an echo in Keith Hart's point (2005) – reviewing his own seminal work on the 'informal economy' (1973) – that, in fact, informal and formal economies cannot really be viewed as separate, because they are mutually constitutive. The informal economy allows the formal economy to stay in place – it props it up.

There is also another issue of scale here, which involves anthropological and other definitions – namely, what we think we are talking about. It is reflected in the range of material covered by the chapters in this volume, as well as in the two works, of Roy and Robertson, cited in the editors' position statement in their original call for papers. Roy talks about situations in which extreme violence, either physical or symbolic/structural, has become 'the ordinary' (see also Agamben 1998; Das 2006). In a discussion reminiscent of Veena Das's (2006) work on the Partition and other periods of violence in India, Roy (2008) shows how familial, patriarchal and domestic violence form a grey area reflecting but also mimicking the general and widespread political violence by which they are encompassed. Robertson (2006), on the other hand, begins by looking at constructions of informality and the behaviours involved in shadow, second or grey economies; citing Keith Hart's work on the slums of Accra, his is a more traditional view of the everyday ordinariness of ambiguous economic practices (Robertson 2006). This is much more similar to the grey areas I have been describing here, where informal dealings and the ambiguities that allow them are not marked by regular, extreme violence, either physical or structural. Robertson goes on to discuss corruption and to call for an anthropological or even phenomenological study of embodied practices of corruption: If it is so widespread, who is doing it, and where and how does it take place? I would add to these questions a further one, which is definitional: Who decides if an act or practice is corruption, particularly when there are so many contradictions between the rule of law and acceptable (if often ambiguous) local practice?

The question of the distinction between corruption and grey activities is a difficult one. The violence portrayed in Roy's work, like that in the work of Das, is of a different order from most (although not all) of the practices discussed by Hart (1973) and Robertson, or those to which I refer in this chapter and elsewhere (see Pine 1999). These different kinds of acts have many elements in common, most strikingly the ambiguities around public and private, state and domestic, legal and illegal, and connections and strangers. But the extent of difference in scale is extreme, and perhaps we should here be asking what we are trying to look at, if the notion of a grey zone, or grey economy, reaches across the entire span. Again, I think we have to ask whether we are talking about degree or scale, or whether we are putting together phenomena that are in fact too different to be placed under a levelling rubric. I am not trying to argue here that we should not make these connections and comparisons, nor that we should avoid problems of scale. But I do think we need to be clear about the distinctions arising from scale, and be explicit about where our data, and our arguments, are located.

Polish Temporalities: Continuities and Change

So, I want to make an argument about three different periods in recent Polish history: late socialism, early postsocialism and EU accession. The point I am making is simple. During the socialist period there was a kind of uneasy truce between the political economy of the state – the formal economy – and the grey economy. The structures of the state and the activities of the grey zones of ordinary life coexisted, to some extent peacefully, because they spilt over into each other and involved many of the same actors and practices, albeit in different contexts. Everybody was involved to some degree in the planned economy – working for the state, relying on state benefits of various kinds, and using state markets as avenues of production (peasants and workers producing for the market) and consumption (citizens from all walks of life purchasing at least some of their consumer goods, both necessities and luxuries, through state outlets). But almost everyone was also involved, in some way or another, in the informal economy, which I have argued was in many ways seen as superior, more efficient, and rooted in intimate relations or relations of trust. In this sense the market for the consumer was not a place as much as it was a set of relations. I have already described how, during the late socialist period, everything and anything could be arranged through networks of *znajomie* (acquaintances; people who are known to one). A very wise old man in the mountain village explained this to me when I first arrived. He told me he was going to the forest to cut me down a Christmas tree. I asked him if that was legal, and he replied: *'Tutaj nic nie jest wolno, ale wszystko jest możliwe'* (Here nothing is allowed, but everything is possible).

During the two periods of acute change, after 1989 and after 2004, however, the symbiotic, if unspoken, relation between the formal and the grey economies shifted. Regime change in 1989 brought with it both a drastic restructuring of the formal economy and a simultaneous retreat of the state from institutions of care and benefit. Following the kinds of rhetorical tropes Sarah Green refers to in her chapter in this volume, capitalism was expected to take a Fordist, modernist form, to add colour and variety and opportunity to dull and stunted lives. Initially it was expected and anticipated that the period of loss and hardship would be about five years – this magic number which, as few people failed to register, was in a rather sinister way reminiscent of socialism's five-year plans. (I say sinister here because everyone knew that five-year plans rarely met their objectives, that the goods produced were altered significantly in order to meet the criteria of quantity,[2] that results were faked, that success depended on illicit agreements between individual directors and distributors, and so forth.) Instead, what emerged in place of the planned economy in many economic domains and spaces was what I have elsewhere referred to as 'cowboy capitalism' (Pine 1996, 152). The old structures were systematically broken down, but frequently what replaced them was not a new system, or any kind of new regulation of labour, market or economy, but a kind of free-for-all, where maverick companies and entrepreneurs from the West built fly-by-night companies, profiting from asset stripping and buying up ridiculously cheap properties and commodities; where suitcase traders flooded in from the East, further destabilising already fragile local markets; and where what had been the grey, informal or semilegal economy expanded to become the main market force, the main ordinary. During this period of regime change I was doing research on the collapse of the textile factories in Łódź, which had, since the nineteenth century, been the biggest centre of textile production in Eastern Central Europe. The kind of fragmented economic processes that are generally taken to be characteristic of neoliberalism proliferated. It was a period of great opportunity for those willing and able to take risks, and of amazing success for those that were lucky, but for most of the population it was a profoundly unsettling and precarious time. While the official economy collapsed under the double pressures of the IMF-imposed conditions for economic restructuring and the Balcerowicz Plan, which put these into practice, the grey economy – the informal market for goods, services and labour – flourished.

Factories closed, workers were unemployed, and cowboy enterprises were set up in old factories by German and Italian entrepreneurs, who hired back a few workers with none of the rights and benefits they were used to from the socialist state. New enterprises grew up in private basements: in a region or town where a major factory or plant had closed down, it was always possible to tell what it had been by the number of prominent signs, on display outside almost every house, announcing the *hurt/detal* (wholesale/ retail) of what the factory had formerly produced – 'tights and socks' in this place, 'machine-embroidered blouses' in that, 'sheepskin coats' in a third. Most striking in this period was the lack of regulation. On the one hand this left the dismantling of the state sector open to massive corruption, manifested most obviously in asset stripping and land and property deals that bypassed public auction or sale and involved various kinds of cronyism and backhanded payments. On the other hand, once the best of the machines and other assets had been creamed off, what remained was sold off to individuals or simply abandoned. The selling off of individual machines, such as computerised sewing machines and other tools of the textile industry, led to the shrinking of big industry into tiny, cottage, family-based enterprises. In other words, the retraction of the state laid the ground for the expansion of the grey zones that already existed – ranging from the selling off of large state-owned assets to foreign companies and local managers for ridiculously small amounts of money, to the individual purchase of a couple of small machines to set up an unregistered and untaxed sweatshop in the basement of the family home. Corruption on a grand scale could no longer be identified as 'elsewhere', but rather seemed to be seeping in everywhere. Furthermore, the extremity of the degree to which the former state sector broke down (in terms of no longer either achieving full employment or providing a range of social and economic entitlements) allowed various forms of grey practices, which had formerly been contained in the more intimate domain of domestic relations and close circles of kin and friends, to expand outwards to fill up the empty spaces. The new economic enterprises, such as basement sweatshops employing former factory workers with no job security and no benefits, often masked extreme exploitation and sometimes violent coercion based on gender and generation – the grey economy seemed no longer to have any checks on it.

On the other hand, it was the grey economy in its more moderate form that provided the flexibility and fluidity to keep the basic structures of ordinary life woven together, and to keep them going. So, though the continuity of the state and its institutions might for a period be in tatters, the process of daily life in the lived world continued to be possible, on the whole, because the grey zones were relatively unaffected. They continued to provide the ordinary, often at a much expanded and more elaborated scale.

Not all of the expansion, or effervescence, of informal markets and practices was negative. In the same period in the early 1990s I went to stay in the mountains, and a close friend, whose house I live in when I am there, told me she was going on vacation – *na wyczeczka* (an outing) – to Odessa. She asked me if I would look after her children while she was gone. I agreed, a bit puzzled about this sudden and totally uncharacteristic urge for a holiday. As I visited other houses in the village, people asked me, 'What's Marta going to take to Odessa?'; I realised that not just Marta but a whole group of women were going. Different women filled in different bits of the picture for me. They were taking a bus from the village to the eastern border, where they were going to board a train and travel through the night to Odessa. Gradually the air of secrecy receded, and they began to discuss among themselves, and with me, what they should take. I came to understand that the *wyczeczka* was in fact a buying and selling trip, a trading expedition, involving cross-border trade with the (still-existing) Soviet Union. It was a rather complex and very clever plan: on the surface, a cultural *wyczeczka* for a group of Polish village women; underneath, a complicated journey involving informal markets and unknown trading partners. I understood the need for secrecy and the fear of the risk involved. Somehow, the risk seemed exacerbated by the fact that Poland was now officially *not* a socialist state, while Ukraine was still very much part of the Soviet Union.

Marta and her sister discussed what to take – what would Ukrainian women want to buy? Perfume, deodorant, make up. Western clothes. The latter presented a problem. Marta had made a pile of their clothes to take to sell, but by their labels they were clearly Polish. Then she came up with a plan. She told me to bring all of my clothes into the kitchen, and together we carefully cut out the labels – Gap, Warehouse, John Lewis, Marks and Spencer – and then sewed them into the Polish clothes in the place of the old labels. Marta now had a new set of Western clothes to sell.

When she returned she told me in great detail about the trip. When they got to the border and left the bus for the train, it was already dark. The bus driver handed some money over to the train conductor, who presumably handed it on to the border guards, because not a single one of the large bags the women were carrying was checked. The train went on some way through the night, and then came to a stop in a forest. Silently, Ukrainian women appeared from the depth of the forest and climbed onto the train. The Polish women displayed their goods in front of them, and the Ukrainian women bought them with rubles, before melting back into the dark cover of the forest. The train then continued on to Odessa, where the village women bought presents for their families, goods that were scarce or more expensive in Poland, and vodka. They went sightseeing, got on the train and returned home. Most of them had made a profit, and returned with rubles to spare and goods to trade and sell.

I love this story, partly because it is a perfect example of the way the grey economy expanded in this precarious period of the retreat of the Polish state and formal economy. This trip took huge orchestration, involving women from about half of the village houses, and enormous coordination. It also involved them in serious risks, from bribing border guards, to smuggling, illegal private selling in the Soviet Union and money laundering. None of this seemed to worry them unduly. But for me what was most striking was the sheer scale of the enterprise. One woman, or even two, might have done a similar trip during the socialist period – in fact several village women were accomplished long-distance traders and smugglers, travelling as far as Turkey to buy gold – but most villagers balanced their state jobs and/or pensions with their informal activities. These activities provided a significant part of their income, but were not anything like as elaborate as this *wyczeczka* scheme.

Over the following decade the Polish political economy gradually stabilised and became reregulated. The grey economy slipped back to a more shadowy or secondary position in many regions, although in some the sense of cowboy capitalism continued. Initially the restructuring programme was imagined in five-year blocks, of which the first block was expected to be the hardest – the tough medicine – followed by a second five-year period of consolidation of the new economic policies. It was thought that after ten years a new free-market democracy, securely based in a democratic state system and a strong civil society, would have emerged. Now, 25 years on, it is clear that this period of precariousness, in which uncertainty and ambiguity are the ordinary, is likely to be indefinite in many regions of the former socialist bloc. While much of western Poland, and several of the larger cities, seem to be settling into economic stability a decade after EU accession, it is certainly true that in some of the areas of eastern and northern Poland, furthest from the centre both geographically and conceptually, this state of precariousness continues (see Joyce's chapter in this volume). And it is undoubtedly the case that throughout the entire region of former socialist countries, certain groups of people – including residents of former one-industry towns that have lost their industry, workers on former collective farms that have been abandoned by the state, and, of course, Roma and other minorities – perceive few opportunities outside the grey social and economic zones they currently occupy.

For most of the Polish population, however, the next big change came with the preparations for EU accession at the beginning of this century, and then with accession itself in 2004. All across the former socialist world the conditions for EU membership targeted two specific problem areas. Firstly,

if former socialist countries were going to be European, they had to clean up
their human rights records and develop new policies or enforce existing ones,
including addressing gay rights and the rights of Roma – both anathema in
several of the countries in question. Secondly, they had to reduce or ideally
eliminate corrupt practices. Interestingly, although we have witnessed an
alarming rise of new right-wing movements that particularly target Roma
in several countries, including Hungary and Bulgaria, in Poland both Roma
rights and gay rights improved during the accession period, with rates of
violence against Roma decreasing and gay pride events eventually being
allowed rather than banned or met with government-approved violence.
But the question of corruption seems to me to be a much more complicated
one, precisely because while challenging what are popularly seen as corrupt
practices on the one hand, the EU also opens up its own possibilities for
new areas of informality, cronyism and influence as soon as it begins to put
its funding, training and bureaucratic institutions into place. Sarah Green has
given us various examples of this in her chapter in this volume. There has
now been a fair amount of anthropological work on access to and exclusion
from EU funding, programmes, etc. in the former socialist bloc. In her work
on Lithuania being in EU-influenced hands, Ida Harboe Knudsen describes
in vivid and meticulous detail the various processes and practices involved
in joining the EU. What she shows, which parallels exactly what I found in
eastern Poland between 2003 and 2006, and which also I heard discussed
in identical terms in Romania at a panel of the Romanian Anthropological
Association in Sibiu in 2013, is how the EU in many ways steps into the gap
left by the socialist state – from centralised and levelling bureaucracy and
regulations to five-year plans. Further, access to funding is limited to those
with particular kinds of skills, know-how and possessions: literacy, the IT
skills necessary to fill in an application form, the connections necessary to
have an application considered, and in rural areas the number of animals, area
of land and size of business necessary to qualify for a grant. What all of the
ethnographic accounts reflect is a potential for big and small corruption to be
implicit in almost all of these rules and regulations, played out through local
gatekeepers and imported EU administrators. In eastern Poland I was given
graphic accounts of grants received for sheep farming by several individual
farmers, who would circulate the same herd of the requisite number of sheep
among their farms to be sure of having sufficient animals present at any
moment of inspection. I heard similar accounts from local agronomists in
Romania; similarly, there are detailed accounts of land being counted twice,
or businesses being registered on paper that do not in fact exist. But what also
seems clear is that the proliferation of rules and regulations and demands for
licences and documentation imposed by the EU creates a space for parallel

practices that exist under its radar – again, I refer back to the example from Harboe Knudsen, which I also myself witnessed in Lublin, that I mentioned at the beginning of this chapter. In both Lithuania and Poland, and I am certain in other postsocialist spaces as well, formally registered stalls in legal market places, clearly demarcated and often covered, are rented by traders meeting EU regulations. At its periphery, outside its boundaries, the official market is surrounded by unlicensed small traders who set up illegal stalls or not quite legal displays on the ground outside the main market space, or who walk about, surreptitiously offering various bootleg goods and commodities from inside their jackets or deep in their copious bags. Interestingly, in Lublin the inside market is referred to as Polish, while the traders who huddle or move about outside the building are known as the Ukrainians.

What ethnographies of the EU suggest is that accession to the union has brought with it a new range of possibilities for expanding the grey zone. It also seems to me, however, that the old grey economy, based on face-to-face exchanges, economies of favour and intimate transactions, continues to be the ordinary for many citizens. As more goods and services become available, as shopping centres and shops expand across the countryside, the economy of shortage is no longer the propelling agent in these grey economy dealings. Rather, what matters increasingly now, I think, is finding something – through a friend, a family member, an acquaintance – at a price that can be afforded: perhaps a local fake of a known international brand, perhaps a cheap product fallen from the back of some lorry, or imported without duty from another cheaper market. Because of the nature of the capitalist markets that are growing in Poland, and I think throughout Eastern Central Europe, and because of the precariousness created by the 2008 European and North American economic crisis, with its resulting high unemployment, particularly of young people, and its increasingly uneven labour markets, it seems to me unlikely that we will see a time in the near future when grey economies cease to be the ordinary.

Conclusion

At the core of this chapter is the contention that in many parts of Poland (and I would argue elsewhere in the former socialist lands and beyond as well), grey zones provide spaces for people to deal with the hardship and exclusions inherent in dominant state and bureaucratic structures, focusing here on the economic. In these instances, while formal legality may often be questionable, local people themselves see these practices as absolutely ordinary, and as the only way often to respond to uncertainty and ambiguity. These economic practices are highly relational, and are understood and contained within local ideologies as not only necessary, but also as moral and positive. At particular critical moments, the balance between the grey zones and the dominant structures shifts, as we saw in Poland after the fall of socialism and again with EU accession. At these critical moments expansion of grey economies can allow different kinds of practices to develop, sometimes based on violence and coercion within the intimate private or domestic domain, sometimes generating new patterns of privilege and exclusion as new forms of gatekeepers and elites develop. These practices come to be viewed by local people as corrupt when they are seen as acts for individual gain, which are either amoral, outside the world of local relations and trust, or immoral, in fact betraying that world. However, throughout each of these periods, although they shift in size and shape, grey economic practices continue to provide a safety net for many people, who in turn continue to view them as moral acts, within the proper order of relations within families and communities.

Notes

1   Meat is a particularly interesting example as, during this time, there was very rarely any meat available to buy except through connections. Butcher shops might display chicken or cheap sausage, but rarely beef or pork. So access to meat in the village was primarily through two means: when meat was (rarely) delivered to the village shop, the shopkeeper immediately packaged it up and held it under the counter for favoured customers; and when a farmer slaughtered a pig or calf (which was also rare, as most people had only one or two of each, if that), the meat and products such as sausage would be distributed to kin, neighbours and people to whom favours were owed or who were part of the same circle of labour exchange.
2   Katherine Verdery (1996, 21) famously refers to the production of tiny shoes that no one could wear in order to make the limited materials like leather and glue extend to the numbers demanded by the plan. In Poland in the late 1970s, *Górale* villagers working in the local shoe factory told me exactly the same thing when they described their work practices to me.

References

Agamben, G. 1998. *Homo Sacer: Sovereign Power and Bare Life*. Palo Alto: Stanford University Press.
Das, V. 2006. *Life and Words: Violence and the Descent into the Ordinary*. Berkeley: University of California Press.
Firlit, E. and J. Chlopecki. 1992. 'When theft is not theft'. In J. R. Wedel (ed.), *The Unplanned Society: Poland During and After Communism*, 95–109. New York: Columbia University Press.
Harboe Knudsen, I. 2012. *New Lithuania in Old Hands: Effects and Outcomes of EUropeanization in Rural Lithuania*. London: Anthem Press.

Hart, K. 1973. 'Informal income opportunities and urban employment in Ghana'. *Journal of Modern African Studies* 11(1): 61–89.

_____. 2005. 'Formal Bureaucracy and the Emergent Forms of the Informal Economy'. United Nations University World Institute for Development Economics Research (UNU-WIDER) Research Paper no. 2005/11.

Kornai, J. 1980. *Economics of Shortage*. 2 vols. Amsterdam: North Holland Press.

Kotkin, S. 1995. *Magnetic Mountain: Stalinism as a Civilization*. Berkeley and London: University of California Press.

Ledeneva, A. V. 1998. *Russia's Economy of Favours: Blat, Networking and Informal Exchange*. Cambridge. Cambridge University Press.

Pine, F. 1996. 'Redefining women's work in rural Poland'. In R. Abrahams (ed.), *After Socialism: Land Reform and Social Change in Eastern Europe*, 133–56. New York and Oxford: Berghahn Books.

_____. 1999. 'Incorporation and exclusion in the Podhale'. In S. Day, A. Papataxiarchis and M. Stewart (eds), *Lilies of the Field: Marginal People Who Live for the Moment*, 45-61. Boulder: Westview Press.

Robertson, A. F. 2006. 'The anthropology of grey zones'. *Ethos* 71(4): 569–73.

Roy, S. 2008. 'The grey zone: The "ordinary" violence of extraordinary times'. *Journal of the Royal Anthropological Institute* 14(2): 316–33.

Verdery, K. 1996. *What Was Socialism, and What Comes Next?* Princeton: Princeton University Press.

Yurchak, A. 1997. 'The cynical reason of late socialism: Power, pretense and the *anekdot*'. *Public Culture* 9(2): 161–89.

Chapter 3

BETWEEN STARVATION AND SECURITY: POVERTY AND FOOD IN RURAL MOLDOVA

Jennifer R. Cash

This chapter examines household economy in rural Moldova as a grey zone. Standard statistical measures are used to render Moldova as 'Europe's poorest country'.[1] According to national measurements, rural households suffer from the highest rates of poverty when measuring incomes against a 'minimum consumption basket'. Such high levels of poverty are frequently used to explain the country's high rates of labour migration. Yet other statistics indicate that Moldova is a 'food secure' country,[2] and empirical studies by agricultural economists suggest that average land holdings are sufficient for provisioning the food needs of rural households. How should such data be understood – are Moldova's rural households starving, or are they food secure?

In this chapter I outline the range of ambiguous and uncertain data that underlie assessments of rural poverty and household wellbeing. The 'greyness' surrounding the issues of land ownership and use, household production and consumption, cultural values, and social networks is extensive and persistent, even at the local level. Even when closely questioned and observed, informants insist that they themselves do not know how they 'make ends meet', deny their participation in numerous economic practices (such as lending and borrowing), and fail to recognise the substantial material contributions that villagers make to one another's welfare. Such greyness tempers my optimism about ethnography's role in revealing a comprehensive account of informality, at least in the case of rural Moldova (cf. Abel and Polese 2014). Nevertheless, an ethnographic investigation of this greyness does begin to reveal the moral narratives and agendas inherent in the national and international development programmes that insist on the unambiguous identification of the country's rural population as 'poor'.[3] No degree of refining the collection of economic data can change the fact that such programmes operate largely independently of the realities of everyday rural life. More importantly, an investigation into the persistence of the greyness surrounding rural household economy helps to reveal how the moral narratives that appear in the guise of poverty assessments have changed rapidly during the postsocialist period.

Poverty in Postsocialist Moldova

When Moldova gained independence in 1991, local and international attention initially focused on the volatility of ethnic relations, problems of nation building, and the new state's political stability. Little attention was given to the country's economic weaknesses, but by the late 1990s it had become clear that these were substantial. Soviet Moldova had primarily supplied agricultural products to other republics; it had little heavy industry and few natural resources other than rich agricultural land. With independence Moldova's economy was deeply crippled, and decollectivisation caused more problems than it solved for the country's new 'farmers', who were deprived of salaries and saddled with land that they could neither work easily and profitably nor sell. By the early 2000s Moldova was identified as 'Europe's poorest country', and the label has stuck without much critical examination, even as the precise nature of the economic problems in the country has shifted and evolved.

Over the following pages I use data drawn from ethnographic research in Moldova to interrogate the predominant narratives that have emerged about poverty in rural areas of the country.[4] During 2009–10 I conducted ten months of fieldwork in the village of Răscăieți in the country's southeastern corner. I chose my fieldsite for many of its representative characteristics, including those relating to its pre-Soviet poverty;[5] near-destruction during World War II; rapid modernisation and improved living standards during the Soviet period; and drastic reimpoverishment and high rates of labour migration during the post-Soviet period. Răscăieți is of medium size for a Moldovan village, with an official population of about 2,500 people living in some 1,200 households. The number of villagers present at any given time is much lower because labour migrants rarely change their registration status; just over half of school-aged children have at least one parent abroad. Compared to the Soviet period, when the village's two farms (one specialising in growing vegetables for seed stock and the other in wine grapes) provided nearly universal employment, there are few employment options today. By my estimates about three hundred individuals have regular employment in the village and another thirty or so have work in the regional centre or other nearby villages.

In the opinion of most villagers, the lack of paid work within the village is a sure sign of the country's recent impoverishment. Yet during fieldwork in 2009 and in earlier years, I have been met often with assertions that households 'have (enough)' and that they are not 'dying from hunger'. Such assertions, combined with others about the 'wealth' and 'richness' displayed in times of celebration and in everyday dress and comportment, led me to a closer consideration of the ascribed poverty of Moldova, and of its rural areas in particular. Importantly, reports on Moldova's poverty frequently combine data about the 'minimum consumption basket' (i.e. the absolute national poverty line), the country's high rates of migration, and remittance spending patterns in ways that produce an image of the country's rural population as being on the brink of starvation. Not only does such an image differ from that which villagers hold of themselves, it is also at odds with other data that confirm that average land holdings are sufficient for villagers to provision their food needs. It is perhaps not surprising that existing forms of statistical data about food (in) security raise as many questions as they answer about household economy and wellbeing. Yet I also found that villagers also render their economic activities 'grey' – obscure, unknown and inexplicable, even to themselves and visiting ethnographers. In the midst of such an impenetrable grey zone around household economy, the emergence of definitive national and international narratives of Moldova's food-related poverty is all the more striking. Closer examination of the grey zone illustrates how quickly a changing global discourse on poverty has worked to obscure both the actual living conditions in rural Moldova and earlier (Soviet) standards of wellbeing that remain important in villagers' self-imagination (see also Kaneff and Pine 2011, 4–6).

Grey Household Economies and Moral Narratives of Poverty

The concept of grey zones within anthropology and related fields is most often connected to the themes of violence and political corruption, particularly with reference to moral and legal ambiguity. These uses of the concept are logical extensions of the concept's highly influential appearance in a reflective essay about German concentration camps by Primo Levi (2008).[6] From this usage, the idea of a 'grey zone' has been particularly useful for identifying gaps in legal codes and the provision of basic rights and securities, as well as for drawing out the range and continuum of ambiguity and uncertainty in human life where desires for survival, dignity and prestige are concerned (e.g. Scheper-Hughes 2007). As the editors of this book explain in their introduction, the concept can be productively expanded to study the perceived ambiguities and uncertainties of Eastern Europe's postsocialist societies, without sacrificing the more specific concerns for regulating violence, establishing morality and ensuring human rights with which it has previously been associated.

In this chapter I have returned to Primo Levi's assertions about the normalcy of both grey (uncertainty) and black and white (certainty) in human life. In the very opening of his essay, Primo Levi asks, 'Have we – we who have returned [from the camps] – been able to understand and make others understand our experience?' (2008, 88), immediately modifying his own question by noting that to 'understand' must mean to 'simplify'. Without simplification, he writes, '[the] world around us would be an infinite, undefined tangle' (Levi 2008, 88), and he speculates that basic human cognition requires distinguishing dichotomies that necessarily also imply moral distinctions: we/they, friend/enemy, winner/ loser. In short, the implication of Levi's analysis is clear: life is grey, but we succeed (most of the time) in making it appear to be black and white, both to ourselves and to others. Much later in his essay, Levi suggests that it is only through abnormal exercises of power, such as those represented by concentration camps, that people remain indefinitely in a 'grey zone', unable to formulate, enact or explain their behaviour according to consistent principles (2008, 199).

If Levi's analysis is expanded beyond its immediate context, then we might expect that persistent grey zones, whether identified in terms of geographical regions (like Eastern Europe) or particular domains of social life (such as economy), appear because some form of power is operating to prevent the emergence of moral (black-and-white) narratives. Yet, by the same token, it is necessary to remember that the emergence of black-and-white narratives also signals the operation of some form of power, bringing cognitive and moral order to an otherwise 'normal' state of grey. Persistently grey zones thus provide an opportunity to explore how both certainty and uncertainty are created, but such an exploration necessarily requires a more sophisticated attention to the kinds and forms of power than Levi himself articulated (cf. Petropoulous and Roth 2006).[7]

Household economy in rural Moldova constitutes a distinctly grey zone. Statistical efforts to ascertain poverty and wellbeing rely on a variety of forms of incomplete and ambiguous data. But villagers also claim that they 'do not know' how they make ends meet, and they routinely fail to observe or report the many values, relations and practices that contribute to the redistribution of food between the houses that have more and those that have less. Some of this greyness is a normal reflection of everyday life; some of it indicates the operation of local ideologies of self-sufficiency, equality and classlessness; and some of it is linked to the very real uncertainties produced in recent years by the disintegration of the Soviet economy, privatisation, decollectivisation and the advent of global market capitalism. Amidst these 'shades of grey', each of which indicates both normality and the operation of different kinds of power in rural life, the emergence of a clear, unambiguous, black-and-white portrayal of rural poverty points to the creation of a new moral narrative in the form of scientific indicators.

New Poverty Narratives

Moldova's official poverty line is calculated in absolute terms according to a 'minimum consumption basket'. The cost of the 'basket', which contains foodstuffs that meet nutritional needs stratified according to age and gender, other necessary items for daily life, and basic utilities, is calculated against individual income levels (Laur 2005). This form of poverty calculation is best designed to track extreme conditions, but is poorly suited to understanding actual living standards or relative levels of inequality (see Betti et al. 2012, 129, 133). In recent decades policy specialists throughout Europe have generally favoured the use of relative poverty indicators for gauging national poverty levels, and composite indices for international comparisons. Moldova, like the USA, therefore represents a case in which poverty specialists continue to be concerned not with relative forms of inequality, but with absolute deprivation. The data on poverty in Moldova thus suggest a particularly stark picture of the first 15 years of postsocialism. From 1993 to 2004 incomes severely lagged behind the level of the minimum consumption basket (Laur 2005, 6–7). The situation deteriorated between the mid-1990s and 1999–2000 – when 90 per cent of the population fell below the poverty line. Since 2004 salaries have been generally adequate for bringing individuals who have them above the poverty line, but the lack of income in rural areas continues to be a major problem (Laur 2005; National Bureau of Statistics 2011).

When combined with other statistics, this suggests that rural Moldovans are on the brink of starvation. For example, the national Household Budget Survey indicates that rural households purchase 51 per cent of their food, and that this percentage has been climbing in recent years (National Bureau of Statistics 2010). Reports of high levels of migration are also often coupled with the information that Moldova has the world's fourth-highest remittance economy relative to GDP (World Bank 2011, 14). Having encountered such combined statistics in development reports and international news features several times, I began to wonder what they really meant. On the surface such statistics seem to tell a familiar moral story about migration: i.e. that the high rates of illegal migration from Moldova are a reflection of a difficult decision to leave the comforts of home behind in pursuit of work abroad, a decision made at the point of starvation or extreme family need. Such stories have already been interrogated by other anthropologists, who have considered how female migrants use such narratives to establish and maintain their moral reputations 'at home' (e.g. Keough 2006), and by economists, who have established that most migrants have treated migration, particularly their choice of destination and thus the issue of legality, as one option among many in sustaining or moderately improving their existing lifestyles, which are primarily of middling means and status (Goerlich and Luecke 2011). These approaches have nevertheless accepted their respondents' claims that migration was necessary. In this chapter, however, I approach the story from a different direction by asking whether or not the poverty statistics accurately depict scenarios of extreme food insecurity in the countryside. The short answer is that they do not; the longer answer is that such an investigation serves as a reminder that all social scientific approaches are limited in their capacity to fully grasp the interplay between the values and practices that surround the production and consumption of food in rural communities and which lead to both food security and starvation.

Are Rural Households Starving?

In the early 2000s most rural households received land during the decollectivisation of former *kolkhoz* (collective) and *sovkhoz* (state) farms. Legislation facilitating decollectivisation in Moldova was passed in 1991 and 1992, but most redistribution in Răscăieţi, as throughout the country, took place through the National Land Program of 1998–2000 (Gorton and White 2003; Csaki and Lerman 2001; Lerman and Cimpoieş 2006). Individually held shares in Răscăieţi are smaller than the national average holding of 1.56–2.0 ha, and combined household shares are also significantly smaller.[8] In the initial distribution of land, current and pensioned farm workers (including those who had been employed in the farms' social services, such as their kindergartens) received full shares, but individuals who had worked for the state (e.g. as school teachers) received partial shares. The average landholding for a household with two farm shares and a house garden in Moldova is 4.21 ha; in this village, it is only 2.56 ha.[9] No one born after 1976 received land in the initial distribution of farmland, but in 2009 most of the village's youngest families (headed by adults in their twenties and early thirties) had inherited, purchased or planned to purchase partial shares.

The privatisation of land in Moldova was designed to protect peasant households from rapacious land markets. New owners received arable land, orchards and vineyards in equal proportions to their neighbours, and legal restrictions on land sales deterred large-scale purchases. Land privatisation also produced configurations of household land ownership that guaranteed most owners the possibility of basic self-provisioning. Pre-Soviet production figures indicate that 3 ha was the minimum amount of land that could feed a household of about four people (see Hitchins 1994, 341). It might well be expected that slightly smaller post-Soviet allotments could feed today's smaller households, even with little cash input for machinery, fertilisers, pesticides or high-yield seeds.

Indeed, a study by Martin Petrick, an agricultural economist, indicates that it is possible for an average farming household to produce most of the food that it needs, and even have some leftover for sale. Petrick (2000) calculates that the average farming household devotes 19 per cent of the harvest from its private lands to feeding livestock, 55 per cent to feeding its members, and still has a remaining 26 per cent (mostly apples, grapes and some milk) to sell (2000, 19).[10] In my own research I found that households in Răscăieţi, even with their smaller than average land allotments, were also able to produce enough grain, meat and milk for their own self-reported needs (Cash forthcoming). Households that succeeded in self-provisioning these staples varied in size, composition, age and access to other forms of income; they also varied in whether they farmed their own land or rented the arable parcels to the local cooperatives. Lack of land was not necessarily a barrier to self-provisioning; among younger families that I surveyed,[11] several that 'had no land' were partially incorporated into a joint household with the parents of one member of the couple. They perceived themselves as two households because the younger couple retained control over their own income; but the joint farming of the older generation's land, and other shared food procurement strategies, produced enough food for at least four adults and a few young children. Some households even produced more food than they needed. One household, for example, produced a wheat surplus of 26 kg/person (almost 23 per cent of the regional average for annual consumption).

Yet in my research, only about a quarter of households actually succeeded in self-provisioning their basic staples. In some cases poor land quality was at fault, but the amounts that households calculated that they needed 'to last' (*a ajunge*) for one year varied in ways that defied easy correlation. For example, one household that produced more than double the regional consumption average of wheat (240 kg/person) reported that it only lasted 6–8 months. The household needed nearly four times what others needed, but there were no obvious factors (e.g. a greater number of livestock) that could account for the difference. When I probed, the head of the household claimed that she herself could not explain why they seemed to need so much more wheat than other families. The probable answer, suggested below, is that she did not account for the substantial quantities of wheat and bread she gave to her five grown children and neighbours.

At a national level rural households seem generally unable to self-provision. Data collected in the national Household Budget Survey indicate that, on average, rural households produce only 35.8 per cent of the cereals they consume, 37.6 per cent of the milk, 50.5 per cent of the meat, 74.5 per cent of the eggs, 40.3 per cent of the potatoes, 51.1 per cent of the vegetables and 72.1 per cent of the fruit (National Bureau of Statistics 2010, 128). How can we understand the gap between what should be possible and what actually happens? If rural households can self-provision, why don't they?

The Grey Zone between Having and Giving

As indicated above, the existing data on household economic decisions in rural Moldova are patchy at best. Averages of 'private' land holdings are often calculated without distinguishing corporate holdings from those of individual owners; the small garden plots of urban dwellers are also often included with the diverse plots produced by decollectivisation. Few statistics track the median age of rural landowners; the specific patterns of land ownership associated with individuals born after 1976 are not tracked; and little attention has been given to the problems of inheritance. Statistical collection seems caught in the immediate moment of decollectivisation, when only questions of ownership and distribution were important. Similarly, data on poverty are trapped by methodologies that foreground absolute poverty over relative poverty, and which focus on calculating whether basic needs (in nutritional terms) can be met through income. Household budget data on food expenditures further suffer from more subtle problems because they do not distinguish food that was purchased out of convenience or preference from that purchased out of absolute need. Nor is food purchased for gifting, feasting or special occasions tracked separately from that purchased for daily consumption. Taken together, available statistical data produce more questions than answers about whether and how rural households survive, and how important land ownership is to household wellbeing.

In this section I turn to an ethnographic sketch of household economy from within the grey zone. Making some sense of the activities that households undertake requires, at the very least, attention to the broader context of social relations and values in which rural households make economic decisions. Perhaps the first point to make is that despite a strongly professed ideology of self-sufficiency (see Cash forthcoming), few individuals actually expect to run a household without access to cash income. Thus, the initial formulation of the question about rural poverty – Why do landowners buy food when they could produce it? – points immediately to the very normal practice of buying food. Ethnographic observation revealed, for example, that purchasing bread is commonplace, even for households that normally bake their own. Even households that produce most of their own food regularly also buy food (including bread, cheese, cold cuts, mayonnaise, eggs and sweets) for the preparation of feasts. Feasts are numerous and celebrated on diverse occasions (see Cash 2011) – any village household easily hosts fifteen feasts or more within a year, and average expenditures per feast are reported at 100 dollars or euros; minimal expenditures by experienced home cooks with well-organised cellars still run to 30 euros per feast. In most years, with the prominent exception of the late 1990s and early 2000s, most people have had access to cash, further underscoring the normality of small-scale purchases of food and other items that could, in theory, be produced at home. In practice few people try to avoid such purchases, and instead find pleasure in the excuse to enter a shop and chat with the salesclerks and other customers.

The prominence of feasting also draws attention to the relationship between having and giving. In rural Moldova, as in many other places of the world, households that have more resources are expected to give more away, but the practices through which such giving occurs are rarely tracked or trackable through standard forms of surveying (see Guyer 2004). In my research informants generally denied the importance of gifts and giving in the context of household management. Almost half of those surveyed denied that they ever borrow objects from others, while others underreported. By my count the household in which I lived lent at least one object per day and were in regular (and largely reciprocal) lending relations with seven other households. Not only did most informants fail to calculate what they gave away, but it was socially unacceptable to remember when some things, especially bread, were given away. Substantial quantities of food – such as potatoes, wine, flour and oil – that households gave to or received from their relatives, friends or neighbours during funeral preparations were never reported on surveys and almost never mentioned in conversation. Similarly, 'poor' people never appeared during funeral processions to claim distributions of bread to which they are ritually entitled (Cash 2013), and on the few occasions when people came to 'ask' for bread, they came at night.

The silence around such practices of giving, lending and receiving render invisible the social mechanics of household provisioning. I was especially intrigued by how one household miraculously escaped being labelled as poor. The household has little, but it gives away much of what it does have in material and symbolic terms, gaining a reputation for generosity. Vera, a widow in her early fifties, lives alone for much of the year while her grown son Petrica works irregularly in Moscow. Prior to decollectivisation Vera held a variety of jobs, including being a brigade leader and beautician. Now she receives a single medical pension, rents her land and occasionally cuts hair at home. Although the household self-reports as successfully self-provisioning and denies receiving gifts, food or assistance from others, this is not the case. The household receives enough wheat and oil (sunflower seeds) from the rented land, but Vera's home garden is barely tended, she raises no animals and she lives largely on rotating store credit between her pension disbursements. Instead, the household receives substantial material support from its neighbours, but through an exchange and flow of goods and services that is minimally tracked by anyone. Although I surveyed this household along with several on which it relies heavily, none of what I documented being given out on an almost daily basis was reported by any of the households. Instead, public attention focused on the help that Vera and her son 'gave' freely and unasked as 'neighbours'.

As the account of Vera's household indicates, unequal flows of food from one neighbour's house into another normally go unremarked in daily social life, and are even less likely to be recorded on questionnaire forms. Ethnographic observation also revealed a variety of situations in which households regularly assumed high 'unavoidable' social costs (such as attending weddings) and debts on behalf of others (as in the case of godparenthood). Although I was told that such 'risks' were assumed as part and parcel of the responsibilities of running a household, these costs were rarely included when respondents detailed their normal household expenses. Respondents readily recounted the monthly costs of fuel, electricity, telephone and satellite television services, insurance and medical treatments, but feigned that they did not know the regular or annual costs of sociability, hospitality or ritual participation, and quickly tired of my efforts to elicit such information. The uncalculated redistribution of food, 'gifts' of labour, loans of small equipment, expenditures on rituals and celebrations, and social debts are entirely commonplace. They are important for maintaining social respect between households of unequal means, but they also create a grey zone around food production and consumption that makes it very difficult for anyone, even villagers themselves, to identify or track poverty.

From a 'Little Piece of Heaven' to Europe's Poorest Country: Informality, Grey Zones and Moral Narratives of Poverty

Poverty statistics for Moldova, calculated primarily in terms of the ability to access food in market terms, do not just conceal the grey zone of household economy that is structured by social values, relations and practices related to food production, consumption and exchange. Such statistics are also implicated in the disjuncture between this grey zone and the moral narrative of poverty that dominates national and international economic development programmes and policies.

In both rural and urban areas of Moldova people discursively deny the story about 'poverty' that is told through national and international statistics. They do not deny the validity of the economic indicators, but they point out that the official figures produce paradoxes that defy logical explanation. Despite insufficient and unstable incomes, people nevertheless appear 'rich'. Women, especially, are well dressed; urban cars are luxurious new models; and lavish celebrations are prominent and ever present, even in the countryside. How can people live so well in a country that is so poor? Locals insist that even they cannot answer this question.

Neither empirical experience and observation nor statistical data seem able to bring definitive resolution and clarity to the mechanics of household economy in rural Moldova. Are all households able to make ends meet without recourse to migration through their various combinations of land, income and social networks, or only some? Is migration driven by need, or by rising aspirations? While such persistent greyness may well be normal, development agencies, social scientists and the media seek more definitive assessments of poverty. Can ethnographers only contribute to answering these questions by refining the methodologies available to clarifying local economic realities? Interrogating greyness allows a more complex intervention.

Much of the material I have presented here might well be subsumed within a study of economic informality. My ethnographic research reveals that most people in the countryside are not exclusively following any of the formal paths imagined for them by state policies: subsistence farming, market-oriented farming or paid labour (combined with limited gardening). Instead, sharing, lending and borrowing, gifting, and redistribution are pervasive but oft-denied informal strategies. As Pine (in this volume) notes in her discussion of scale, practices such as these, which are part and parcel of social relations with neighbours, friends and relatives, hardly seem to merit consideration in the same category as the legally dubious and illicit practices that have been so oft-discussed in the postsocialist area. Nevertheless, these practices now form part of the new, mutually constituted formal and informal sectors of Moldova's economy. One might imagine that improved research methodologies that assume high levels of informality would make it possible to ascertain what rural individuals and households actually consume and how they do it. With better methods we might arrive at a more accurate assessment of local poverty, especially in food-based terms.

Yet to focus exclusively on capturing the dynamics of informality is an exercise in making the grey zones transparent without apprehending the greyness itself. Grey zones are such because of the operation of both power and morality. Thus we can also ask, what is possible because of the grey? What would happen if the grey were resolved into clearer patterns of black and white? In villages the greyness of household economy is important for masking and levelling status differences between households. Even households that are not able to produce or purchase enough food for their own consumption can appear to 'have enough' – and perhaps even as much as their more successful neighbours – because no one counts or tracks the movement of resources too carefully. In such a context only socially alienated households are in any real danger of starvation. At the same time, the lack of careful accounting of all that is taken and given means that households that might well be 'richer' in fact appear to be – and perhaps become – on more equal standing with their neighbours.

Current directions in the study of informality seem to be heading towards exactly such an interest in greyness for its own sake. For example, Morris and Polese (2014) criticise the modernist teleologies, Anglo-American democratic biases and Western European/American centrism inherent in most discourses about informality that continue to insist that it is a barrier to successful transition, and/or that informality will disappear with the successful establishment of democratic/capitalistic political, legal and market institutions. Recently Yalçın-Heckmann (2014) has also suggested that instances of informality in post-Soviet spaces might be productively approached as entry points for understanding local moral economies. Perhaps it is no accident that one of the editors of this volume (Harboe Knudsen) and Yalçın-Heckmann both contributed to the Morris and Polese volume.

Recent efforts to clarify Moldova's poverty levels have in fact created new moral narratives that never quite match the realities of everyday life. In Moldova the disjuncture is recognised by villagers themselves, who make use of the Soviet narrative of the countryside's 'wealth' and progressive development to contest the new narrative of food-related poverty. In the countryside informants point out that the climate is favourable, the land is fertile and food is easily abundant. 'We are not dying of hunger,' they insist, drawing an implicit contrast to the famines that accompanied war and Soviet collectivisation, as well as to the self-image they hold from Soviet Moldova's role as a major agricultural producer. During the Soviet period, particularly under Brezhnev, Moldova was known as a 'little piece of heaven', a land of plenty and a favoured destination for military personnel and others who could choose where to live or retire. In this context villagers rhetorically ask why they themselves are now fleeing such a favourable place. The only answer they venture displaces responsibility to the state. The country, they say, is poorly run: if only there were regular cash salaries and a few more infrastructural amenities (e.g. indoor plumbing and trash collection), the countryside would again be a good place to live.

In this chapter, however, I have used the concept of the grey zone to show how multiple types of information come together to produce an image of poverty in rural Moldova that defies explanation, contestation and solution. The story of how Moldova so rapidly changed from a 'little piece of heaven' in the 1980s into 'Europe's poorest country' in the early 2000s is thus only partly a story of actual economic decline. It is equally a story of changing discourses about economy and poverty, international political relations and forms of statistical measurement. With closer interrogation of this second story, we come closer to understanding how moral narratives of poverty operate independently of the constraints and realities of daily life, yet ultimately come to shape people's assessments of their life circumstances, options and necessary actions.

Notes

1 For example, the introduction of the report on Moldova's poverty produced by Elena Laur begins: 'Moldova remains the poorest country of Central and Eastern Europe, and one of the poorest in the world (according to the Human Development Index, Moldova held 104 place in 1999 and 108 in 2003)' (2005, 1). Laur's use of the Human Development Index (HDI) is an interesting choice because the index is a composite that does not measure poverty per se; moreover, Moldova has a ranking of Medium Human Development. Read carefully, however, her point is that Moldova was falling on the list during the 1999–2003 period; indeed, it continued to fall in the subsequent decade, ranking 114th in 2014, and it remains the lowest-ranked country in continental Europe by a significant degree (Albania, the next lowest, is ranked 95th) (UNDP 2014, 159). Moldova is indeed the poorest country in Europe according to the UN's Multidimensional Poverty Index, but the results are not so stark: 0.2 per cent of the population are deemed to be in 'severe poverty' and 5.2 per cent near this level. Rates in other southeastern European countries ranked much higher in the HDI are similar, for example Albania (0.1/7.2 per cent), Bosnia-Herzegovina (0/3.2 per cent) and Montenegro (0.5/1.3 per cent). Moldova's Multinational Poverty Index is also significantly less drastic than the countries ranked just above it in the HDI, e.g. Bolivia (7.8/17.3 per cent) and Gabon (4.4/19.9 per cent). See http://hdr.undp.org/en/content/table-6-multidimensional-poverty-index-mpi (accessed 30 November 2014).

2 'Food insecurity' can be broadly defined as an inability to access, physically or economically, food that meets dietary needs and preferences. See the explanation of the concept provided by the World Health Organization, as agreed at the 1996 World Food Summit – available at: http://www.who.int/trade/glossary/story028/en/ (accessed 27 October 2013).

3 Examples of official reports that stress Moldova's status as the 'poorest country in Europe' include, for example, those by the Ministry of Economy (2012) and the World Bank (2004); the International Monetary Fund report interestingly modifies the country's status to 'one of the poorest in Europe' (2013, 3). As indicated above, this status is not ascribed incorrectly. Rather, what I want to stress is the degree to which the country's poverty is dramatised to shockingly 'un-European' levels within Europe. A separate paper would be necessary to elaborate this argument.

4 Research during 2009–10 was undertaken in the context of the Research Group on Economy and Ritual at the Max Planck Institute for Social Anthropology. Earlier periods of relevant field research were funded by the International Research and Exchanges Board (IREX) and the National Endowment for the Humanities (NEH) through the

American Council of Teachers of Russian/American Council for Collaboration in Education and Language Study (ACTR/ACCELS, now collectively the American Councils for International Education). I gratefully acknowledge the support of each of these institutions; the responsibility for the data and interpretations presented here remain mine alone.

5 For descriptions of the main features of Bessarabia's pre-Soviet poverty, including landlessness, food scarcity, disease and high rates of illiteracy, see Kaba (1919), Livezeanu (1995) and Hitchins (1994).

6 The essay was originally published by Levi in *The Drowned and the Saved* (New York: Vintage Books, 1988).

7 My analysis is guided by Eric Wolf's (1999) delineation of four modalities of power. In my reading, Levi implicitly addresses the first three (i.e. innate capacities of an individual; the ability of one individual or group to assert its will over another; and the forces that delimit behaviour in any given situation), but does not quite address the fourth modality ('structural' power), in which ideas are operationalised in and through structures. Yet this fourth modality is crucial for understanding the subtle relationship between grey zones and black-and-white cognitive and moral schema, because it enables an understanding of how the 'relations that command economy and polity, and those that shape ideation interact to render the world understandable and manageable' (Wolf 1999, 5–6).

8 The low figure of 1.56 ha is provided by a paper published by cadastral experts in the Ministry of Agriculture (Guțu, Gorgan and Guțu 2009, 2) who advocate a new land redistribution programme that would overcome the process of excessive plot fragmentation in many locales. A UN report (2012, 7) calculates the average as 1.8 ha, but notes that a full 25 per cent of private owners hold less than 1 ha. This report records an average garden allotment of 0.21 ha, which is slightly smaller than the allocations made in Răscăieți during the 1980s, but nearly double the 0.12 ha currently available to new households. Yet another study (Petrick 2000, 12) indicates that the median size of a private plot is 2 ha. Although all three sources use official data, the differences arise because there is no formal differentiation in official statistics between the private landholdings of large agricultural firms, individual commercial farmers, allocations to former farm workers and the holdings of people who have land but did not receive shares during decollectivisation. Petrick (2000, 12) provides the best discussion.

9 Until 2007 newly formed families were eligible for 0.15 ha allotments for housing and gardens, but the allotment size has since been decreased to 0.12 ha in accordance with national law. In the 1980s the parcels were even larger – 0.25 ha, which may explain to some extent why young families find it appealing to buy existing houses, rather than accept the free allotments from the mayor's office. In some years families received additional allotments for each child as well.

10 Petrick's research turned up a different level of inconsistency: the income generated by farming was not enough to cover costs related to the use of machinery or pesticides. Under such conditions he would have expected fewer households to farm than actually did. Like my informants, he claimed to be unable to explain how or why they could afford farming.

11 In addition to extended participant observation, I conducted a household survey with 25 households. Although the sample was small, it was representative (see Cash forthcoming for details); more importantly, it provided quantified information for trends and patterns that appeared in other qualitative forms.

References

Betti, G., F. Gagliardi, A. Lemmi and V. Verma. 2012. 'Subnational indicators of poverty and deprivation in Europe: Methodology and applications'. *Cambridge Journal of Regions, Economy and Society* 5: 129–47.

Cash, J. R. 2011. 'Capitalism, nationalism, and religious revival: Transformations of the ritual cycle in postsocialist Moldova'. *Anthropology of East Europe Review* 29(2): 181–203.

_____. 2013. 'Charity or Remembrance? Practices of Pomană in Rural Moldova'. Max Planck Institute for Social Anthropology Occasional Paper no. 144.

_____. Forthcoming. 'How much is enough? Household provisioning, self-sufficiency and social status in rural Moldova'. In S. Gudeman and C. M. Hann (eds), *Oikos and Market: Explorations in Self-Sufficiency after Socialism*. New York and Oxford: Berghahn Books.

Csaki, C. and Z. Lerman. 2001. 'Land Reform and Farm Restructuring in Moldova: A Real Breakthrough?' The Hebrew University of Jerusalem, Department of Agricultural Economics and Management Discussion Paper 5.01. Available at: http://departments. agri.huji.ac.il/economics/en/publications/discussion_papers/2001/index.htm (accessed 28 February 2013).

Goerlich, D. and M. Luecke. 2011. 'International labour migration, remittances and economic development in Moldova'. In D. Kaneff and F. Pine (eds), *Global Connections and Emerging Inequalities in Europe: Perspectives on Poverty and Transnational Migration*, 57–78. London: Anthem Press.

Gorton, M. and J. White. 2003. 'The politics of agrarian collapse: Decollectivisation in Moldova'. *East European Politics and Societies* 17(2): 305–31.

Guțu, V. G., M. Gorgan and D. Guțu. 2009. 'Privatizarea – Premisă obiectivă a creării sistemului cadastral' (Privatisation – The objective premise for creating a cadastral system). *Studia Universitatis* 28(8): 50–67.

Guyer, J. 2004. *Marginal Gains: Monetary Transactions in Atlantic Africa*. Chicago: University of Chicago Press.

Hitchins, K. 1994. *Rumania 1866–1947*. Oxford: Clarendon Press.

International Monetary Fund (IMF). 2013. 'Republic of Moldova: Poverty Reduction Strategy Paper – Joint Staff Advisory Note'. IMF Country Report no. 13/270. Available at: http://www.imf.org/external/pubs/ft/scr/2013/cr13270.pdf (accessed 11 November 2014).

Kaba, J. 1919. *Politico-economic Review of Basarabia*. Hoover Commission for Roumania.

Kaneff, D. and F. Pine (eds). 2011. *Global Connections and Emerging Inequalities in Europe: Perspectives on Poverty and Transnational Migration*. London: Anthem Press.

Keough, L. 2006. 'Globalizing "postsocialism": Mobile mothers and neoliberalism on the margins of Europe'. *Anthropological Quarterly* 79(3): 431–61.

Laur, E. 2005. 'The Brief Characteristic of Creating and Developing the Poverty Monitoring and Analysis System in the Republic of Moldova'. Paper prepared for the International Seminar on Poverty Measurement at the National Institute of Statistics and Economic Studies, Paris, 30 November–2 December. Available at: http://www.insee.fr/en/insee-statistique-publique/default.asp?page=colloques/pauvrete/pauvrete.htm (accessed 11 October 2012).

Lerman, Z. and D. Cimpoieș. 2006. 'Land consolidation as a factor for rural development in Moldova'. *Europe-Asia Studies* 58(3): 439–55.

Levi, P. 2008. 'The Gray Zone'. In A. Jones (ed.), *Genocide*, vol. 3, 188–206. London: Sage.

Livezeanu, I. 1995. *Cultural Politics in Greater Romania: Regionalism, Nation Building and Ethnic Struggle, 1918–1930*. Ithaca, NY: Cornell University Press.

Ministry of Economy of the Republic of Moldova. 2012. 'Poverty Report: Republic of Moldova, 2010–2011'. Available at: http://www.mec.gov.md/sites/default/files/poverty-report-republic-of-moldova-2010-2011.pdf (accessed 11 November 2014).

Morris, J. and A. Polese. 2014. *The Informal Post-socialist Economy: Embedded Practices and Livelihoods*. London: Routledge.

National Bureau of Statistics of the Republic of Moldova. 2010. Household Budget Survey. Available at: http://www.statistica.md/pageview.php?l=en&idc=263&id=2206 (accessed 28 February 2013).

_____. 2011. 'Minimul de existență în anul 2010'. Press release, 6 April. Available at: http://www.statistica.md/newsview.php?l=ro&idc=168&id=3367 (accessed 11 October 2012).

Petrick, M. 2000. 'Land Reform in Moldova: How Viable are Emerging Peasant Farms?' Institute of Agricultural Development in Central and Eastern Europe (IAMO) Discussion Paper no. 28. Available at: http://www.iamo.de/dok/dp28.pdf (accessed 28 February 2013).

Petropoulous, J. and J. K. Roth (eds). 2006. *Gray Zones: Ambiguity and Compromise in the Holocaust and its Aftermath*. New York: Berghahn Books.

Scheper-Hughes, N. 2007. 'The gray zone: Small wars, peacetime crimes, and invisible genocides'. In A. McLean and A. Leibing (eds), *The Shadow Side of Fieldwork: Exploring the Blurred Borders between Ethnography and Life*, 159–84. Malden, MA: Blackwell.

United Nations. 2012. 'Rapid Food Security and Vulnerability Assessment – Moldova'. Available at: http://www2.un.md/drought/2012/RapidAssessmentMoldova2012Final.pdf (accessed 28 February 2013).

United Nations Development Programme (UNDP). 2014. *The Human Development Report 2014 – Sustaining Human Progress: Reducing Vulnerabilities and Building Resilience*. New York: UNDP. Available at: http://hdr.undp.org/en/2014-report (accessed 11 November 2014).

Wolf, E. R. 1999. *Envisioning Power: Ideologies of Dominance and Crisis*. Berkeley: University of California Press.

World Bank. 2004. 'Recession, Recovery and Poverty in Moldova'. Europe and Central Asia Region, Human Development Sector Unit, report no. 28024-MD. Available at: http://www-wds.worldbank.org/external/default/WDSContentServer/WDSP/IB/2006/02/09/000160016_20060209172255/Rendered/PDF/280240ENGLISH0Recession0PAen01PUBLIC1.pdf (accessed 11 November 2014).

_____. 2011. *Migration and Remittances Factbook 2011*. Washington DC: World Bank. Available at: http://data.worldbank.org/data-catalog/migration-and-remittances (accessed 4 November 2014).

Yalçın-Heckmann, L. 2014. 'Is Informal Economy a Euphemism for Moral Economy? Thoughts on Azerbaijan's Moral Society and Informal State'. Talk given at the 'Ethnology Workshop' at the Max Planck Institute for Social Anthropology, Halle, 21 January.

Chapter 4

BROKERING THE GREY ZONES: PURSUITS OF FAVOURS IN A BOSNIAN TOWN

Čarna Brković

Jelena, a twenty-something law student from Bijeljina, a town in Bosnia and Herzegovina (hereon: Bosnia), told me one day in 2009 that if she ever got pregnant, she would ask Amela for help during the delivery. Amela was a medical doctor and her acquaintance living in Tuzla, a Bosnian town located less than an hour's drive away from Bijeljina across the Inter-Entity Boundary Line (that is, the internal Bosnian administrative border). Jelena's personal relationship with Amela was forged during several seminars on civil society and peace building they attended together. Discussing her lack of enthusiasm for Bosnian public healthcare, Jelena half-jokingly said: 'Naturally, I'll go to see Amela, I don't want these people here in Bijeljina to mutilate me.' Jelena did not really think there was a danger of being 'mutilated' during the future potential delivery, but she was convinced that a personal relationship with a medical doctor was a 'must' (*moranje*) in order to access decent healthcare. If something went wrong, Jelena said, Amela would do everything she could to help her because they were friends. This personal relationship carried more weight for Jelena than the fact that she and Amela lived in different Bosnian entities,[1] that they belonged to different ethnonational groups,[2] or that Jelena would most probably have to pay, officially, for the service out of her own pocket, because her official healthcare insurance did not cover procedures in Tuzla.[3] It went almost without saying that she would also give a gift to Amela, as a token of gratitude and as a mark of their friendship.

   Most people during my fieldwork in Bijeljina, conducted in 2009–10, similarly claimed that a personal relationship with doctors (as well as with social workers, municipal officials, state bureaucrats and so forth) was the most important thing for getting anything done with a degree of quality. It seemed that whenever people in Bijeljina needed to access a public service (a healthcare treatment, social welfare provision, an official document, a job and so on) they followed institutional procedures *and* utilised personalised relations. These personalised relations are called *veze* (singular: a *veza*, literally meaning 'relation', as well as 'connection') or *štele* (singular: a *štela*, literally meaning 'a relation that needs to be fixed'). My interlocutors also complained about the 'system' and the state, which pushed them to rely on such pursuits – they frequently talked about the local welfare systems and Bosnia itself as being dysfunctional, clientelist and corrupt. Bijeljinci (residents of Bijeljina) repeatedly claimed that *'ne možeš naći posao bez veze'* (you can't get job without relations), *'ne možeš se liječiti bez veza'* (you can't get healthcare treatment without relations), *'kod nas sve može i ništa ne može'* (here, everything is possible and nothing is possible), *'u ovoj državi ništa ne radi'* (nothing works in this state) and so forth.

Taking the notion of grey zones as an analytical prism, this chapter does not interpret *veze/štele* as remnants of Yugoslav socialism or as side-effects of a stalled postwar and postsocialist transformation. Instead, it approaches these relations 'as something in and of themselves' (see Harboe Knudsen and Frederiksen's introduction to this volume) – as relationships that allow people to actively negotiate the best possible welfare in the grey zone that marks the boundary between Bosnian 'state' and 'society'. Taking a cue from Alexander's (2002) emphasis on brokering as a practice of negotiating among different sets of knowledge and experience, this chapter suggests that Bosnians' widespread pursuit of *veze/štele* can be understood as an attempt to 'personalise the state'. That is, *veze/štele* include an active effort by people to locate themselves at the 'intersections', rather than 'interstices', of shifting and shrinking networks linking people to the state (Alexander 2002). Welfare arrangements, in Bosnia as elsewhere, are ambiguously positioned between a legal obligation of the state and the personal compassion of socially located persons. By pursuing welfare through *veze/štele*, Bijeljinci confirmed their (unequal) sociopolitical positions and senses of self, while navigating their way through the grey zones of intersections and interstices of the state and society.

The Grey Zones of Welfare

There was a widespread impression among Bijeljina's residents that practically everybody pursued *veze/štele*, for oneself or for someone else. In a piece of United Nations Development Programme (UNDP) research from 2008–09, 95 per cent of over sixteen hundred people across Bosnia said that *veze/štele* were required for access to public, state-run services (Nixon 2009, 79). The participants of the UNDP research identified job searching and healthcare as two key fields in which *veze/štele* were important. In the eyes of my interlocutors from Bijeljina, Bosnia appeared largely to be a 'network state', a state in which semiformal connections and clientelist networks 'can be found both *outside* the state institutions but also incorporated *within* and *passing though* institutional divisions such as ministries and administrative hierarchies' (Kononenko and Moshes 2011, 6, emphasis added). They claimed that *veze/štele* worked through the state institutions, not just separately from or outside of them.

Furthermore, *veze/štele* have also come to be an important element in the work of various international actors in Bosnia. The international community has been present in the country since the 1992–95 war, and consists of various humanitarian and developmental organisations, nongovernmental, governmental and intergovernmental agencies, and so forth. Its role in the country is personified by the Office of the High Representative (OHR).[4] The international community has been guided by a set of goals that include the development of civil society and the return of displaced persons and refugees to their former homes, in order to create a workable, multiethnic state with a pluralistic, democratic and market-based system (Bougarel, Helms and Duijzings 2007). Bougarel, Helms and Duijzings emphasise that, in attempting to reach these goals, 'the international community places strong political pressure on nationalists, but at the same time indirectly contributes to the financing of their clientelistic networks' (2007, 28; see also Deacon and Stubbs 1998 and Pugh 2003). New research indicates that the international organisations and actors in Bosnia even tend to use a '*štela*' way of relating in their internal affairs and decisions about employment (Koutkova forthcoming).

Numerous reasons exist for such fusion of personal relationships with the work of public actors, especially in the field of welfare. On the one hand, over the past two decades Bosnia has been undergoing postwar transformation alongside postsocialist transformation (Gilbert 2006). Under the close supervision of – and with financial assistance from – the international community, Bosnian state authorities and various international and local, public and private actors have engaged, with various degrees of success, in peace reconciliation processes (Duijzings 2007; Helms 2003), the reversal of war-related ethnic cleansing (Jansen 2011), the reconstruction and privatisation of public property (Jansen 2006), the construction of civil society (Stubbs 2007), state building and Europeanisation (Coles 2007; Helms 2006), and so forth.

The profound transformations of Bosnia have redefined the relationship between the state and society in ways that are hard to predict and control. However, attempts to personalise the state should not be understood as the results of the inconsistencies that abounded in the Bosnian postwar and postsocialist transformations. In other words, *veze/štele* should not be understood as reasonable and sensible strategies that people use to overcome the faults of 'improper' markets or 'aberrations' in a developing democracy – because such an interpretation implicitly defines how politics and economy ought to work in a 'proper' state.

Instead, if we take them as 'something in and of themselves', the very need to broker access to public welfare and to personalise the state could be understood as a contextually specific way of enacting globalised changes in what the state is, how it relates to society and what it should be responsible for. Politics of survival and wellbeing are increasingly changing shape across the world (Fassin 2012; Fraser 2003; Ticktin 2011). In many contexts healthcare and social protection are increasingly moving away from something that the state is legally obligated to provide to all its residents and towards self-responsibility, flexibility, compassion and moral duty (Clarke 2004; Rose 2006; Stubbs and Zrinščak 2011). Du Gay demonstrates that new models of public management in UK welfare include sidelining traditional bureaucratic indifference in favour of an 'ethic of care for the other' (2008, 342), which means encouraging officials to conduct their administrative duties with a sense of compassion. In Italy responsibility for survival and wellbeing has gradually shifted from a legal obligation of the state to a matter of personal moral duty and humanitarian sentiment (Muehlebach 2012). Various actors that merge private economic and political interests with public interests are redefining the roles and responsibilities of the state, in the West as much as in Eastern Europe (Wedel 2009).

Similar changes can be traced in the welfare reforms in Bosnia as well. Public welfare has been continually changing in Bosnia since the early 1990s, as a part of broader postwar and postsocialist transformations. Efforts to 'build' the Bosnian state went hand in hand with attempts to redefine its meanings and practices. The state did not withdraw from people's lives, as much as it altered its roles, functions and relations with nonstate actors. Informed by persistent global modifications of the politics of survival and wellbeing, the internationally supervised reforms of the Bosnian public welfare system redefined the state's roles and responsibilities for people's survival and wellbeing (Deacon and Stubbs 2007). As a result, in the grey zone of Bosnian welfare arrangements, 'transformations have created a taken-for-granted reality of ambiguity' (Frederiksen and Harboe Knudsen, this volume). Instead of attempting to create a welfare system that evenly targets all Bosnian citizens, the reforms conducted within the complex administrative division of Bosnia have led to a situation where Bosnian state institutions provide some welfare services to only some citizens, based on their territorial residence (Maglajlić and Rašidagić 2007), as well as on the basis of personal relationships between public officials and citizens (Brković

2014). The 'uneven allocation of citizenship, which confers particular rights on some whilst denying those rights to others' (Stubbs and Zrinščak 2011, 6), is as much a consequence of the postsocialist reforms informed by various neoliberal policies as of clientelist politics or legacies of Yugoslav socialism. Leaving more than 25 per cent of Bosnians without any healthcare insurance (Maglajlić and Rašidagić 2011), the reforms have pushed many to cultivate social relations with 'the right people' when looking for healthcare. In such a context *veze/štele* provide a locally specific, historically meaningful way to actively manage one's own survival and wellbeing. By enabling people to be both citizens and socially located persons, *veze/štele* offer a way to navigate ambiguous conditions of the politics of survival and wellbeing in Bosnia.

Lack of Formal Consistency

Pursuits of *veze/štele* in Bosnia do not lend themselves easily to anthropological theorising, even though 'routing relations through persons [has become] the substance of anthropological empiricism' (Strathern 1995, 12). Speaking in very general terms, one of the most prominent analytical moves in social anthropology is to expose social relations and historically grounded practices by which the state, sex, gender, kinship, nation, body or the economy are produced and, through that, to undermine their presumable natural and self-evident qualities. The challenge with *veze/štele* is that it is almost vulgarly explicit that they are relations – they are literally called 'relations' in Bosnia – and that they are involved in reproduction of personhoods, of the social order and of the state (cf. Dunn 2004; Humphrey 2012). But *how exactly* they do this is often blurred when looked at through anthropological lenses. Such informal relations may challenge boundaries between 'corruption' and 'friendship' (Haller and Shore 2005), or 'commodities' and 'gifts' (Rivkin-Fish 2005; Stan 2012). *Veze/štele* have different degrees of formality and are not institutionalised, but they operate throughout institutions (Ledeneva 2006). They shape people's sense of self, but the systems that work through *veze/štele* may be despised – as is the case in Bosnia. And so forth.

Miller (2007) suggests that there are very few anthropological analytical tools through which social relations themselves can be looked at. Miller's argument is that anthropologists increasingly use the term 'relationship' without specifying what they mean by it. He suggests that the concept of a 'social relationship' contains a 'basic contradiction between its own normative aspect […] and the actual entity that constitutes that person at the time', and argues for a dialectic approach that focuses 'upon the discrepancy between this diversity of practice and the retained formality of [the] ideal', of what a relation ought to be (Miller 2007, 552). Similarly, Strathern (1995) shows that there are two disparate senses of relation – between ideas (its normative, formal sense) and between persons (its concrete, experiential sense) – and argues that anthropology draws conclusions about one (the abstract) from the other (the concrete).

This is where the challenge I have mentioned lies. Concrete pursuits of *veze/ štele* do not reveal an abstract, formal consistency, since, in my experience, they depended on the person who was making the pursuit and the people he or she could get in touch with. Similarly to *blat* in Russia, what one *veza/ štela* (relationship) entails another *veza/štela* does not have to (cf. Ledeneva 1998). For instance, it made sense for Jelena to plan to ask a person of a different ethnonational background (such as Amela) for help, because Jelena was very critical towards the widespread ethnonational politics in Bosnia (see Husanović 2011; Mujkić 2007). However, very few of my other interlocutors made similar assertions, while some explicitly stated that, taking into account war-related experiences and resentments, it was best not to expect Bosnian Serbs, Bosnian Croats and Bosniaks to provide favours 'to one another'. Thus, *veze/štele* sometimes reproduce ethnonational categories and people's sense of who they are as ethnonational beings – but this is not the case always and for everybody. As we will see, for Marija (another of my interlocutors, whose pursuit will be addressed in more detail later on) ethnonational identity was almost irrelevant in her attempt to secure a desired medical treatment for her mother. However, gendered relations gained importance in her pursuit, visible in the fact that her mother's doctor started flirting with Marija and that she was not sure what to do about this. Thus, *veze/štele* can involve sexist expectations – but, again, not always and not for everybody.

With regard to *blat* in Russia, and taking a cue from Wittgenstein, Ledeneva (1998) calls this 'family likeness' or 'family resemblance'. In this 'family likeness' type of relationship, entities we consider to be related do not have to have a single defining feature; instead, there is 'a complicated network of similarities and relationships overlapping and criss-crossing' (Ledeneva 1998, 38). The same can be said about *veze/štele* – these terms do not refer to a single, distinct type of a relationship, but to a broad sum of similar and criss-crossed relations.

In order to go beyond such a lack of formal consistency, this chapter looks at what *veze/štele* do 'in and of themselves', as an element of a grey zone between the state and society. Instead of addressing how *veze/štele* in postsocialist Bosnia may be theorised 'for critiquing fundamental concepts in western social science' (Rogers 2010, 13), including the 'state', 'market' or 'corruption', my aim is to explore how these relations work in everyday dealings with public welfare. In the ambiguous, grey zone between the state and society, *veze/štele* can be understood as a form of brokering practice. If they do not fit into distinct domains, it is precisely because *veze/štele* enable different people to cross domains – they allow Bosnians to actively work on getting as good a welfare provision as possible by negotiating different sets of knowledge and experience implicated in Bosnian welfare. As complex and recursive as any other kind of a relation is (Strathern 1995), *veze/štele* offer a contextually specific way to actively pursue ambiguous forms of welfare protection.

Different People Broker in Different Ways

For my interlocutors, engagements with public welfare, such as a visit to a doctor, often involved a lot of effort and sometimes a transferral of trust and knowledge. For instance, Marija contacted a large number of people – her family and friends, work colleagues and acquaintances – trying to find someone who could personally link her to relevant doctors. She had no prior clientelist bond in this context; rather, she got in touch with all the people who might have been helpful in finding one. In general, even when they could not find an appropriate *veza/štela*, Bijeljinci attempted to personalise the public healthcare system. When my interlocutors discussed their healthcare issues, one of the most prominent topics in conversation were persons. People did not necessarily talk at length about the symptoms of a medical condition or about the details of a treatment, but they avidly discussed medical doctors, nursing staff, their spouses, children and so forth. Oftentimes, people even remembered the names of former professors and mentors of medical doctors. Such efforts to personalise the relationship with an institution, preferably through a *veza/štela*, are very similar to the practice of brokering.

In her discussion of relationships between the state and society in eastern Turkey, Alexander (2002) suggests that brokering presents the practice of coordinating between related (but distinctive) orders of knowledge and meaning in a way that secures the highest benefits for the broker and the actors he or she represents. In Erzurum, a city in eastern Turkey, different orders of knowledge and meaning included local village social worlds, the state apparatus at the periphery and the more centralised manifestations of the state:

> Systems of meaning in villages coexist with central and local state constructions. Without a broker adept in making each system of meaning understandable to the others, villagers risk being caught in the interstices rather than the intersections of networks of communications that might connect them to the state. (Alexander 2002, 150)

The broker's role in this context was to navigate and translate across unpredictable and complex separations and comings together of the state apparatus and local sociality, in a way that enabled villagers to establish links with the state. The brokering role was institutionalised, in the sense that the broker was nominally a salaried state official, as well as a person appointed by village election, whose payment came from the contributions of villagers.

In Bijeljina, on the other hand, the broker was not a single person; most of my interlocutors pursued *veze/štele*. Everybody seemed to broker something, for oneself or someone else. Despite their lack of formal consistency, *veze/štele* had something in common – they allowed people to actively negotiate as good a provision of public welfare as possible, by translating the language of citizenship and legal obligation into a language of personal relations and moral duties, and back again. In the grey zone of quickly transforming relations between the state and society, *veze/štele* enabled people to personalise public welfare and healthcare systems and to be 'proactive', both as citizens and as socially located persons.

The work of Edmund Leach is useful for thinking about the practice of brokering. Leach (1993) makes a distinction between metonymical and metaphorical relations. In his terminology, a *metonymical link* between the entities A and B exists when A and B belong to the same 'code', or the same 'order'. The link between written musical notes is metonymical, since they belong to the same code of music notation. The link between the letters B and C is also metonymical, since they belong to the same 'context' of the English alphabet. On the other hand, a *metaphorical link* between the entities A and B exists when A and B do not share the same context, or the same order. The relation between musical notes written on a paper and the finger movements of a musician is metaphorical, since these two do not belong to the same code but require the translation of one (notes) into the other (finger movements).

In Leach's terms, *veze/štele* are metaphorical relations (rather than metonymical): people use *veze/štele* to translate the bureaucratic language of citizenship into the language of personalised relations and social positions, and back again. While nationalist Bosnian politicians often merge the two, discussing statehood in terms of kinship, the everyday dominant language in many public bureaucracies is one of 'socially produced indifference' (Herzfeld 1993) – that is, until one can find a *veza/štela* within a public institution. *Veze/štele* allow Bosnian inhabitants to actively pursue welfare not just as citizens, but also as gendered, ageing, nationalised, racialised beings. In my experience people constantly attempted to make metaphorical links: to be recognised by the state actors as citizens as well as socially located persons.

This is why people used to say that *everything is possible and nothing is possible*: what matters at one point for one person does not have to matter at another point for a different person. The grey zone at the boundary of the Bosnian state is not blurry, but rather moving and changing, depending on the person making the pursuit and the people being pursued. This might seem like a small difference, but I think it is important. 'Blurry' suggests a lack of distinction and a lack of shape. However, as we will see, Marija's pursuit of healthcare was quite distinctive in comparison with the pursuits of most men: she had to kiss someone in order to get what she needed. The kind of *veze/štele* people are able to pursue depends on their social position and location. Getting access to public resources through *veze/štele* is *different for different people*. People's social positions, personal histories and knowledge shape the ways in which they can broker access to public welfare. Keeping that in mind, let us turn to another pursuit of *veze/štele* in the town of Bijeljina.

Marija's Pursuit

One late and warm June afternoon in 2010, I was having a drink with Marija, a 28-year-old retail worker, and Marko, a 32-year-old bank employee. Marija and I had come to Marko's new home to congratulate him on deciding to move away from his parents and to rent a nicely furnished one-bedroom apartment. While we were drinking coffee, the discussion revolved around our parents and, inevitably, Marija's mother, who had recently had two heart attacks in a row. Since she was at a high risk of having a third and possibly fatal heart attack, Marija's mother was on the agenda of the next *konzilijum*. The *konzilijum* was a regular meeting of medical practitioners working in the same hospital, who made decisions about demanding cases. The *konzilijum* had to decide whether Marija's mother would stay in Bijeljina's local hospital or go to Tuzla or Belgrade for a surgical procedure.

Marija saw this as a matter of life or death of her mother – she did not want her to stay in Bijeljina's hospital, so she was frantically looking for a *veza/štela* to the members of the *konzilijum*. This task was difficult, since she did not know who those people were. Marija knew that her mother's doctor was in the *konzilijum*, but she was not sure he would recommend her for a procedure beyond the boundaries of the local healthcare system. Marija said that, although the doctor was married, he flirted with her without subtlety, and that she was not sure what to do about it. As we were chain-smoking and listening to Marija's ordeal, Marko mentioned that his mother had a cousin who was married to a doctor employed in Bijeljina's hospital. This piece of information changed the atmosphere in the room. Marija calmly, but firmly, asked Marko to call his mother and ask for the cousin's phone number. The next hour was spent in phone conversations between Marko and his mother, Marija and Marko's mother, Marko and his cousin, and Marija and the cousin. The cousin said her husband was away, but promised she would let him know about Marija and her mother.

By that point, we reasoned that even if the cousin's husband was not in the *konzilijum* (and thus not a direct *veza/štela*), he knew who the *konzilijum* members were. The smallest possible benefit of this afternoon event would be gaining this information about who the members were; the largest possible benefit would be influencing the *konzilijum* to send Marija's mother to another hospital. Not knowing what would happen, Marija called Marko several times over the following days, while Marko kept calling his cousin until he reached her husband, who promised to do whatever he could to help Marija's mother.

Marko was not the only person helping Marija to find a *veza*. When Marija took her mother to Bijeljina's hospital for the first time, she called friends to keep her company while she was waiting in front of the hospital. One of those friends called me to join them. While we were sitting on the bench in the hospital's yard, Marija made a dozen phone calls to her friends and work colleagues to let them know about her mother and to ask whether they had a strong *veza* in the hospital. Some of those people had some sort of a *veza/štela* in the hospital and Marija pursued those *veze/štele* further.

In the end Marija's mother was sent to Tuzla for a surgical procedure – which was an excellent solution in Marija's opinion. Marija bought a painting for her mother's doctor as a token of gratitude and, after a couple of months, she mentioned that, once, she almost kissed him on the lips.

Don't Blame the Player, Blame the Game: *Veze/Štele* and Their Discontents

Being different for different people, *veze/štele* refer to a wide array of criss-crossed social relations, from relations between close family and the closest friends, to those between people who do not know one another personally but through someone else. As we have seen, the relations Jelena planned to pursue were different from those brokered by Marija. To put it simply, Jelena and Marija had to broker in different ways because their social locations were different; they were different people. However, there was something that was the same for both Jelena and Marija. They had to actively work on brokering among different orders of knowledge and experience in order to get the healthcare they desired, while the exact shape of this brokering – the 'codes' and 'paths' that were available to them – depended on who and where they were socially.

Arguing against an interpretation of favours as a primarily economic activity, Humphrey (2012) suggests that the 'veering' way of doing things in Mongolia and Russia persists because it shapes people's senses of self. Favours among Mongolians and Russians 'bring into being indefinitely lasting relationships and circles of relations, and they confer a sense of self-worth within these arenas' (Humphrey 2012, 37). In this, she follows the direction of Dunn's (2004) argument that the system of favours in Poland, called *znajomości*, offers a way to interpret personhood as a composite of social relations. When people engage in *znajomości*, they reproduce their personhoods as entities embedded in and constituted from multiple links with other human beings (see also Auyero 2001; Auyero, Lapegna, and Page Poma 2009; Morris and Polese 2014). Alexander also suggests that understanding how people connect to one another requires 'a parallel exploration of personhood' (2002, 22) – because personhood, as a sociohistorically situated sense of self, emerges from sets of relationships. In a similar manner *veze/štele* in Bosnia cannot be encapsulated by the field of economic activity. The pursuits discussed in this chapter were more than economic strategies, for they shaped who people were and how they perceived one another. *Veze/štele* recreated people's social positions, subjectivities and unequal power relations. But, there is an important difference from Humphrey's case, located in the widespread criticism people directed towards the state for necessitating that things had to be done in a veering way.

Humphrey notes that in Mongolia, people 'are used to, prefer, and value highly acting in this [veering] way' (2012, 24). However, people do not need to appreciate or like the strings that shape them in order to be shaped by them (cf. Larson 2008). Rather than valuing it, in Bijeljina my interlocutors criticised the state, which pushed people to pursue jobs and healthcare through *veze/štele*. They discussed *veze/štele* as a strategy one used when one had to, and they criticised the 'system' for such 'abnormality'. This criticism was, indeed, a way to remove the responsibility for *veze/štele* from oneself to the system, the state or society. It can be summarised by the idea to 'not blame the player, but blame the game'. Still, this criticism revealed that while the Bosnians I spoke to may have been shaped by *veze/štele*, they did not like pursuing them. Instead, they expressed yearnings for a 'normal state' – that is, for predictability and certainty in everyday life (Jansen 2015).

Therefore, I suggest that *veze/štele* persist in Bosnia not because people prefer getting things done through them, but because *veze/štele* are implicated in the reproduction of power relations and, through that, subjectivities. The kinds of *veze/štele* you can access reveals how powerful you are – they illuminate the social worlds through which you can broker and reproduce your position within them.

Conclusion

This chapter has approached *veze/štele* as a form of brokering. These relations offer people a historically meaningful way to actively work on protecting their own survival and wellbeing, and thus to ensure they will be located at the intersections, rather than the interstices, of the Bosnian state apparatus. I have used Leach's terms to suggest that *veze/štele* are not metonymical relations, those which connect entities of the same order and the same code. They are, rather, metaphorical relations that enable people to broker across state and society and to navigate various personal expectations and institutional requirements.

Among my interlocutors the success of the pursuit of *veze/štele* depended on many things – on the kind of a favour one needed (a permanent job in a state institution, a visit to a doctor, a passport, to be included on the list of welfare recipients); on the kind of already-existing relationship between the pursuer and his or her *veza/štela* (how close they were, how well connected they were, how much they appreciated one another); on the respective social positions of the pursuer and his or her *veza/štela*; on the prior relations among people connecting them, and so forth. There was no recipe for *veze/štele*, but rather a variety of possibilities. For instance, it was impossible to know with certainty whether the *konzilijum* would have made the decision to send Marija's mother to another healthcare centre without any external influence, or which of the *veze/štele* Marija pursued was the most useful. In order to increase her mother's chances of survival, Marija had to be a broker who translated institutional rules and procedures of eligibility into personal fondness and willingness to help. Marija's ordeal does not indicate a 'recipe' for a successful outcome as much as it illuminates the importance of the pursuit itself.

I have suggested that these pursuits of relations were resilient to change not because people prefer conducting them – indeed, my interlocutors openly criticised the system working in the veering way. Instead, they persist because they are implicated in power relations and the reproduction of senses of self.

That such efforts to 'personalise the state' have significant effects on the distribution of public resources reveals that the boundary between the state and society in Bosnian welfare is a grey zone, a context where 'the emergence of such forms of suspicion, doubt, uncertainty and ambiguity may gain a sense of *ordinariness*' (Frederiksen and Harboe Knudsen, this volume). In the Bosnian 'welfare assemblages' (Lendvai and Stubbs 2009) exceptions and ambiguities abound, reflecting not just residues of local historical legacies – or complexities of postwar administrative divisions to entities, cantons, and the district – but also neoliberal ideas about the state's responsibility for welfare (cf. Collier 2011; Stubbs 2014). Although *veze/ štele* are certainly shaped by legacies of Yugoslav socialist bureaucratic systems (cf. Horvat 1969), they should not be understood as traces of the 'local' and the 'culturally specific', hidden within the (internationally supervised) modernisation of the Bosnian state. Instead, they allow Bosnians to enact, in a locally meaningful way, various new ideas about self-responsible, proactive and flexible citizenry, created during the postwar and postsocialist transformation. *Veze/štele* turn the exceptional into the rule and the indefinable into the norm – and this is where their contemporary importance should be looked for.

Getting welfare protection often depends on someone's personal will, compassion and judgement. The inability to know whether the desired state services and funds will be available – and if so, in what way – has become a rule, rather than an exception. Brokering access to healthcare and social welfare in Bosnia enables a clientelist modality of power to flourish: some people can decide whether or not to grant access to public resources to other people on the basis of good will and personal judgement. Navigating the 'net', that is, pursuing all people who can potentially be a *veza/štela*, is the way to deal with this uncertainty – although it recreates uncertainty every step of the way.

Notes

1 The state of Bosnia and Herzegovina consists of two entities officially created at the end of the 1992–95 war: the Republic of Srpska and the Federation of Bosnia and Herzegovina. Bijeljina is located in the Republic of Srpska, while Tuzla is located in the Federation of Bosnia and Herzegovina.

2 Jelena sometimes talked about herself as a Bosnian Serb and sometimes as a Bosnian citizen who does not want to have any ethnonationality, while she saw Amela as a Bosnian citizen and, ethnonationally, as a Bosniak (Bosnian Muslim).

3 Bijeljina and Tuzla belong to different healthcare systems within Bosnia – Bijeljina is a part of the healthcare system of the Republic of Srpska, while Tuzla is a part of the healthcare system of the Tuzla canton in the Federation of Bosnia and Herzegovina. Bosnia has 13 different healthcare systems, which coincide with its internal administrative entity, cantonal and district boundaries.

4 The OHR is an international institution set up after the 1992–95 war to oversee the implementation of the peace agreement in Bosnia and Herzegovina. It has strong governmental functions, which include the potential to enact laws and to remove elected officials from state positions.

References

Alexander, C. 2002. *Personal States: Making Connections between People and Bureaucracy in Turkey*. Oxford: Oxford University Press.

Auyero, J. 2001. *Poor People's Politics: Peronist Survival Networks and the Legacy of Evita*. Durham, NC: Duke University Press.

Auyero, J., P. Lapegna and F. Page Poma 2009. 'Patronage politics and contentious collective action: A recursive relationship'. *Latin American Politics and Society* 51(3): 1–31.

Bougarel, X., E. Helms and G. Duijzings (eds). 2007. *The New Bosnian Mosaic: Memories, Identities and Moral Claims in a Post-war Society*. Aldershot: Ashgate.

Brković, Č. 2014. 'Scaling humanitarianism: Humanitarian actions in a Bosnian town'. *Ethnos: Journal of Anthropology*. Available at: http://www.tandfonline.com/doi/abs/10.1080/00141844.2014.912246?journalCode=retn20#.VF_RC_msV2J (accessed 9 November 2014).

Clarke, J. 2004. *Changing Welfare, Changing States: New Directions in Social Policy*. London: Sage.

Coles, K. 2007. *Democratic Designs: International Intervention and Electoral Practices in Postwar Bosnia-Herzegovina*. Ann Arbor: University of Michigan Press.

Collier, S. J. 2011. *Post-Soviet Social: Neoliberalism, Social Modernity, Biopolitics*. Princeton and Oxford: Princeton University Press.

Deacon, B. and P. Stubbs. 1998. 'International actors and social policy development in Bosnia-Herzegovina: Globalism and the "new feudalism"'. *Journal of European Social Policy* 8(2): 99–115.

_____ (eds). 2007. *Social Policy and International Interventions in South East Europe*. Cheltenham: Edward Elgar.

Du Gay, P. 2008. '"Without affection or enthusiasm": Problems of involvement and attachment in "responsive" public management'. *Organization* 15(3): 335–53.

Duijzings, G. 2007. 'Commemorating Srebrenica: Histories of violence and the politics of memory in eastern Bosnia'. In X. Bougarel, E. Helms and G. Duijzings (eds), *The New Bosnian Mosaic: Identities, Moralities and Moral Claims in a Post-war Society*, 143–66. London: Ashgate.

Dunn, E. C. 2004. *Privatizing Poland: Baby Food, Big Business, and the Remaking of Labor*. Ithaca, NY: Cornell University Press.

Fassin, D. 2012. *Humanitarian Reason: A Moral History of the Present*. Berkeley: University of California Press.

Fraser, N. 2003. 'From discipline to flexibilization? Rereading Foucault in the shadow of globalization'. *Constellations* 10(2): 160–71.

Gilbert, A. 2006. 'The past in parenthesis: (Non)post-socialism in post-war Bosnia-Herzegovina'. *Anthropology Today* 22(4): 14–18.

Haller, D. and C. Shore (eds). 2005. *Corruption: Anthropological Perspectives*. London: Pluto Press.

Helms, E. 2003. 'Women as agents of ethnic reconciliation? Women's NGOs and international intervention in postwar Bosnia-Herzegovina'. *Women's Studies International Forum* 26(1): 15–34.

_____. 2006. 'Gendered transformations of state power: Masculinity, international intervention, and the Bosnian police'. *Nationalities Papers* 34(3): 343–61.

Herzfeld, M. 1993. *The Social Production of Indifference: Exploring the Symbolic Roots of Western Bureaucracy*. Chicago and London: University of Chicago Press.

Horvat, B. 1969. *An Essay on Yugoslav Society*. New York: International Arts and Sciences Press.

Humphrey, C. 2012. 'Favors and "normal heroes": The case of postsocialist higher education'. *HAU: Journal of Ethnographic Theory* 2(2): 22–41.

Husanović, J. 2011. 'Upravljanje životom kroz biopolitičke/tanatopolitičke režime u Bosni i Hercegovini: Bauci emancipativne politike' (Governing life through biopolitical/ thanatopolitical regimes in Bosnia and Herzegovina: The spectres of emancipatory politics). In D. Majstorović and V. Turjačanin (eds), *U okrilju nacije: Etnički i državni identitet kod mladih u Bosni i Hercegovini* (In the nation's embrace: Ethnic and state identity among youth in Bosnia and Herzegovina), 266–78. Banja Luka: Centar za kulturni i socijalni popravak.

Jansen, S. 2006. 'The privatisation of home and hope: Return, reforms and the foreign intervention in Bosnia-Herzegovina'. *Dialectical Anthropology* 30: 177–99.

———. 2011. '*Refuchess*: Locating Bosniac repatriates after the war in Bosnia-Herzegovina'. *Population, Space and Place* 17: 140–52.

———. 2015. *Yearnings in the Meantime: 'Normal Lives' and the State in a Sarajevo Apartment Complex*. Oxford: Berghahn Books.

Kononenko, V. and A. Moshes (eds). 2011. *Russia as a Network State: What Works in Russia When State Institutions Do Not?* New York: Palgrave Macmillan.

Koutkova, K. Forthcoming. '"The king is naked": Internationality, informality and *k'o fol* state-building in Bosnia'. In S. Jansen, Č. Brković and V. Čelebičić (eds), *Negotiating Social Relations in Bosnia and Herzegovina*. London: Ashgate.

Larson, J. L. 2008. 'Ambiguous transparency: Resumé fetishism in a Slovak workshop'. *Ethnos: Journal of Anthropology* 73(2): 189–216.

Leach, E. 1993. *Culture and Communication: The Logic by which Symbols are Connected*. Cambridge: Cambridge University Press.

Ledeneva, A. V. 1998. *Russia's Economy of Favours: Blat, Networking and Informal Exchange*. Cambridge: Cambridge University Press.

———. 2006. *How Russia Really Works: The Informal Practices That Shaped Post-Soviet Politics and Business*. New York: Cornell University Press.

Lendvai, N. and P. Stubbs. 2009. 'Assemblages, translations, and intermediaries in South East Europe'. *European Societies* 11(5): 673–95.

Maglajlić, R. A. and E. K. Rašidagić. 2007. 'Bosnia and Herzegovina'. In B. Deacon and P. Stubbs (eds), *Social Policy and International Interventions in South East Europe*, 149–66. Cheltenham: Edward Elgar.

———. 2011. 'Socio-economic transformation in Bosnia and Herzegovina'. In M. Stambolieva and S. Dehnert (eds), *Welfare States in Transition – 20 Years after the Yugoslav Welfare Model*, 16–40. Sofia: Friedrich Ebert Foundation.

Miller, D. 2007. 'What is a relationship? Is kinship negotiated experience?' *Ethnos: Journal of Anthropology* 72(4): 535–54.

Morris, J. and A. Polese. 2014. 'Informal health and education sector payments in Russian and Ukrainian cities: Structuring welfare from below'. *European Urban and Regional Studies*. Available at: http://eur.sagepub.com/content/early/2014/03/30/096977641452 2081.abstract (accessed 9 November 2014).

Muehlebach, A. 2012. *The Moral Neoliberal: Welfare and Citizenship in Italy*. Chicago: University of Chicago Press.

Mujkić, A. 2007. 'We, the citizens of Ethnopolis'. *Constellations* 14(1): 112–28.

Nixon, N. 2009. *Veze među nama: Društveni kapital u Bosni i Hercegovini. Izvještaj o humanom razvoju za Bosnu i Hercegovinu* (The ties that bind: Social capital in Bosnia and Herzegovina. National human development report). Sarajevo: Razvojni program Ujedinjenih nacija (UNDP) u Bosni i Hercegovini.

Pugh, M. 2003. 'Protectorates and spoils of peace: Political economy in South-east Europe'. In D. Jung (ed.), *Shadow Globalization, Ethnic Conflicts and New Wars: A Political Economy of Intra-state War*, 47–69. London: Routledge.

Rivkin-Fish, M. 2005. 'Bribes, gifts and unofficial payments: Rethinking corruption in post-Soviet Russian health care'. In D. Haller and C. Shore (eds), *Corruption: Anthropological Perspectives*, 47–64. London: Pluto Press.

Rogers, D. 2010. 'Postsocialisms unbound: Connections, critiques, comparisons'. *Slavic Review* 69(1): 1–15.

Rose, N. 2006. *The Politics of Life Itself: Biomedicine, Power, and Subjectivity in the Twenty-First Century*. Princeton: Princeton University Press.

Stan, S. 2012. 'Neither commodities nor gifts: Post-socialist informal exchanges in the Romanian healthcare system'. *Journal of Royal Anthropological Institute* 18(1): 65–82.

Strathern, M. 1995. *The Relation: Issues in Complexity and Scale*. Cambridge: Prickly Pear Press.

Stubbs, P. 2007. 'Civil society or Ubleha?'. In H. Rill, T. Šmidling and A. Bitoljanu (eds), *20 Pieces of Encouragement for Awakening and Change: Peacebuilding in the Region of the Former Yugoslavia*, 215–28. Belgrade and Sarajevo: Center for Nonviolent Action.

_____. 2014. 'Thinking Reform Otherwise in the Semi-periphery: Agency, Flexibility and Translation'. Presentation at the Interpretative Policy Analysis panel 'Thinking and Performing "Policies Otherwise": Towards an Ethics and Politics of Policy Translation', Wageningen, Netherlands, 3–6 July.

Stubbs, P. and S. Zrinščak. 2011. 'Rethinking Clientelism, Governance and Citizenship in Social Welfare: The Case of Croatia'. Paper presented at the ninth annual ESPAnet conference 'Sustainability and Transformation in European Social Policy', Valencia, 8–10 September.

Ticktin, M. 2011. *Casualties of Care: Immigration and the Politics of Humanitarianism in France*. Berkeley: University of California Press.

Wedel, J. R. 2009. *Shadow Elite: How the World's New Power Brokers Undermine Democracy, Government, and the Free Market*. New York: Basic Books.

Part II

BORDERS

Chapter 5

GOOD NEIGHBOURS AND BAD FENCES: EVERYDAY POLISH TRADING ACTIVITIES ON THE EU BORDER WITH BELARUS

Aimee Joyce

The first time I encountered the Polish–Belarusian border I passed beyond it without realising. The marker was in the demesne of a church and something about its haphazard placement in the landscape did not resonate with my expectations of an international border. I had fallen into the trap of thinking of borders as they are drawn on maps: absolute, clear lines across space and place. But they are not. They are – as this book proposes – grey zones, blurred and imprecise, nebulous, difficult to locate, contradictory and insecure. The border is a physical place and also a process, one which has multiple inputs often called 'conceptual borders': history, landscape, economics, governance and culture (Kaneff and Heintz 2006; Paasi 1999). In my fieldsite in eastern Poland understanding the border as a place and process resonated strongly. Each of the conceptual borders above had their own boundary line and together they ensured that the frontier on which my fieldsite stood was far from unchanging. The marker on the church lands was just the latest in a number of signs intended to draw a clear line where none existed. In what follows I posit that one of the processes destabilising the idea of a singular, static and timeless border in my fieldsite was that of alternative, supplementary and peripheral trading practices. How these practices were undertaken and discussed was part of a constantly constructed, refined and reconstructed border grey zone where the concept of the 'inside' remained potent (Green 2005; Perera 2007, 2009).

My particular approach to grey zones emerges from the work of anthropologists interested in corruption and informal networks, particularly Wolf (1966) and Robertson (2006). In an article called 'Kinship, friendship and patron–client relationships in complex societies' Wolf explores the resources and organisations that exist in those zones perceived as the 'grey areas of the map' by the 'key centres of control' and the relationships between these two categories (1966, 6). Robertson draws on the existing literature on moral ambiguity and grey zones (Levi 2013 [1986]), approaching corruption as an 'epistemological puzzle' that, despite ethnographic inquiry, is 'still adrift in Cartesian ambiguities', caught unproductively in discussions of legality/ illegality or formal/informal networks (2006, 11). His tentative solution to the puzzle seems to hinge on a renewed anthropologically engaged and body-aware approach to the areas that corruption operates within, an approach that privileges how people undertake and speak about corruption and do not seek to impose discursive categories in a top-down manner.

This chapter situates itself between Wolf's interest in how informal structures can run parallel to the state while concurrently shaping and being shaped by it, and Robertson's call to focus on processes and practices, and not just the relationship between the informal and formal (Wolf 1966; Robertson 2006). To achieve this I look at the stories of traders and local residents and some of the practices of trading that were employed in a constant drawing and redrawing of the 'inside' group. Of specific interest is my respondents' frequent use of the word *dobrosąsiedztwo* (good neighbourliness) when discussing cross-border trade with Belarus and Ukraine. If the border is a dialectical process, constantly being formed in the interaction between conceptual and literal boundaries (Kaneff and Heintz 2006), what role do ideas of neighbourly relations with non-EU states play? Bruns and Miggelbrink define small-scale trade and smuggling as primarily depending on the 'exploitation of differences in prices and exchange rates over time and space via circulation activities' (Williams and Baláž 2002, 323, cited in Bruns and Miggelbrink 2012, 2). I intend to demonstrate that of equal importance is the creation and maintenance of social and kin relations across time and space, which are at the centre of cross-border trade in the Polish–Belarusian borderlands. In doing this I will also be asking if trading practices based on a refusal to recognise the validity of the new EU border are proof of simple alienation from the project of state maintenance in Eastern Europe, or if they represent an attempt to overcome a state-led production of border-space.

Methodological Considerations

Haller and Shore begin their edited book on corruption with the assertion that few anthropologists start fieldwork intending to research corruption. Instead the anthropologist begins to research corruption as it is of interest to their respondents or a practice they encounter as part of their day-to-day life in the field (Haller and Shore 2005). This was most certainly the case with my own focus on cross-border trade. While conducting my primary research on religion and landscape I met and got to know people involved in cross-border trade. Alongside this, despite the fact that most of the town's residents were not involved in trading, smuggling was a practice that was widely talked about.

This chapter is based on data collected during a year of fieldwork (2011–12) in a small town located between two of the official border crossings from Poland to Belarus. The research is broadly based on the anthropological long-term participant observation model (Russell Bernard 2006). Throughout my time in the village I conducted interviews and attended the various events that created the cyclical rhythm of the town. I also interviewed members of local government and studied the town's history. However, when it came to researching cross-border trade and smuggling my methods were more haphazard. Most of the interviews were conducted around the kitchen tables of my respondents or their acquaintances. While I frequently observed and talked to people when the goods arrived in the town, I never managed to observe the journey across the border. The traders I knew felt uncomfortable with the idea of my presence, firstly because I was a researcher and secondly because I was someone without any of the practical skills of a trader. I did frequently travel to the large open-air market near to the train station and border crossing in Terespol, as there I was able to meet and speak with traders about their practices. I decided against researching the legal aspects of cross-border trade in this area, instead basing my discussions of legality on what interviewees and respondents said and practised. As such, throughout my face-to-face interviews I made a point of not asking people if they were legally or illegally transporting goods. I was interested in how people understood the relationship between trading, the border and the state from the perspective of day-to-day life in the town.

The topic of this chapter has also impacted how I have presented my data. As Robertson makes clear, the legal status of corruption is often an obstacle to writing up the research we do (2006). I have made the decision to obfuscate where the information presented was gathered. The people quoted and discussed have been anonymised, no real background on how we met is given, and frequently when I found myself writing about people who were too easily recognised, I combined aspects of their narratives with those of other respondents to ensure that they are unidentifiable.

Some Theoretical Considerations

What first encouraged me to pay closer attention to the stories and practices of importing goods in my fieldsite was the ordinariness that suffused the topic. Growing up in an Irish harbour village I had heard tales of smugglers before, but they were steeped in the heroic folklore tradition. I was in the town to research everyday religion and I found myself confronted with a kind of everyday smuggling, conceived of as cross-border trade by my respondents. When I speak of 'the everyday' I am not just concerned with the ordinary. The phrase contains implicit references to the cyclical nature of the ordinary, to the uncatalogued, habitual and routine nature of life, how so much of what we do is left unexamined or is almost impossible to grasp outside of its context (Elden 2004; Lefebvre 2008a [1947], 2008b [1961], 2008c [1981]). Cross-border trade was deeply embedded in the habitual activities of the town. People smoked Russian cigarettes and drank Belarusian vodka when they visited one another's homes. The local Eastern Orthodox church had hymn books from Ukraine and the clothes in the town's small second-hand shop had Cyrillic tags. A positive local attitude to the ideal of a borderland identity was apparent in the ubiquity of non-Polish goods in the town. Cross-border trade was not an issue of legality or illegality; it was about *dobrosąsiedztwo*, good neighbourliness. In this case the neighbours were Belarus and, sometimes, Ukraine. Defining these countries as neighbours implies they are part of the same community and discreetly challenges the demarcation that defines both as outsiders (to the EU and to the Polish state).

When the idea of a 'fieldsite' was first challenged by many, including Gupta and Ferguson, there was a call for a focus on borderlands and other 'hybrid' or marginal spaces (1997). This seemed to hark back to the work of Barth (1969), who in approaching the study of identity and ethnicity in transborder regions helped to spur the initial interest in borderlands. Approaches to border studies have continued to multiply recently. Donnan and Wilson (2012) created a companion guide to border studies that asked for approaches to the border which saw it as a process as much as a product. Kaneff and Heintz have also drawn attention to the dialectic nature of the border, stating that 'literal borders and conceptual boundaries [are] complementary processes that sometimes reinforce each other, sometimes subvert each other' (2006, 8). More recently Mezzadra and Nielson (2013) have used this struggle over the production of the border as a method to explore questions of global capital. This focus on the border as a process, production and method agrees with my own understanding of borderlands, which initially grew from Pine and Pina-Cabral's *On the Margins of Religion* (2008) and Sarah Green's *Notes from the Balkans* (2005). Pine and Pina-Cabral's understanding of marginality as a dynamic process and of the capacity for peripheral practices to become hegemonic or to disappear altogether prompted them not to speak of borders but of grey zones (2008). Green's work focuses on how marginality is constituted and understood in borderlands and their grey zones from the perspective of those who live there (2005). She brings the importance of 'indeterminacy' to the fore: how a place can be fractal, lacking edges, beginnings or ends (Green 2005, 135). Her dual focus on the ordinariness and the ambiguity of borders was particularly applicable to my own data on the border and interest in everyday life. Such approaches remind us that the state still has a controlling role in the maintenance of the 'nation', but that its project is incomplete when lived as a part of everyday life (Mezzadra and Nielson 2013).

This idea of 'ordinariness' is at the centre of my discussion of cross-border trade. The trading researched here was an everyday practice. As I stated earlier in this section, I tend to avoid discussions concerning trade law in Poland and the EU to avoid replicating the unhelpful binary of illegal/legal. I opt instead to explore the nuanced relationships embedded in trading practices (F. von Benda-Beckman, K. von Benda-Beckman and Wiber 2006; Hart 1973). When I use the term legal in this piece it is as an emic term and its meaning changes dependent upon the context in which it is used.

Traders' Relations to the Border

Tomasz has an eventful past, which includes a position in the Russian Soviet Army, a short and brilliant career as an entrepreneur in East Germany, and a rebirth in the 1990s as a travelling trader. Finally, now older and ostensibly retired, he has returned to Poland. When I met him during my fieldwork he was getting by through an assemblage of erratic, short-lived construction jobs and trading. His experience as a trader in the initial postsocialist period was serving as a valuable inroad for his latest, even more questionably legal profession. In late June the weather is glorious in this part of Poland, and everywhere is saturated with pastoral greens and blues, which attract hundreds of tourists every year. I am sitting on the bench under the apple tree with my landlady and Tomasz, who is talking to us about the local economy. Earlier in the week I had been palmed off by the provincial council secretary when I asked her about the formal economy of the *gmina*.[1] As we sit in the sun trying to enumerate the spheres of economic interest within the town, Tomasz begins to expound on his favourite subject, Poland after the fall of socialism. The narrative is pure 'Wild West', trading and cheating your way to the newfound wealth the opening up of Poland had made available. There are stories of madcap midnight car journeys down back roads to avoid official border crossing. Not to mention Tomasz's ability to recollect perfectly the comparative prices of goods in Poland, Belarus and Ukraine at the time. It is an idealised past, which for Tomasz means one free of government interference (Boyer 2010). Tomasz's nostalgia, his contradictory longing for something lost and desire to return to it (Boym 2001), is not for socialist Poland but a very short-lived and specific period just after 1989, when gaps in governance allowed a vast grey zone to develop where semilegal economies flourished. He sees this period as a time when the future seemed newly opened up to opportunity and the ease with which goods moved through the town was an example of a new way of living. Now that is gone, Tomasz's nostalgia for this time is recognition that it is an 'impossible past', a comment on current Polish politics and a tacit acceptance of the politics of post–EU accession Poland (Creed 2010).

Poland's eastern border has a long history of movement. After World War II the decision was made to run the new postwar state border of Poland along the River Bug. To run the border along such a long-standing environmental divider makes it appear a natural and organic boundary. But as stated before, the Polish border has not always been here; it has shifted east and west. The Polish state disappeared completely in 1795, again in 1848 and once more between 1939 and 1945 (Snyder 2003). The border is not just a state border: it is also presented as a religious one. The perception that Poland is the 'most Catholic country in Europe' (Puhl 2012) is reiterated by the official promotional state website of Poland, which states that 'the Catholic Church in Poland is an institution which has always been associated with the concept of Polish statehood' (Polska n.d.). This reiteration has the effect of drawing a border around Poland that separates it from the Orthodoxy of Ukraine and Belarus, this border being especially clear on the eastern side. Again, the official website tells us that the Orthodox in the country are concentrated in the east and represent a Belarusian minority. Newspapers and official television stations (most recently Poczobut 2013) also draw a 'democracy' border along the east of Poland, contrasting Poland to the dictatorship of Łukaszenka in Belarus and the disharmony and corruption in post–Orange Revolution Ukraine. This was a particularly obvious during my fieldwork, when TVP Info, the public broadcast news station, was filled with stories of Yulia Tymoshenko's imprisonment,[2] along with the secret execution of two suspects in the Minsk Metro bombings.[3] Then there is the border of Europe, first imagined in the medieval period after the first Polish king converted his subjects to Christianity in 966, and again a popular motif since Poland joined the EU in 2004 (Zarycki 2007, 2011). It is among all these borders that the locals of my fieldsite have tenaciously built an identity as *po granica*, meaning 'from (or on) the border'. There have been, historically, official attempts to counter this tendency and Polonise the area, such as the 1947 Akcja Wisła (Operation Vistula), which transported a large number of Orthodox and Ukrainian Poles to the west of the country (Misiło 2012). Despite these actions, the town and surrounding area remain religiously diverse, and throughout my time there many people emphasised to me their connections to Belarus and occasionally to Ukraine. The practice of smuggling or grey zone trading was strongly associated with the idea of the border by many of my respondents. Trading and travelling traders have a long history in this part of Poland, and the ways people shared this history draws our attention to how locals chose to orientate themselves to an imagination of the borderlands that defied state control and alienation (Hobsbawm 1969). At first glance the local cross-border traders appeared to have much in common with Hobsbawm's 'social bandits'; they seemed to be antistate rebels supported and celebrated by the peasants they continued to live alongside (Hobsbawm 1969). In nomenclature this resistance to the 'outside', whether Polish, European or 'Russian', was apparent. My respondents referred to themselves frequently and playfully as *tutujszki*, meaning 'from here'. They did not use the term *kresy* (simply 'borderlands') often applied to this region, because it was negatively associated with areas of high sectarian tension on the border, and with Ukraine (Naumescu 2007; Hann 2009).

Talking and Practising Cross-border Trade

The local economy was an ad hoc assemblage of market exchange, house holding, barter, cross-border trading and gifting. Yet the apparent cacophony seemed to be ruled by a set of shared principles. The first of these was that the area was special and those perceived to be 'inside' or 'local' were fortunate.

Gifting was a significant part of the local economy, and was based on notions of kinship and neighbourly relations that extended beyond the strict geographical confines of the town. Family members in the big city, especially sons and daughters, were incorporated into this gift network. In this way the 'inside' of the town was extended to include those kith and kin separated by distance but considered relationally close. This strengthening of kinship ties in the face of economic uncertainty has also been observed by Pine (2001, 2002) in central and southern Poland. There were a number of minibuses that made daily or weekly journeys from the town to the local small city and from there on to the large cities of Poland. When the buses pulled into the town there would be a queue of women holding bulging, well-packed boxes and bags of foodstuffs, 'Russian' (a catch-all term for any former Soviet country) cigarettes, homemade decorations and small luxury items. For a nominal fee the driver would pack these gifts into the back of the bus and under seats. When he arrived at his destination he would be met by the intended recipients. I often asked the women I knew why they sent these gifts and was always told it was because the food from the town was better than anything you could buy in the big cities (see Pine 2002), or that the recipient did not know how to make a palm or other decorative object, or that Russian goods could only be purchased in the borderlands. This generation of women far from the centres of the Polish economy were concerned with helping their kin to live well. In the cities young people had come to rely on the baskets from the countryside, resituating the family as a vital form of social security (see Harboe Knudsen 2012, who has explored outcomes of this generational aspect of reliance on kin structures in Lithuania). The gifts circulating out into Poland tucked under the seats of minibuses did more than just build a safety net, they incorporated their recipients back into the town and reinforced the knowledge that the town was a source of nourishment not matched in the outside world.

Likewise the import of goods across the border drew on ideas of family and neighbours, but there were two separate discourses about trading linked to the different actors and methods of trafficking. The one I was most familiar with was small-level cross-border trading. This type relied on having a family member or close friend who lived in Belarus. On New Year's Eve I took a break from party preparations to stop for tea in a house that was eagerly awaiting the arrival of Belarusian kin. They appeared mid-afternoon, two older ladies laden with bags of all kinds, dressed in the recognisable *babcia* (grandmother) style. Over sweet tea, even sweeter Russian cakes and a variety of alcohols they began to unload their bags. Packed under tights and undergarments, wrapped carefully in old socks, were packs and packs of Russian cigarettes. Next they took out innocuous-looking water flasks and began to decant them into empty vodka bottles provided by their host. Finally, from the bottom of a bag filled with cheap plastic toys, they pulled out a bottle of expensive Belarusian liquor carefully deposited in the back of the packaging of a baby doll.

Getting to observe this arrival of goods happened late in my fieldwork when I knew the women involved well. The manner in which people closely guarded their methods of bringing goods over the border was reflected in the ambiguity around the legality of this trading. Traders never discussed the law unless directly asked. Even then there were a range of answers, but most told me you could bring in as much as you liked as long as you went to the right customs official. While this was a purposefully flippant response, it indicated how specialised a field the traders operated in. The skills they utilised had been built up over years, and although sometimes passed on by word of mouth, vitally, they were not widely known. It was commonly recognised that I was an anthropologist and as such sharing a skill or technique with me would render it useless as I might write about it. Conversely, because this grey zone trading was associated with a high degree of cunning, people loved to tell me stories about it. I was told how old women would tape the cigarettes to their waists and wear woolly jumpers to hide the bulges, or hide bottles of alcohol wrapped in undergarments among other 'unmentionables'. Even the trains were subject to this clever hide-and-seek operation. Cushions were pried off seats and hollows cut in the foam to hide bottles. Doors were broken so that they could be opened mid-journey. It is hard to tell how many of these examples were exaggerated. I was never on a train as it crossed the border at Terespol, though I frequently sat on trains heading there with doors flung wide open. Through speaking with my respondents, especially those not involved at all in this kind of trade, I began to see that the methods and stories I heard about were likely the kinds of trading practices widely known and practised only when customs officials were unlikely to be encountered. Once techniques were common knowledge it had to be assumed that border officials, often from the local area, were aware of them too. So using certain techniques required a combination of skill and a willingness to take a gamble. Approaching the right border official sounds straightforward, yet it is hard to imagine how you would know what 'approach' meant, or even how to figure out whom the 'right kind of official' was, without further knowledge or skill. Grey zone trading was a delicate act of conceal and reveal, and the story telling and exaggerated tales were part of this performance.

My favourite example of an exaggerated trading tale was about the smuggling of vodka. Twice I was told by respondents, with straight faces, that during the high summer vodka bottles were shoved into wooden barrels and floated down the River Bug. To make sure they did not stray they were tied to a rope that occasionally was tied to the Polish riverbank; at these points a man would sit fishing, and as the barrels arrived he would take out the correct number of bottles and send the barrel off down the next section of the river. When I repeated this story later I was roundly ridiculed for taking it seriously. There is undoubtedly an element of the comic to these stories, and whenever I heard them I thought of coyote or fox, those cunning but flawed tricksters of myth and proverb, who as often as not come out poorly in the stories told about them. The grey zone cross-border trade that some of the townspeople were involved in seemed to be morally understood as a playful and necessary act. I hesitate to call it smuggling, as such a title stresses its illegality, an aspect that I found was barely discussed by my respondents.

The jovial tales of traders stopped when people discussed large-scale smuggling. According to my respondents, these men were cut-throat operators. Stories of 'bad smugglers' were rarely told; they lacked the thick description and the gender equality of local-level efforts, with the perpetrators (always male) and their methods even more vaguely alluded to. It was hard for me to know whether people knew of the bad smugglers or if they simply spoke of them according to commonly recognised narratives of bandits from outside the local area. There was a very clear line drawn between the morality of cross-border traders who worked for the interests of local people and the town, and those who worked without regard for it. Often local animosities crept in to tales of outsider smugglers; they were not Polish and Belarusian smugglers, but Russian and Ukrainian ones. This delineation of traders based on ethnic origin also demonstrated that there was a nested understanding of outsiders and insiders, with the Russians at the very edge. No one knew what goods they smuggled; the borderlands were not the destination, merely a waypoint. Previously I had taken my newly inherited ancient Russian-made bike on a five-hour trip to a nearby beauty spot, only to return to an anxious chastisement from my landlady. 'What road had I used?' she asked, and looked visibly relieved when I told her I had taken the main roads only. 'Good, don't go by the forest roads,' she commanded, 'only use those roads in the tourist season.'[4] When I asked why, she informed me that the forest roads were used by smugglers in the winter and I did not want to see anything by accident.[5] I began to imagine these men as the 'big bad wolves' to the residents' 'cunning foxes'; they carried guns, hid in the forests and attacked unfortunate townsfolk.

This division of fox and wolf, which I make here, was expressed by my respondents through an insider/outsider discourse. In reality such a division is a crude line separating practices that often blur into one another and lose their clarity. Between the kindly *babcie* and the gun-carrying people traffickers are a range of other traders of differing shades of morality. Even those people who slot neatly into the archetypes are not necessarily fully contained by them. But that sense of getting one over on the authority figures included in the insider/ outsider binary is important. The town was presented as the centre of rude health and good fortune. Those inside the town physically and relationally were proffered as clever and adept at getting around outside forces threatening them, trying to curtail them or merely hampering them with unnecessary rules and regulations. The inside was a porous concept. It stretched beyond the town and into Krakow and Minsk, and it also excluded many of the inhabitants who did not fit certain criteria. The inside was constantly shifting and reshaping itself in relation to who was involved and what activities were undertaken. For cross-border trading the inside relied on the concept of the borderland. The town straddled the edge of the Polish state because of its physical location. Officially its interactions with those east of the River Bug were defined and controlled through the state's border practices. Engaging in illegal activities to overcome these practices does not directly challenge the alienation they beget. Rather the illegality of such acts moves the actor even further from the idea of the state and the citizen. In taking this alienation seriously we can see the traders are not social bandits in any significant sense. The rationale for cross-border grey zone trading was not a direct challenge to the state's power; the traders

I researched were not the rebel peasants of Hobsbawm's book (1969). Instead cross-border trading was motivated by a sense that those areas of Belarus close to the Polish border were closer to the town than the governments in Warsaw or Europe. This whole borderland region was one large grey zone, insecure and ambiguous. When I began to pay attention to trading I was surprised to find that my respondents had clearly oriented themselves to the East and not to the EU. This was despite the fact that many children and grandchildren now worked in EU states and that Poland was drawing closer and closer to 'Europe' at a national level. But the town's traders still considered the inhabitants of the Belarusian and Ukrainian frontiers their true neighbours: part of a borderland community, kith and kin relations that grew in the shadow of the state borders even as they expanded beyond them. All trading in the town was associated with *dobrosąsiedztwo*: good neighbourliness. The further you felt from the nation and its political and administrative centres the closer you felt to your neighbours, the cousins in Minsk and the childhood friends just the other side of the Terespol border crossing. While my respondents may remain removed from or subject to the Polish state's practices of bordering, the kind of grey zone trading discussed here enabled them to form closer ties to borderland neighbours and served to emphasise the primary importance of these ties. It is such closeness and the refusal to see the border as a division, instead making it part of a shared transnational borderland identity, that begins to challenge the state's bordering practices.

Conclusion

In light of the effects of the Balcerowicz Plan, Polish accession to the EU was presented not just as a mark of success: it was also envisioned as a way to guarantee economic stability and security (Hann 1994). However, this was not the reality for the people on the Polish border. Rather, it was continued poverty, large levels of youth emigration and a new set of regulations making legal cross-border trade more difficult. Despite recent efforts to encourage investment in the region, increasingly it is on the edge of the officially preferred centres of economic activity. Joining the EU meant money was to stay in the EU, even if this required people to buy the more expensive Polish goods. Such a situation is easily disempowering. However, as always in periods of economic insecurity, cross-border trade has become a way to avoid the uncertainty of poverty through the cultivation of neighbourliness, a way to mobilise social relationships against impersonal economic forces. When I asked respondents directly about the morality of trading in these grey zones, I was frequently told Belarus was a neighbour, and when dealing with money you ought to trust your neighbours.

Notes

1   *Gmina* roughly translates as 'municipality' or 'commune'.
2   Tymoshenko, the former prime minister of Ukraine and coleader of the Orange Revolution, was imprisoned in October 2011 for abuse of power. The trial was condemned as politically motivated by outside observers such as the Helsinki Committee on Human Rights. Throughout 2011 and 2012 the media reported frequently on Tymoshenko's ill health and ongoing trials.
3   After the 2011 Minsk Metro bombings two young men, Dmitry Konovalov and Vladislav Kovalyov, were quickly arrested. Belarusian authorities convicted them on problematic evidence and confessions that activists, including Konovalov's mother, claim were the result of torture. Both men were executed by a shot to the back of the head. Their families and the media were informed only after the executions were carried out.
4   '*Dobry. Nie jedź przez drogi leśna. Możesz używać tej drogi tylko w sezonie turystycznym.*'
5   From my personal fieldnotes, May 2012.

References

Barth, F. (ed.). 1969. *Ethnic Groups and Boundaries: The Social Organisation of Cultural Difference*. London: Little, Brown & Co.

Benda-Beckman, F. von, K. von Benda-Beckman and M. G. Wiber (eds). 2006. *Changing Properties of Property*. New York and Oxford: Berghahn Books.

Boyer, D. 2010. 'From *algos* to *autonomos*: Nostalgic Eastern Europe as postimperial mania'. In M. Todorova and Z. Gille (eds), *Post-communist Nostalgia*, 17–28. New York: Berghahn Books.

Boym, S. 2001. *The Future of Nostalgia*. New York: Basic Books.

Bruns, B. and J. Miggelbrink. 2012. 'Introduction'. In B. Bruns and J. Miggelbrink (eds), *Subverting Borders: Doing Research on Smuggling and Small-Scale Trade*, 12–20. Wiesbaden: VS Verlag für Sozialwissenschaften.

Creed, G. W. 2010. 'Strange bedfellows: Socialist nostalgia and neoliberalism in Bulgaria'. In M. Todorova and Z. Gille (eds), *Post-communist Nostalgia*, 29–45. New York: Berghahn Books.

Elden, S. 2004. *Understanding Henri Lefebvre: Theory and the Possible*. London: New York: Continuum.

Green, S. F. 2005. *Notes from the Balkans: Locating Marginality and Ambiguity on the Greek–Albanian Border*. Princeton: Princeton University Press.

Gupta, A. and J. Ferguson (eds). 1997. *Anthropological Locations: Boundaries and Grounds of a Field Science*. Berkeley, Los Angeles and London: University of California Press.

Haller, D. and C. Shore (eds). 2005. *Corruption: Anthropological Perspectives*. London: Pluto Press.

Hann, C. M. (ed.). 1994. *When History Accelerates: Essays on Rapid Social Change, Complexity and Creativity*. London: Athlone.

_____. 2009. 'Does ethnic cleansing work? The case of south-east Poland'. *Cambridge Anthropology* 29(1): 1–25.

Harboe Knudsen, I. 2012. *New Lithuania in Old Hands: Effects and Outcomes of EUropeanization in Rural Lithuania*. London: Anthem Press.

Hart, K. 1973. 'Informal income opportunities and urban employment in Ghana'. *Journal of Modern African Studies* 11(1): 61–89.

Hart, K., J.-L. Laville and A. D. Cattani (eds). 2010. *The Human Economy*. Cambridge: Polity Press.

Hobsbawm, E. J. 1969. *Bandits*. London: Weidenfeld & Nicolson.

Kaneff, D. and M. Heintz. 2006. 'Bessarabian borderlands: One region, two states, multiple ethnicities; guest editor's note'. *Anthropology of East Europe Review: Central Europe, Eastern Europe and Eurasia* 24(1): 6–16.

Lefebvre, H. 2008a [1947]. *The Critique of Everyday Life, Volume I: Introduction*, trans. J. Moore. London: Verso.

_____. 2008b [1961]. *The Critique of Everyday Life, Volume II: Foundations for a Sociology of the Everyday*, trans. J. Moore. London: Verso.

_____. 2008c [1981]. *The Critique of Everyday Life, Volume III: From Modernity to Modernism*, trans. J. Moore. London: Verso.

Levi, P. 2013 [1986]. *The Drowned and the Saved*, trans. R. Rosenthal. London: Abacus.

Mezzadra, S. and B. Nielson. 2013. *Border as Method: Or the Multiplication of Labor*. Durham, NC: Duke University Press.

Misiło, E. 2012. *Akcja Wisła 1947: Dokumenty i materiały* (Operation Vistula, 1947: Documents and materials). Kiev: Archiwun Ukraińskie.

Naumescu, V. 2007. *Modes of Religiosity in Eastern Christianity: Religious Processes and Social Change in the Ukraine*. Berlin and London: LIT Verlag.

Paasi, A. 1999. Boundaries as social practice and discourse: The Finnish–Russian border'. *Regional Studies* 33(7): 669–80.

Perera, S. 2007. 'A Pacific zone? (In)security, sovereignty and stories of the Pacific borderscape'. In P. K. Rajaram and C. Grundy-Warr (eds), *Borderscapes: Hidden Geographies and Politics and Territory's Edge*, 201–30. Minneapolis: University of Minnesota Press.

_____. 2009. *Australia and the Insular Imagination: Beaches, Borders, Boats, and Bodies*. New York: Palgrave Macmillan.

Pine, F. 2001. '"Who better than your mother?" Some problems with gender in rural Poland'. In H. Haukanes (ed.), *Women in Post-communist Societies*, 51–66. Bergen: Institute of Gender Studies.

_____. 2002. 'Retreat to the household? Gendered domains in postsocialist Poland'. In C. M. Hann (ed.), *Postsocialism: Ideas, Ideologies and Practices in Eurasia*, 95–113. London: Routledge.

Pine, Frances and João de Pina-Cabral (eds). 2008. *On the Margins of Religion*. New York: Berghahn Books.

Poczobut, A. 2013. 'Białoruś patrzy na Ukrainę. Władza milczy, opozycja zazdrości' (Belarus looks to Ukraine. Power is silent, the opposition of jealousy). *Gazeta Wyborcza*, 2 December. Available at: http://wyborcza.pl/1,75477,15060425,Bialorus_patrzy_na_Ukraine__Wladza_milczy__opozycja.html (accessed 14 January 2014).

Polska, Official Promotional Website of the Republic of Poland. n.d. 'Churches and religious life in Poland'. Available at: http://en.poland.gov.pl/Churches,and,Religious,Life,in,Poland,397.html (accessed 14 January 2014).

Puhl, J. 2012. 'Crisis of faith: The Catholic Church's fading influence in Poland'. *Der Spiegel*, 11 July. Available at: http://www.spiegel.de/international/europe/influence-of-catholic-church-on-the-decline-in-poland-a-843694.html (accessed 15 January 2014).

Robertson, A. F. 2006. 'Misunderstanding corruption'. *Anthropology Today* 22(2): 8–11.

Russell Bernard, H. 2006. *Research Methods in Anthropology: Qualitative and Quantitative Approaches*. Lanham, MD: Alta Mira Press.

Shields, R. 2005. *Lefebvre, Love and Struggle: Spatial Dialectics*. London: Routledge.

Snyder, T. 2003. *The Reconstruction of Nations*. New Haven: Yale University Press.

Williams, A. and V. Baláž. 2002. 'International petty trading: Changing Practices in Trans–Carpathian Ukraine'. *International Journal of Urban and Regional Research* 26(2): 323–42.

Wilson T. M. and H. Donnan (eds). 2012. *A Companion to Border Studies*. Malden, MA: Wiley-Blackwell.

Wolf, E. R. 1966. 'Kinship, friendship and patron–client relationships in complex societies'. In M. Banton (ed.), *The Social Anthropology of Complex Societies*, 1–22. London: Routledge.

Zarycki, T. 2007. 'History and regional development: A controversy over the "right" interpretation of the role of history in the development of the Polish regions'. *Geoforum* 38(3): 485–93.

_____. 2011. 'Eastern Poland in a center–periphery perspective'. In M. Stefański (ed.), *Strategic Issues of the Development of the Lublin Regioni*, 95–112. Lublin: University of Economy and Innovation in Lublin.

Chapter 6

BOSNIAN POST-REFUGEE TRANSNATIONALISM: A GREY ZONE OF 'POTENTIALITY'

Maja Halilovic-Pastuovic

The aim of this chapter is to situate Bosnian post-refugee transnationalism in relation to post-Dayton Bosnia. The chapter focuses on Bosnian migrants who entered the Republic of Ireland in 1992 as programme refugees and who were, from the moment of their arrival, participants in a lengthy reception and resettlement programme. This programme was coordinated by the Irish government and its main objective was the long-term successful integration of Bosnian refugees in Ireland.

However, despite the fact that more than two decades have elapsed since their arrival, Bosnians do not feel part of Irish society (Halilovic-Pastuovic 2007). Yet rather than repatriating and moving permanently back to Bosnia, they have chosen to cross borders on an annual basis and divide their time between the two countries. They spend most of the year in Ireland, but during the summer months migrate to Bosnia with their families.

My overall research interrogates the specificities of Bosnian post-refugee migrations between Ireland and Bosnia. However, the focus of this chapter is on Bosnia only.[1] I apply two theoretical lenses in my research – theories of transnationalism and Goldberg's (2002) racial state theory. As a result, I conceptualise Bosnian post-refugee transnationalism as being a grey zone of 'potentiality'.

As this volume shows, the notion of a grey zone can be very useful in highlighting misleading dichotomies, everyday complexities and the sense of the 'in between' in Eastern Europe. The Bosnian migrants that this chapter describes have created such a zone for themselves by refusing to shape their existence in one state only. Instead, they cross borders that they are not meant to cross on a regular basis, often live parallel lives in both places, and have created a situation where notions of home and belonging are fluid and multifaceted.

In understanding transnationalism as grounded (Smith and Guarnizo 1998), this chapter explores the reasons behind the scarcity of Bosnian migrants permanently returning to post-Dayton Bosnia.[2] It demonstrates that factors such as ethnic reification and the politicisation of nationalism, which characterise the divided society of post-Dayton Bosnia, contribute to Bosnian migrants choosing transnationalism over a permanent return. Ethnically segregated postconflict Bosnia is a very different place to the one that the Bosnians lived in prior to 1992, before the conflict began. As such, I argue that in some cases forced migration leads to enforced transnationalism. This chapter is based upon in-depth interviews with Bosnian migrants who participate in post-refugee transnationalism, which were conducted between 2006 and 2008, along with ethnographic data collected during my stays in Bosnia in the summers of 2007, 2008 and 2009.

Grounding Bosnian Post-refugee Transnationalism

In the 1990s the emerging field of transnational studies presented transnationalism as a useful conceptual tool to deal with the twin forces of mass migration and electronic mediation that characterise the current period of globalisation. Born out of a workshop in 1990 led by the anthropologists Linda Basch, Nina Glick Schiller and Cristina Szanton Blanc, the concept aimed to elucidate the 'processes by which immigrants and refugees forge and maintain multistranded social relations that link together their places of origin and places of settlement' (1994, 7). This followed the observation that an increasing number of people are able to live dual lives where

> participants are often bilingual, move easily between two cultures, frequently maintain homes in two countries, and pursue economic, political and cultural interests that require presence in both. (Portes 1997, 812)

The work concerning transnational activities has been vast, leading to a problem, not uncommon with theorisations of 'novelty' phenomena, where the concept is fraught with inconsistencies in meanings and usage. Furthermore, its swift movement across the different disciplinary boundaries of anthropology, sociology, political science and geography, to name but a few, has added to its increasing conceptual ambiguity.

In trying to disentangle the discursive ambiguity of the concept, Nolin (2006) has proposed differentiating between two streams of typologies with regard to transnationalism, identified by Glick Schiller (1997) and Mahler (1998) respectively.

Glick Schiller has identified the currents of transnationalism as transnational cultural studies, transnational migration studies and transnational communities studies. According to Glick, within the first stream the concepts of unboundedness (Basch, Glick Schiller and Szanton Blanc 1994), postnation/transnation (Appadurai 1996) and cultural hybridity (Bhabha 1994) are explored in largely abstract theoretical terms. On the contrary, transnational migration studies, being grounded in empirical research, are focused on more tangible effects of population movement and 'double consciousness' (Mahler 1995; Smith and Guarnizo 1998). Finally, transnational communities studies are focused on binational households and communities and transnational social relations (Goldring 1998; Levitt 1998; Portes 1996a, 1996b).

Mahler (1998) has differentiated between two main strands of transnational studies: transnationalism from below and transnationalism as transmigration. According to Mahler, transnationalism from below is generated by grassroots politics and social movements that resist and disrupt the workings of transnationalism from above, which is represented by structural elites, processes and international bodies that influence the reconfiguration of global capital (such as the International Monetary Fund, the World Bank or the nation-state). On the other hand, transnationalism as transmigration focuses on the migratory process itself and the impact it has on the communities concerned.

Despite the diversity of currents within the field of transnationalism, which continue to the present day, Smith and Guarnizo (1998) have highlighted and questioned the totalising emancipatory character that is present across many approaches.

In warning us against this celebratory vision, Smith and Guarnizo focus their analytical lens on different thematics relating to transnationalism from below, including, among others, the need for a grounding of transnationalism.

In proposing an understanding of transnational actions as grounded, they call for transnational migrants, viewed as 'deterritorialized, free-floating people [...] "neither here nor there"' (Smith and Guarnizo 1998, 11), to be reconceptualised, by focusing on the locality of transnationality, on actual border-crossing activities, since

transnational practices, while connecting collectivities located in more than one national territory, are embedded in specific social relations established between specific people, situated in unequivocal localities, at historically determined times. (Smith and Guarnizo 1998, 11)

In following Smith and Guarnizo's theorisation of transnationalism as grounded, in this chapter I ground Bosnian post-refugee transnationalism within the two societies the Bosnian migrants currently live in. On the one hand there is Ireland, into whose politics of interculturalism the migrants were inserted from the beginning, and where they feel racialised and marginalised. On the other hand there is the changed, post-Dayton Bosnia, characterised by the politicisation of nationalism and ethnic reification. The latter is the focus of this chapter.

Post-Dayton Bosnia as a Racial State

In addition to viewing Bosnian post-refugee transnationalism as being grounded in the conditions of the two aforementioned nation-states, I follow Goldberg's (2002) conceptualisation of modern nation-states as racial states.

While producing a comprehensive philosophical archaeology of racial conceptualisation –commencing with Hobbes and moving forward to Rousseau, Kant, Marx, Hegel, Mill and others – and through exploring the work of postwar European intellectuals such as Zygmunt Bauman and Michel Foucault, as well as expanding on the work of racial state pioneers Eric Voegelin, Michael Omi and Howard Winant, Goldberg developed a comprehensive theory of modern nation-states as racial states in which race and state are intrinsically interconnected and defined through each other. Goldberg links the Enlightenment's preoccupation with classification and order with liberalism, hence situating the discourse of race and racism as 'one of the central conceptual inventions of modernity' (Voegelin 1997 [1933], 3).

Goldberg posits that every modern state is a racial state, albeit each in its own specific way, not only because of their passive denial of the inherent heterogeneity of the populations they border, but also because of their active role in constructing and naturalising homogeneity.

Goldberg argues that it is possible to define the nation-state as a more or less coherent entity in two related ways: as a series of state projects underpinned and rationalised by a self-represented history as state memory, and as state power(s). It is precisely the power that the state has, or that the state is, which enables the state to define and carry out projects and to authorise official narrations of historical memory. The state has 'a power to define the terms of its representations and to exercise itself and those over whom the authority is claimed in light of these terms' (Goldberg 2002, 8). By using different techniques of governance such as constitutions, border control, policymaking and the law, modern states exercise their power to categorise and exclude or include in racially ordered terms.

The idea of the racial state is often difficult to digest. The opponents of the concept have voiced their concern regarding its reductive nature and expressed their worry at the overarching impact it proposes, particularly when society today is often described as postracial. Yet two important issues need to be clarified. The first is that race and state are both modern phenomena and historically interlinked. The idea of race was deeply embedded in the development of the modern state and has strengthened the advancement of nationalism (Lentin 2008).[3] Traces of the idea, albeit in different discursive manifestations, are still present today. Secondly, the process of racialisation that racial states utilise in order to enact the imperative of homogeneity – whether it is for the dominant state ethnicity(s) or the other ethnicities present within the state – needs to be understood beyond the black-and-white issue. Some time ago Miles defined racialisation as a 'process of categorisation, a representational process of defining an Other (usually, but not exclusively) somatically' (1989, 75). Arguably today, while race is by no means absent from society, this process centres largely around culture and ethnicity.

Post-Dayton Bosnia is a clear example of a racial state. Built through the Dayton Agreement reached in Ohio in 1995 by members of the international community and three presidents of former Yugoslavia,[4] the Bosnia of today is a divided country where ethnoreligious identities have been (re)constructed, homogenised and foregrounded in both public and private spheres. The Dayton Agreement ended the Bosnian conflict by creating two ethnonationalist geopolitical entities: the Federation of Bosnia and Herzegovina, which controls 51 per cent of the geographical region of the state of Bosnia and consists mainly of Bosnian and Croat populations, and the Republika Srpska, which controls the other 49 per cent of the territory and where the majority of the population is of Serb origin. Two decades after the Dayton Agreement the state of Bosnia remains ethnically polarised. It is 'subject to separatist political agendas, the government is constantly deadlocked and ethnic and religious chauvinism are still common' (Richmond and Franks 2009, 17). In other words, the racialising techniques that the Dayton Agreement implemented in Bosnia are still in effect.

Most of the interviewees I spoke to refuse to return permanently to such a demographically changed and divided country, and opt instead for annual summer visits. Later in the chapter I discuss the major changes that have occurred in post-Dayton Bosnia, but first I briefly refer to the issue of post-refugee transnationalism.

From Forced Migration to Enforced Transnationalism

In recent times there has been intense interest in refugee issues, particularly among politicians and the media in the 'West', leading to what Stedman and

Tanner (2003) have called 'the pattern of refugee manipulation'. Indeed, falling figures in refugee applications have been viewed by the majority of European states as a reflection of a successful strategy of delivering a neoliberal dream of prosperity and peace. Interestingly, despite the overblown concern about refugee matters, there has been a lack of systematic work on forced migration, there being 'a huge gap between ill-informed and often highly charged official discourses of the refugee' and research and analysis carried out as 'the basis for a considered approach to refugee issues' (Marfleet 2006, 7). Furthermore, even within the field of refugee studies, which has grown since the 1990s, attempts to consider forced migration on a global scale have been scarce: since the pioneering work of Zolberg, Suhrke and Aguayo (1989) there has been only sporadic analysis of refugee issues in international and transnational contexts (notable exceptions to the rule include Al-Ali, Black and Koser 2001; Al-Ali 2002; Canada Centre for Refugee Studies n.d.).

One of the reasons for the lack of research on refugee transnationalism is that migrant transnationalism has been typically associated with voluntary migrants, with its conceptual reliance being on mobility and regular circulatory connections between the host society and the point of origin. Despite the initial migratory pattern of fleeing home, refugees have often been viewed as a relatively 'immobile' category of migrants, due to their lack of financial resources, lack of social networks and the obvious inability to go back, at least for a certain amount of time. Also, for a while within the field of transnational studies the focus has been on the movement of persons rather than other transnational activities such as sending remittances or transnational communication, which possibly more aptly epitomise refugee transnational behaviour, particularly at the beginning of the refugee process. Also, while the human consequences of forced migration at the personal, social, economic, cultural and political levels differ from situation to situation, under the conceptual framework of the term 'refugee experience', which has been widely used within the field of refugee studies (Ager 1999), only a few discrete phases have been identified, namely preflight, flight, temporary settlement and resettlement/repatriation (Desjarlais et al. 1995). Notably, this rigid nomenclature, still relevant today, does not allow for a transnational option in the refugee experience.

Although the policies of managing forced migration, particularly in the European context, vary slightly from one state to another, for most of them the refugee cycle is perceived as having an end, either through repatriation home or through integration into the host society.

In relation to Bosnian refugees in Europe, some countries such as the Netherlands, Finland and France decided to grant 'temporary residence permits' to the people fleeing the conflict, whereas other countries opted to provide 'temporary displaced person status' (Belgium) 'collective protection' (Norway) or 'tolerated status' (Germany) (Joly, Kelly and Nettleton 1997). Notwithstanding the fact that the particular reactions of these countries with regard to details of protection were diverse, they shared the common thread of 'temporality' in their responses, where the main agenda relating to the nature of the assistance given revolved around offering help for as long as the conflict continued. Once it was over the refugees were supposed to go back home. Indeed, the very call by the United Nations High Commissioner for Refugees (UNHCR) in July 1992 for a 'temporary response' to the Yugoslav conflict could in itself be viewed as an indicator of the nature of the help sought (ECRE 1993).

A small number of countries had a different approach, promptly recognising refugees as 'permanent residents', as in the case of Sweden (Joly, Kelly and Nettleton 1997), or as 'ethnic minorities of tomorrow', as in Ireland (O'Neill 2001). However, despite the variation of the responses, transnationalism was not perceived as a possible outcome of Bosnian forced migration.

Though responses to the refugee experience have been split in terms of favouring repatriation or resettlement, repatriation has been, and arguably continues to be, the preferable option.[5] The 1990s have been declared the decade of repatriation (Collyer 2006), and different strategies for postconflict return have been tested, such as the United Nations Development Programme's TOKTEN project (Transfer of Knowledge through Expatriate Nationals) and the International Organization of Migration's MIDA programme (Migration for Development in Africa). The case of Bosnia represents the largest repatriation movement in Europe since World War II (Koser and Black 1999).[6]

Consequently, research carried out with regard to refugee movements at the 'end of the cycle' of the refugee process traditionally centred on issues of integration in the host society or reintegration back 'home'. It was not until the ninth conference of the International Association for the Study of Forced Migration, held in Sao Paulo in Brazil in January 2005, that the significance of transnational perspectives with regard to forced migration was acknowledged and added as a third durable solution, apart from repatriation and resettlement, to the refugee question.

While transnationalism is being acknowledged, albeit slowly, as a part of the refugee process, it is important to distinguish refugee transnationalism from other transnationalisms.

The main (and most obvious) distinction between refugee and other population movements is that refugees do not want to leave but are forced to, often with little notice. As Marfleet argues, refugees are 'produced by a complex of factors: economic, political, social, cultural and environmental. Their lives are shaped by political and legal structures and by both official and popular ideas of nation and nationalism, citizen and alien, "race" and ethnicity' (Marfleet 2006, 7). They are people outside the borders of their own countries unable or unwilling to gain the protection of their own governments. Becoming 'refugees' transforms their movements into a political and legal category framed by international discourses.

Additionally, when discussing forced migration it is helpful to revisit Kunz's (1973) distinction between anticipatory refugee movements and acute refugee movements. In the former, refugees have time to prepare to leave their homeland and migrate before the situation prevents their departure. In the latter, refugees have no time to prepare since their departure arises from sudden political changes and military activities. Also, refugees often operate with no foresight with regard to choosing their host country.

Therefore, refugee transnationalism particularly stemming from acute refugee movements has a different dynamic to other transnationalisms. As Nolin (2006) argues, refugee transnationalism incorporates a conceptual shift from a focus on *connections* to a focus on *ruptures and sutures* in the sense of belonging. It offers a 'possibility to grapple, in a critically analytical way, with the entanglements of refugee actions and narrations as well as with government declarations and policy changes' (Nolin 2006, 182). There are two significant elements to this course of ruptures and sutures that characterises refugee transnationalism.

The first is the initial rupture, a critical juncture, a dislocation point after which contextual certainty comes into question. While acknowledging that dislocation is an intrinsic part of every movement, the volume and rapidity of external change with regard to the political and social circumstances in the country of embarkation marks the initial stages of refugee transnationalism as different to other types of transnationalism.

The second relates to the first visit back 'home' after an amount of time in exile. Most of my respondents reflected upon this juncture and stated that Bosnia upon their return 'was not Bosnia as it used to be'. Yet again, while changes in the country of origin inevitably occur and are noticeable upon return for all migrants, the degree and quality of changes are drastically different for those returning after movements arising from ethnic conflict situations.

Both of these ruptures, as well as subsequent ones – which need to be located within the social and political changes that characterise postconflict societies – contribute to refugee and post-refugee transnationalism being processually different from other transnationalisms. It could be argued that forced migration leads to enforced transnationalism (Al-Ali, Black and Koser 2001).

However, it is important to distinguish that such a conceptualisation does not involve understanding enforced transnationalism as either a state (or states) forcing its (their) will on migrant populations, or as the simple opposite of voluntary transnationalism. Rather, it is an acknowledgment of the realisation that 'state policy, the context of flight, historical antecedents', and/or 'the dominance of the particular ideological, moral or cultural positions' can combine to push transnational activities in a certain way (Al-Ali, Black and Koser 2001, 595). Highlighted as such, the notion of enforced transnationalism is particularly useful in conceptualising forced migrations originating from 'ethnic' conflicts where there are rapid sociopolitical changes occurring in the society of origin.[7]

The policy of the racial state of postconflict Bosnia, based on the parameters of the Dayton Agreement, has racialised the population and produced conditions in the country that did not exist before. Namely, as I demonstrate below, it has i) politicised nationalism that was prohibited during the socialist times of the former Yugoslavia, and ii) homogenised, reified and geopolitically segregated the region's ethnicities. Ethnic groups were much more multifaceted and porous prior to the conflict.

I argue that the racialised conditions of post-Dayton Bosnia deter Bosnian migrants from returning 'home' permanently, and contribute to Bosnian post-refugee transnationalism.

Post-Dayton Bosnia: Ethnic Reification and the Politicisation of Nationalism

This is how three of my interviewees described present-day Bosnia and Herzegovina:

In both entities [Republika Srpska and the Federation]...in the whole territory of the state, a very small number of people are concerned with the economy, for example. Everybody is concerned with politics, and I mean nationalistic politics, and that is it. Everything is about nationalism, everything is divided, everything has to have a representative from the first, second and third nation [*naroda*]... starting with sports, culture, arts, etc. Everything...absolutely everything.

It is a fact that before life was better down there [in Bosnia]. Much better than now...now it is like a circus. I am thinking...when I look at the news and hear politicians talking...it is...I feel disgusted... It is very nationalistic...well, yes...still, that nationalistic element is still there... I don't understand why.

Then it was Yugoslavia, we were all Yugoslavs and that was it. But now, if you go to Banja Luka [in Republika Srpska] and if you sit down somewhere and ask somebody what they feel they are, nobody is going to say they belong to the state of Bosnia and Herzegovina, nobody, absolutely nobody. Everybody is going to say this is Serbia...that is their state now, that is their homeland and as long as that way of thinking exists there will be no Bosnia and Herzegovina... unfortunately. It has gone too deep and too far...it took roots, I don't know...

All three interviewees arrived in Ireland at the beginning of the conflict in Bosnia and travelled back annually to spend summers there. All three had thought about returning but had decided against it. After spending a number of summers there they felt disappointed with the extent to which nationalism was still present in Bosnia. They kept comparing the Bosnia they left behind when they migrated to the Bosnia of today, and were not prepared to return and partake in the nationalistic divisions.

In his theorisation of the collective experience of a different past in relation to Bosnia and Herzegovina, Jansen (2005) argues that a clear line exists between 'that before' and 'this now'. This distinction goes beyond the chronological tool used for structuring narration; rather, there is a collective event, a turning point, something that happened outside the will and power of the Bosnian people, that overshadows individual life stories. As Jansen notes, 'despite the differences within, all the life pathways shared the collective past that was very different from present circumstances' (2005, 13). This 'that before' does not simply correspond to the temporal dimension of before the war, it corresponds to the set of understandings of what being part of Yugoslav times meant. Most of my respondents had found it difficult to adjust to the changed Bosnia they found upon their return, particularly the nationalistic element of it, and kept referring to the time before the conflict as a time when greater cohesion was felt among people.

In terms of national belonging, Yugoslav socialist ideology was a variation of the classical theme of modernisation: it dictated that, because of the homogenising strength of industrialisation, antifascism and socialist class solidarity, national (or rather nationalistic elements) would cease to exist. Indeed, following the constitution of 1946 the equality of all people in the territory of the former Yugoslavia was determined by law. Also, the category of 'Yugoslav' was introduced in 1950 to debase nationalistic primordial belonging. In other words, the national question of the former Yugoslavia was resolved through politics of balance and compromise with a long-term prohibition of the politicisation of nationalism (Jansen 2005).[8]

In terms of discussions regarding differences between 'that before' and 'this now', this is one of the most significant changes. The taboo of politicising nationalism was broken by the politics of the conflict, institutionalised through the international community's involvement in the conflict,[9] and finally constitutionalised by the Dayton Agreement.[10]

In contemporary Bosnia 'there is little room for anyone who does not follow a national agenda' (Friedman 2004, 84). The ethnically defined political parties control decision making within the administrative, judicial and economic institutions. All three major ethnic groups have taken steps to maintain cultural distance from each other. Each ethnic group maintains its own schools with curricula that reinforce ethnic hatred, blames the other groups for segregation and glorifies its own mythology. Advantage is to be found in alliances with one's 'own' ethnic/national group and in competition with other ethnic groups. If people from another national group manage to return and regain their former land, competing ethnic groups believe that their own power may be compromised. This has been one of the major difficulties for returnees trying to re-establish themselves in areas that are currently occupied by other ethnic groups – so-called minority returnees. Many minority returnees end up exchanging property and moving to where their ethnicity is dominant. This has resulted in Bosnia being more ethnically clustered at present than prior to the conflict, as recognised by my interviewees:

> Bosnia has gone backwards…it should be different, there should not be…how would you say it…there should not be…people are divided…people are divided now, it is not how it used to be, those times are gone…now it is 'I am a Muslim, you are a Serb, he is Croat'…everybody is keeping a distance, keeping a distance from one another. They say he is a Muslim, run away from him…

> Bosnia will never again be Bosnia, not the way it used to be when it was a part of Yugoslavia. Now we have a totally different state. It is divided, you know, people are spending time with their own group more.

The ethnic segregation of present-day Bosnia is the direct consequence of the racialised policies of the Dayton Agreement, which have legitimised exclusivist projects by conflating 'ethnic' with 'national' and by producing schisms along ethnic lines (Pasic 1995; Vulliamy 1998). The agreement in effect created boundary lines within the territory of Bosnia and Herzegovina along the ethnic lines popularised by the conflict, and as such, through politics of 'security through separation' (Dahlman and Ó Tuathail 2005) – authorised ethnic segregation. The accords created 'de facto partitions of Bosnia and Herzegovina', splitting the country into 'ethno-nationalist entities that both acknowledged and effectively rewarded ethnic cleansing' (Robinson and Pobric 2005, 237). This further led to the reification of ethnicity and the interrelated politicisation of nationalism that persists to this day in postconflict Bosnia.

A Grey Zone of 'Potentiality'

Back in 2001 Al-Ali, Black and Koser pointed out that theories of transnationalism need to pay more attention to variations between receiving and sending states, as the social and political developments in those states shape refugees' strategies and practices. In agreeing with this call to action, and in line with my understanding of transnationalism as grounded, this chapter argues that the politics and policies of post-Dayton Bosnia, pushed, or rather forced, Bosnian migrants to seek out 'ways of being' in which they could negotiate and accommodate these politics and policies. I argue that annual summer migrations in particular, but also other transnational activities they are involved in, provide them with an evolving 'space of possibility', where they can negotiate the changes, ruptures and sutures of everyday life.

There are numerous ways of being that Bosnian migrants negotiate and are involved in on a daily basis with regard to both countries. Some are related to more material, practical and financial matters, such as organising flights for summer migrations, maintaining accommodation in two places, remittances, and other financial transactions. Other ways of being are related to more intimate issues in connection with sentiments, memories and personal histories.

In the original paper that discussed transnationalism as a 'space of possibilities' for migrants from Eastern Europe, Morokvasic (2004) stressed that migrants engaged in transnational activities in order to gain (in the case of her study) access to extra income to enable them to maintain a certain quality of life at home. Morokvasic researched gendered migration in postcommunist societies and explored how women found ways to supplement their family income by engaging in short-term periods of work abroad. Morokvasic focused on what migrants gained directly through their involvement in transnational activities. My research focus is on what migrants have lost, and I wish to suggest that post-refugee transnationalism provides Bosnian migrants with a 'space of possibility' where that which has been lost can be regained and rearticulated.

'That which was lost' is mostly linked to the country that the migrants lost: the former Yugoslavia. This country had multiethnic marriages and multiethnic schools; it was a place where you did not need exchange your property to move to a more ethnically homogenous zone to avoid your children getting beaten up on the street. In that place my respondents could get a job regardless of their ethnicity and there were no religious obligations put upon them. They had lots of celebrations of Yugoslav diversity and everyone was welcome, my interviewees explained. Different ethnicities, foods, drinks and songs were celebrated. Nostalgia for those Yugoslav times was almost tactile at moments during my interviews. One woman had a picture of Tito on her shelf in her flat, and during the interview she got up, brought the picture to the table and told me, while holding it, how much better Bosnia was during his time.

In his book *Potentialities: Collected Essays in Philosophy* (1999) Agamben discusses the concept of potentiality as a *possibility that exists*. He traces the concept back to Aristotle, who distinguishes two kinds of potentialities: generic potentiality and existing potentiality. Generic potentiality is common potentiality – an almost universal potentiality where, for example, we can say that anyone can become a head of state. Thinking in terms of generic potentiality, most human beings have the potential to achieve that status. Existing potentiality is potentiality grown out of a specific ability or knowledge. Agamben gives the example of a poet or an architect, since they already have the knowledge and ability to write poems or build objects. Most straightforwardly, for existing potentiality to become an actuality there is no need for an alteration, whereas with generic potentiality an alteration needs to happen before potentiality can achieve its actualisation. I suggest that Agamben's theorisation of existing potentiality is very useful for understanding Bosnian post-refugee transnationalism as a 'space of possibility'.

Bosnian post-refugee transnationalism – characterised by summer migrations, multiple belongings and rearticulations of the Yugoslav past – becomes, I argue, a grey zone of potentiality that provides Bosnian migrants with a space where the former Yugoslavia can be enacted in their lives while maintaining their transnational existence.

Conclusion

In this chapter I have demonstrated that the ethnic reification and politicisation of nationalism that currently characterise post-Dayton Bosnia have influenced Bosnian refugees in Ireland to opt for post-refugee transnationalism rather than a permanent return 'home'. I have argued that the racialising politics and policies of the Dayton Agreement have produced the divided society of postconflict Bosnia.

The racial state of post-Dayton Bosnia, attained by means of the politics of 'security through separation', largely orchestrated by the international community, is an ethnically divided state where ethnic and religious identities have taken on a political significance that was not present prior to the conflict, and where the politicisation of nationalism and the reification of ethnicity have been institutionalised and constitutionalised through the Dayton Agreement. This is not a Bosnia to which my respondents want to return.

While acknowledging discontinuity and change as principal parts of all migration processes, post-refugee transnationalism – stemming from ethnic conflicts in particular – can incorporate such significant social and political changes that it may become enforced (Al-Ali, Black and Koser 2001). In other words, state policies, historical contexts and/or particular political configurations can constrain or push transnational activities in certain directions. In these cases forced migration may lead to enforced transnationalism. However, rather than being a negative condition characterised by a lack of adjustment to changed circumstances, I posit that Bosnian post-refugee transnationalism is a 'space of possibility' (Morokvasic 2004) that Bosnian migrants have carved out for themselves in order to respond to the conditions of the racial state of post-Dayton Bosnia. I further posit that it is a grey zone of 'potentiality'. In addition to earlier theorisations by Primo Levi and others that investigate grey zones in the sphere of moral ambiguity, I propose an extension to the understanding of this concept. I view Bosnian migrants as post-refugee transnational subjects who are creating a grey zone of potentiality as a 'space of possibility', and, as such, enacting their power beyond the rigid nature of the racial nation-state.

Notes

1 Due to constraints of space I do not discuss the politics of ethnicity of the racial state of Ireland in this particular chapter. To read more see Halilovic-Pastuovic (2007).

2 The Dayton Agreement (also known as the General Framework Agreement for Peace in Bosnia and Herzegovina) was reached in Dayton, Ohio, in 1995, and put to an end the Bosnian conflict that broke out during the breakup of the former Yugoslavia. The agreement divided Bosnia and Herzegovina into two political entities: the Federation of Bosnia and Herzegovina and the Republika Srpska.

3 Eric Voegelin (1997 [1933]) distinguishes between the concept of race and the idea of race. He sees the concept of race as a scientific concept composed of a set of false notions with no basis in provable scientific fact. The idea of race, on the other hand, refers to a well-ordered system of political dogmas.

4 The Serbian president Slobodan Milošević, the Croatian president Franjo Tuđman and the Bosnian president Alija Izetbegović.

5 It has been noted that even when the period of temporary protection became prolonged, certain states still refused the resettlement option to people in limbo. For example, more than 6 million of the almost 10 million refugees in the world in 2003 had been displaced for more than five years, displacement described by UNHCR as 'protracted', yet no long-term solution was offered to them towards resettlement. This problem has been described and criticised as a 'warehousing' of refugees (Collyer 2006).

6 It has to be noted that there has been a slight change in policy orientation since 2004, as resettlement is beginning to be more seriously considered as a long-term answer to the refugee question.

7 Prevailing theoretical and media opinion blames the breakup of the former Yugoslavia on the ethnic conflict between the Serb, Croat and Bosnian Muslim populations, which was based on their inability to live together peacefully, particularly within the territory of Bosnia and Herzegovina. Not only has such an approach reified ethnic differences between these populations, it has also largely neglected the influence of other factors preceding the conflict, namely the impact of economic forces in the Yugoslav transition from socialism to the European market economy as well as the international community's involvement in the region.

8 This is particularly relevant with regard to Bosnia and Herzegovina, since it was the most mixed republic of the six republics of the former Yugoslavia. The last census before the conflict shows that 44 per cent of the population identified themselves as Muslim, 31 per cent as Serb, 17 per cent as Croat and 8 per cent as Yugoslav (Filipovic 1997).

9 The extent of the international community's involvement in the reconstruction and 'democratisation' of Bosnia and Herzegovina has been extraordinary, leading to views of Bosnia as a neocolonial protectorate rather than a sovereign state (Zivkovic 1999).

10 The Constitution of Bosnia and Herzegovina is Annex 4 of the Dayton Agreement.

References

Agamben, G. 1999. *Potentialities: Collected Essays in Philosophy*. Stanford: Stanford University Press.

Ager, A. (ed.). 1999. *Refugees: Perspectives on the Experience of Forced Migration*. London: Continuum.

Al-Ali, N. 2002. 'Gender relations, transnational ties and rituals among Bosnian refugees'. *Global Networks* 2(3): 249–62.

Al-Ali, N., R. Black and K. Koser. 2001. 'The limits to "transnationalism": Bosnian and Eritrean refugees in Europe as emerging transnational communities'. *Ethnic and Racial Studies* 24(4): 578–600.

Appadurai, A. 1996. *Modernity at Large: Cultural Dimensions of Globalization*. Minneapolis: University of Minnesota Press.

Basch, L., N. Glick Schiller, C. Szanton Blanc (eds). 1994. *Nations Unbound: Transnational Projects, Postcolonial Predicaments and Deterritorialised Nation-States*. Langhorne, PA: Gordon & Breach.

Bhabha, H. 1994. *The Location of Culture*. New York: Routledge.

Canada Centre for Refugee Studies. n.d. http://www.yorku.ca/crs/ (accessed 12 December 2013).

Collyer, M. 2006. 'Citizens without borders? Discussions of transnationalism and forced migrants at the ninth conference of the International Association for the Study of Forced Migration, São Paulo, Brazil, January 2005'. *Refuge* 23(1): 94–100.

Dahlman, C. and G. Ó Tuathail. 2005. 'The legacy of ethnic cleansing: The international community and the return process in post-Dayton Bosnia-Herzegovina'. *Political Geography* 24: 569–99.

Desjarlais, R., L. Eisenberg, B. Good and A. Kleinmann (eds). 1995. *World Mental Health: Problems and Priorities in Low-Income Countries*. Oxford: Oxford University Press.

European Council on Refugees and Exiles (ECRE). 1993. *Asylum in Europe: An Introduction*, vol. 1. London: ECRE.

Filipovic, M. 1997. *Bosna i Hercegovina: najvaznije geografske, demografske, historijske, kulturne i politicke cinjenice* (Bosnia and Herzegovina: The most important geographical, demographical, historical, cultural and political facts). Sarajevo: Compact.

Friedman, F. 2004. *Bosnia and Herzegovina: A Polity on the Brink*. London: Routledge.

Glick Schiller, N. 1997. 'The situation of transnational studies'. *Identities: Global Studies in Culture and Power* 4(2): 155–66.

Goldberg, D. T. 1993. *Racist Culture: Philosophy and the Politics of Meaning*. Oxford: Blackwell.

_____. 2002. *The Racial State*. Oxford: Blackwell.

Goldring, L. 1998. 'The power of status in transnational social fields'. In M. P. Smith and L. E. Guarnizo (eds), *Transnationalism from Below: Comparative Urban and Community Research Volume 6*, 165–96. New Brunswick: Transaction Publishers.

Halilovic-Pastuovic, M. 2007. 'The "Bosnian project" in Ireland: A "vision of divisions"'. In B. Fanning (ed.), *Immigration and Social Change in the Republic of Ireland*, 153–68. Manchester: Manchester University Press.

Jansen, S. 2005. *Antinacionalism: Ethnografija otpora u Beogradu i Zagrebu* (Antinationalism: Ethnography of resistance in Belgrade and Zagreb). Belgrade: Biblioteka XX Vek.

Joly D., Kelly, L. and C. Nettleton. 1997. *Refugees in Europe: The Hostile New Agenda*. London: Minority Rights Group.

King, H. 2004. 'Has Dayton Facilitated the Building of a Multi-ethnic Bosnia? An Examination of Refugee Return and Reintegration after the Dayton Accords'. MSc thesis, Kingston University, London.

Koser, K. and R. Black. 1999. *The End of the Refugee Cycle? Refugee Repatriation and Reconstruction*. Oxford: Berghahn Books.

Kunz, E. F. 1973. 'The refugee in flight: Kinetic models and forms of displacement'. *International Migration Review* 7(2): 125–46.

Levitt, P. 1998. 'Social remittances: Migration driven local-level forms of cultural diffusion'. *International Migration Review* 32(4): 926–48.

Lentin, A. 2008. *Racism: A Beginner's Guide*. Oxford: Oneworld.

Levi, P. 1988. *The Drowned and the Saved*. London: Michael Joseph.

Mahler, S. 1995. *American Dreaming: Immigrant Life on the Margins*. Princeton: Princeton University Press.

_____. 1998. 'Theoretical and empirical contributions toward a research agenda for transnationalism'. In M. P. Smith and L. E. Guarnizo (eds), *Transnationalism from Below: Comparative Urban and Community Research Volume 6*, 64–103. New Brunswick: Transaction Publishers.

Marfleet, P. 2006. *Refugees in a Global Era*. New York: Palgrave Macmillan.

Miles, R. 1989. *Racism*. London and New York: Routledge.

Morokvasic, M. 2004. '"Settled in mobility": Engendering post-Wall migration in Europe'. *Kruh I Ruze* 28: 30–45.

Nolin, C. 2006. *Transnational Ruptures: Gender and Forced Migration*. Burlington, VT: Ashgate.

O'Neill, J. 2001. 'Integration of refugees in Ireland: Experience with programme refugees 1994–2000'. In C. Harvey and M. Ward (eds), *No Welcome Here? Asylum Seekers and Refugees in Ireland and Britain*, 94–102. Belfast: Democratic Dialogue.

Pasic, A. 1995. *The Old Bridge in Mostar*. Istanbul: IRCICA Press.

Portes, A. 1996a. 'Transnational communities: Their emergence and significance in the contemporary world system'. In M. Castro (ed.), *Transnational Realities and Nation-States: Trends in International Migration and Immigration Policy in the Americas*. Miami: North-South Center.

_____. 1996b. 'Global villagers: The rise of transnational communities'. *American Prospect* 7(25): 74–77.

_____. 1997. 'Immigration theory for a new century: Some problems and opportunities'. *International Migration Review* 31: 799–825.

Richmond, O. and J. Franks. 2009. 'Between partition and pluralism: The Bosnian jigsaw and an "ambivalent peace"'. *Southeast European and Black Sea Studies* 9(1–2): 17–38.

Robinson, G. and A. Pobric. 2005. 'Nationalism and identity in post-Dayton Accords: Bosnia and Herzegovina'. *Royal Dutch Geographical Society* 97(3): 237–52.

Smith, M. P. and L. E. Guarnizo (eds). 1998. *Transnationalism from Below: Comparative Urban and Community Research Volume 6.* New Brunswick: Transaction Publishers.

Stedman, S. and F. Tanner. 2003. *Refugee Manipulation: War, Politics and the Abuse of Human Suffering.* Washington DC: Brookings Institution Press.

Voegelin, E. 1997 [1933]. *Race and State.* Baton Rouge: Louisiana State University Press.

Vulliamy, E. 1998. 'Bosnia: The victory of appeasement'. *International Affairs* 74: 73–92.

Zivkovic, A. 1999. 'Building peace in Balkans: The protectorate, a way to dominate'. *Le monde diplomatique.* Available at: http://mondediplo.com/1999/07/04balk (accessed 13 December 2013).

Zolberg, A., A. Suhrke and S. Aguayo. 1989. *Escape from Violence: Conflict and the Refugee Crisis in the Developing World.* Oxford: Oxford University Press.

Chapter 7

'HOMELAND IS WHERE EVERYTHING IS FOR THE PEOPLE': THE RATIONALE OF BELONGING AND CITIZENSHIP IN THE CONTEXT OF SOCIAL UNCERTAINTY

Kristina Šliavaitė

In this chapter I describe the way that members of the ethnically mixed Russian-speaking community in Visaginas, Lithuania, view their relationship with the Lithuanian state. Anthropologists and other social researchers have demonstrated that the perception of citizenship is not universal and is shaped by sociocultural context(s) (Bloch 2013; Dagnino 2006; Stack 2012; Yalçın-Heckmann 2012). The community where I conducted my research was formed in the Soviet period and its livelihood has been closely linked to the vitality of the nearby Ignalina Nuclear Power Plant. The majority of Visaginas's population moved to Lithuania during Soviet times when the plant and settlement were being built, and many of them believed in the ideas and the future of the socialist modernisation project (Šliavaitė 2005). During the Soviet era the Russian-speaking community in the settlement were like an 'island' in the eastern part of Lithuania, as they had few social connections with the surrounding population (Kavaliauskas 2002; Šliavaitė 2005). When the Soviet Union broke up, Lithuania granted citizenship to all the permanent residents of the country who applied for it. However, I will argue that formal citizenship does not necessarily guarantee that new citizens will develop a sense of belonging and attachment to the national community, or that they will have common perceptions of citizenship and similar expectations of the state. After the events in Ukraine in 2014, with the annexation of Crimea by Russia, Lithuanian journalists rushed to Visaginas to interview the local residents and ask them if they thought a similar scenario was possible in this predominantly Russian-populated part of the country. The concern expressed by these journalists reveals that there is a perception among the general public in Lithuania that the Visaginas community's feelings of civic and national belonging could be ambiguous.

Residents of Visaginas have faced the situation of social uncertainty for more than a decade, starting with negotiations with the EU regarding the eventual shutdown of the nuclear power plant. I first came to Visaginas in 2000 as a PhD student in anthropology. My aim was to listen to local people and to observe everyday situations in order to become acquainted with their perceptions of the disintegration of the Soviet Union and the upcoming shutdown of the nuclear power plant. At that time the residents of Visaginas were highly concerned with how the proposed shutdown of the town's main industry would affect their everyday lives and the local economy. I heard numerous stories about economic and social decline in post-Soviet Lithuania, social uncertainty and insecurity, rising unemployment and the moral degradation of the community (Šliavaitė 2005). Nearly ten years after my initial research I returned to Visaginas to do a follow-up study on the socioeconomic consequences of the shutdown on the local people. I wanted to find out how the residents of Visaginas had adapted to these changes. Between November 2011 and June 2012 I visited regularly with a colleague. During my first visit we walked through the town as I looked for signs of change or stability. The most visible change was the two-storey supermarket in the centre of the town, which had numerous shops, a beauty salon and cafés; it was a popular place of meeting and shopping for the local people. Informant interviews were still dominated by the themes of uncertainty, social insecurity and economic decline, this time caused by the world economic crisis of 2008 and the closure of Ignalina Nuclear Power Plant in 2009.

In this chapter I argue that socioeconomic insecurity and uncertainty as well as feelings of ambiguity about civic and national belonging shape people's perceptions of the state and considerations about citizenship. The concept of citizenship commonly includes the dimensions of community members' legal status, identity and civic activity (Kymlica and Norman 2010 [2000], 30–31). Numerous pieces of research have demonstrated that different projects of citizenship are developed in the same political community by different actors (Dagnino 2007; Stack 2012), and that notions of citizenship are moulded by sociocultural contexts and historical developments (Bloch 2013; Dagnino 2006; Mataradze 2011; Yalçın-Heckmann 2012). Anthropologists and other social researchers question the universal understanding of notions such as 'democracy' and 'citizenship' and emphasise the necessity of investigating what meanings local population(s) attach to these globally circulating concepts (Robins, Cornwall and Lieres 2008). Citizenship presupposes citizens' rights and duties in a certain political community, and this raises questions about changing notions of citizenship in the period of globalisation and intensified migration (O'Byrne 2005; Ong 2000; Soysal 2000). Researchers emphasise the need to perceive and analyse citizenship in relation to social inequality (Kipnis 2004; Shachar 2009). In this chapter I focus on the ways my informants construct their relation to the nation-state and the emic meanings they attach to the notion of citizenship. The ways my informants construct their relation to a state are often ambiguous and situational; I perceive their relationship as a grey zone where boundaries between we/they, official/unofficial and acceptable/unacceptable are negotiated. At the same time, along with many other social researchers I argue that the stories described in this chapter point to a general change in notions of citizenship and belonging in the period of globalisation and migration.

Some Contextual Information and Methodological Notes

Visaginas was built during the Soviet period as a settlement for Ignalina Nuclear Power Plant employees and their families. During the Soviet period the town was named Sniechkus, after the Lithuanian Communist Party leader; it was renamed Visaginas in the 1990s. The construction of the town started in 1975 and was supported by the Soviet authorities in Moscow (Kavaliauskas 1999, 2003). The people who were involved in the construction of the town and the plant were high-level professionals working under the rule of a special ministry responsible for the construction and management of nuclear objects in the Soviet Union (Kavaliauskas 2003). The majority of these professionals had worked at other Soviet nuclear industry sites prior to being assigned to Sniechkus (Kavaliauskas 2003). As the construction of the power plant was a project of key importance to the Soviet Union it provided high-quality construction supplies, and the residents' personal and family economies steadily improved (Kavaliauskas 2002, 2003; Šliavaitė 2005). The population of the settlement increased from 2,395 in 1978 to 31,579 in 1989 (Kavaliauskas 1999, 34–35). After Lithuania gained independence in 1991, a portion of Visaginas's population emigrated from the town and from Lithuania altogether (Kavaliauskas 1999, 51). In 2001 the population of Visaginas was 29,554, and the majority of the inhabitants were Russians (52.4 per cent); Lithuanians were the second-largest group (15 per cent), followed by Belarusians (10 per cent) and Ukrainians (5 per cent) (Lietuvos Statistikos Departamentas 2002). By 2011 the population of Visaginas had fallen to 22,091, a decrease of 25 per cent since 2001 (Lietuvos Statistikos Departamentas 2011). This could be a reflection of general demographic processes in Lithuania during this period, which were characterised by low birth rates and increased emigration (Stankūnienė 2011; Lietuvos Statistikos Departamentas 2011).

The nuclear plant, the symbol of the community, was closed in 2009. Its closure was a major point of discussion in Lithuania's accession negotiations with the EU (European Commission 2008). The Lithuanian government made the decision to close the first reactor of the plant before 2005 and the second before 2010 (European Commission 2008). The plant was closed because it was considered unsafe: Ignalina's reactors were of the RBMK type, the same type as those at Chernobyl (European Commission 2008). However, the nuclear power plant remains an important industry and job provider for the inhabitants of the city, even after its closure, as it employs people in decommissioning works.[1] The number of registered unemployed individuals in the municipality of Visaginas was 1,700 in 2009 (9.4 per cent of the local workforce) and 2,700 (15.2 per cent) in 2010, but dropped to 2,100 (13.9 per cent) in 2012.[2] The level of unemployment in the municipality in 2012 was lower than levels in the municipalities in nearby regions (Utenos Teritorinė Darbo Birža 2012). This could be explained by high emigration rates as well as employment provided by the plant through decommissioning works.

This chapter is based on empirical data collected in Visaginas between November 2011 and June 2012. These investigations were part of the larger research project 'Social Challenges for Ethnic Minorities and New Immigrant Groups in Lithuania after Joining the EU' carried out by the Lithuanian Social Research Centre. In total 17 in-depth interviews were conducted with members of the Russian, Belarusian and Ukrainian ethnic groups. The interview and participant observation data collected during my first piece of fieldwork in Visaginas in 2000–02 provided me with a solid foundation for developing this study (Šliavaitė 2005). Both projects were conducted during periods of social uncertainty for the inhabitants of Visaginas, in terms of the closure of the plant and the world economic crisis.

In this chapter I focus on two informants representing two different generations. The stories of Volodia and Taras contain similar themes to many interviews I conducted with other respondents from my sample group.[3] However, the interviews with Volodia and Taras were more extensive, both informants being open, talkative and providing rich data on the issues of interest to this chapter. Volodia belongs to what I call the older generation of Visaginas's residents: like many others he moved to Visaginas during the time when the plant and the settlement were under construction and the town was in need of a larger workforce. Taras is a member of what I call the 'middle' generation: he was born at the end of the Soviet period and his youth passed during times of political, economic and social transformation. An important thread that continues throughout Volodia's story is the importance of citizenship in the job market during periods of uncertainty. Taras's story centres around the issues of social protection and social security provided by the state. Both stories reveal notions of citizenship and the interconnection between issues of citizenship and socioeconomic concerns.

Citizenship and the Job Market: Volodia's Story

I use the story of Volodia to show how some residents of Visaginas who moved to Lithuania in the Soviet period to work at the plant faced the challenge of having to reconsider their civic and national belonging after the dissolution of the Soviet Union. As my interview material reveals, choices of civic and national belonging are in some ways pragmatic, being based on socioeconomic interests and fuelled by feelings of emotional attachment or detachment regarding the political community. Volodia and other people in similarly disadvantageous socioeconomic situations balance different levels of attachment, the most conceptually challenging being their selection of citizenship, in order to minimise social risks and the consequences of unemployment. This story encourages us to rethink the perception of citizenship as being based on common identity and emotional attachment. Volodia does not perceive citizenship and identity as different sides of the same coin, which brings us to Yasemin Nuhoglu Soysal's argument that an increasing separation of rights and identities is characteristic of current notions of citizenship (2000, 1). Volodia does not perceive common identity as an important aspect of civic belonging. Instead, he develops his story around the issues of citizenship and employment.

I made contact with Volodia through a 'snowball' sampling strategy in 2012. We met for an interview in his flat, which is in a five-storey apartment house built during the Soviet period. Volodia is a thin and quiet man who talks slowly, but he made his points clearly. His calm demeanour came as a contrast to that of his friend Inokentii, who was also present during the interview and who interrupted our conversation a number of times in order to express his opinion on different issues. Inokentii was very emotional and emphasised his disappointment with the Lithuanian state whenever he could. Volodia and Inokentii are Russians and both came to Visaginas in the Soviet period. Inokentii is now retired and gets a pension; Volodia has been unemployed for some years. Both men perceive their status as having deteriorated in post-Soviet Lithuania in terms of their economic and social wellbeing. Both men emphasised that they were not needed by anyone anymore: neither in Lithuania nor in Russia. The main interviewee was Volodia, and I focus on the story he provided.

At the time of the interview, Volodia was 55 years old. He is unemployed. His wife is unemployed as well. They both receive social allowance, which, according to Volodia, is not sufficient to meet everyday needs. He and his wife came to Visaginas from Russia in 1980 because their daughter had some health problems and they were looking for a place more favourable to her health. Over the years Volodia has not learned Lithuanian; he is a Russian and he considers Russia his homeland since he was born and spent his youth there. He mentioned briefly that Lithuania is also important for him since he has lived there for so many years; however, he used the expression 'a foreigner' (Russian: *все равно я считаюсь иностранцем у вас*) when he referred to his situation in Lithuania.[4] By this Volodia not only showed his discontent with his legal status as a permanent resident in the country, he also indicated that he does not feel a part of the society, that he is an outsider. His words were echoed by Inokentii, who added emotionally that they both 'have no status in Lithuania now' (*сейчас мы никто*). Gerli Nimmerfeldt has conducted research among the Russian population in Estonia, suggesting that it is important to address 'the feeling of being at home and being accepted by and part of society' (2011, 205). Volodia is one of those who does not feel a part of the larger Lithuanian community in any sense: culturally, socially or economically. His attachment to Lithuania is ambiguous and not based on a common identity or a sense of commonality, but is instead shaped almost exclusively by socioeconomic issues.

When Lithuania gained its independence, Volodia was employed at Ignalina Nuclear Power Plant. He needed Lithuanian citizenship to keep his job because only citizens of Lithuania could be employed at an establishment of such strategic importance to the state. As Volodia described, keeping the job at the plant was the main reason why he applied for Lithuanian citizenship then. However, a few years later Volodia lost his job at the plant and decided to apply for Russian citizenship instead. He described his decision as being based on the necessity of finding a job, and he believed that he would be more successful in the Russian job market than in the Lithuanian one.

> The thing is that unemployment was killing me slowly [*эта безработица меня убивала*], I was thinking about emigration. Since my mother was still alive, I had a right to gain citizenship [of Russia]. As long as my mother was alive. [...] I was responsible for the family [to provide material support for his family in Visaginas].

Volodia was granted Russian citizenship and relied on his relatives when searching for a job in Russia. However, Volodia did not have positive experiences in his native land. As a result of his failure to find a well-paid job in Russia, he stated that he felt a stranger there as well.

> You know, the situation was such that I was not needed there [in Russia] either. I mean, my age, it was coming to the end [*возраст уже свой у меня*

истек практичестки], you know? […] I was a stranger among strangers, or a stranger among my own people [*чужой среди чужих или чужой среди своих оказался*].

Volodia again referred to his feeling of being a stranger (*чужой*) in Russia and belonging neither to Russian nor to Lithuanian society. He perceives his unsuccessful job search as being related to his age: he was over forty years old when he moved to Russia hoping to find a job. He believes that his age was the most important factor in his failure to find a job. Anthropologist Hilary Pilkington has investigated the process of Russian migration back to Russia from the former Soviet Republics in the early 1990s, documenting a number of social, economic and cultural challenges that migrants encountered upon their return (Pilkington 1998). Volodia's hardships in Russia could have been related to the country's social and economic constraints as well as its limited resources.

Volodia had to return to Visaginas. His wife had stayed in Visaginas and is a citizen of Lithuania. Volodia does not have Lithuanian citizenship anymore, and he is now perceived as a foreigner who can apply only for a permanent residence permit. He can apply for Lithuanian citizenship but would have to go through certain procedures, which include an exam on the Lithuanian language, the country's constitution and its history. Volodia speaks only a basic level of Lithuanian. During the interview Volodia described his decision to reject Lithuanian citizenship as a mistake. Now he considers it an advantage when searching for a job in EU countries. However, he will not attempt to apply for Lithuanian citizenship since he does not think he can pass the test in Lithuanian to the required level. He said: 'I have missed my time and it does not matter if I used to be a citizen of Lithuania or not'. Ayelet Shachar suggests that citizenship serves a 'gate-keeping' function (2009, 23) for certain social guarantees and economic rewards, and that the denial of citizenship by a wealthier country creates 'extreme inequalities in life prospects' (2009, 22). Volodia considers citizenship a resource that opens up possibilities of employment. Currently Lithuanian citizenship could open the doors to the EU job market, but Volodia's earlier decisions closed off these possibilities.

As the issues of economic wellbeing and belonging came up a number of times during the interview, a boundary between we/they was constructed. Volodia and Inokentii discussed social support for citizens provided by the state, both in Lithuania and Russia. Inokentii stated emotionally and abruptly that he did not receive any compensation from the state for his participation in the liquidation works after the Chernobyl catastrophe and related this injustice to his Russian citizenship: 'Yes. A Lithuanian receives [a compensation] because he was in Chernobyl. I also was there [in Chernobyl] but I do not get anything.' Whatever the reason for this situation, the interpretation presented by Inokentii reveals the prevailing feeling of vulnerability among certain groups within the Russian population in independent Lithuania and their perception of themselves as 'others' or 'strangers'. The fieldwork material I gathered in Visaginas between 2000 and 2002 led me to the conclusion that some people in Visaginas considered the post-Soviet transformations of the country as certain deviations from the Soviet path of modernisation; my senior informants clearly saw themselves as part of the soviet modernisation project (Šliavaitė 2005). Both Volodia and Inokentii are representative of the older generation of Visaginas's population, and their sense of vulnerability is shaped by a general disappointment with the post-Soviet transformations and their changing status in society.

Rather ambiguous boundaries are constructed between what are considered official and unofficial economic practices. Citizenship can be successfully exploited to get an additional, unofficial income. Volodia gets unemployment cheques from the Lithuanian state. Even though this social support is small, he values it very much. However, this support does not cover his basic needs, especially during winter time when expenses for heating consume most of his family income. From time to time Volodia earns unofficial money by driving newly bought cars from the EU to Russia. He explains that as a Russian citizen he can pass the border without paying taxes – which he estimates as amounting to up to 30 per cent of the price of a car. His last trip to Russia occurred during the incredibly cold winter days a few weeks before our interview. Volodia received 100 euros in cash for his services and considered this to be a profitable side-business. This kind of income should be considered as informal, and it is perceived as illegal by state authorities because it avoids tax. In addition, officially Volodia cannot collect any other income if he wishes to continue getting state unemployment support. However, the 100 euros gained for this small unofficial affair are almost equal to the monthly unemployment cheque he receives from the state. Volodia successfully explores his twofold legal status: as a citizen of Russia he is able to earn unofficial money; as a person who has a residence permit in Lithuania and a history of employment in the country he is entitled to social allowance from Lithuanian state. State institutions would perceive his activities as being illegal and unacceptable, but this is the only way for him to survive economically.

Citizenship entails certain individual rights in a political community (Shachar 2009). Therefore, citizenship may offer a variety of pragmatic rights and privileges such as access to government-funded jobs and certain social provisions. Volodia exploits his citizenship in a variety of ways in order to gain some economic security and profit. He has found himself in a situation of social uncertainty and ambiguity, and so he explores all the resources available to him to find economic solutions. His citizenship documents are one such resource.

Volodia does not complain much about the lack of social security provisions, nor does he ask for more from the state. Instead, he uses all options available to him in dealing with socioeconomic difficulties and is determined to find solutions. Anthropologist Sherry B. Ortner defines human agency as explicit goals and plans that are 'socially embedded' in the surrounding sociocultural context to achieve certain aims (2006, 129–37); Volodia demonstrates this agency. Volodia belongs to the part of society that is most vulnerable to economic and social challenges. However, he demonstrates agency and applies any resources available to him to survive constant transformations in both local and transnational conditions – including the more specific recent economic decline triggered by the closure of the nuclear power plant.

Social Insecurity, State Protection and Citizenship: Taras's Story

Taras's story further supports my claim that access to social provisions is an important factor in considering citizenship. Taras evaluates citizenship of any country first of all according to the social security it provides. Taras's case points to the importance of social provisions and guarantees from a state in building citizens' attachment. Anthropologist Teona Mataradze in her discussions of citizenship in postsocialist Georgia has demonstrated that citizens there merge the concepts of 'social citizenship' and 'social security', and argues for the separation of these concepts (2011, 472). Building her argument on the work of prominent social scientists, Mataradze argues that the concept of 'social citizenship' refers to certain social rights of each member of a political community and entails the state's formal support for its citizens, while the concept of 'social security' is limited to the most vulnerable groups and includes informal provisions as well (2011, 474). As Mataradze suggests, Georgian citizens' claims for universal state support could be explained by the state–citizen relationship formed during the socialist period (Mataradze 2011). I argue that Taras-like attitudes toward the state could be further fostered by the processes of globalisation and migration, when citizens of former socialist republics have new opportunities for employment and state support in economically better-off countries. As Lale Yalçın-Heckmann has suggested, 'freedom of movement has become a criterion for differentiating and judging between the national state and the social state, and between political citizenship and social citizenship' (Yalçın-Heckmann 2012, 1736).

Taras introduced himself as an ethnic Ukrainian. He was born in the 1980s; the same year his family moved to Lithuania. He lived in Sniechkus, attended a local elementary school and completed the first four grades. In 1990–91, when he was nine years old, all of his family moved to Ukraine as his maternal grandparents lived there. The family kept Lithuanian citizenship and had a residence permit in Ukraine. In Ukraine Taras completed nine more years of schooling and gained a certificate as a professional driver, working in the country for a number of different companies. In 2000 the family returned to Lithuania: they had heard that the economic situation in the country was improving. All members of the family had kept their Lithuanian citizenship and this eased their return. Taras explained that citizenship of Lithuania granted them a right to travel without visas in a bigger part of Europe and consequently offered better job prospects:

> We had Lithuanian passports [...] and we heard that there are better job opportunities in Lithuania, it is possible to travel abroad... If you had a Lithuanian passport you did not need visas...nothing...you could go abroad.

Taras was in his twenties at the time and did not know the Lithuanian language since he had lived in Ukraine for the previous decade. Within a month of his return he was asked to serve in the Lithuanian army. Taras learned Lithuanian in the army and he is proud of that. However, his language skills have deteriorated since then because he did not speak Lithuanian after his service was completed. His poor language skills diminish his chances of finding a job in other regions of Lithuania. After serving in the army he married and stayed in Visaginas. He has a child who needs constant medical assistance and therefore his wife cannot work; she receives a social allowance from the state. Taras said that before the economic crisis he worked at a local company and that his family's economic situation was stable due to the combination of official and unofficial income he received there.

Like Volodia, Taras described common Lithuanian economic practices that reveal ambiguous boundaries between official and unofficial incomes. When Taras worked he received an official salary, which he described as being 'higher than minimum wages'. The employer paid taxes to the state. However, he told me that his paycheque was not enough to meet his family's needs. However, supplemental unofficial income was also available. First of all, as a part of his monthly paycheque the same private company also paid him unofficially, i.e. 'in an envelope' (Lithuanian: *vokelyje*). Secondly, he provided additional services to the clients of the company, and the clients paid him in cash without paying any taxes to the state. The official money, which was taxed, and the unofficial money, paid in cash by the employer and the clients, made the family's economic situation satisfactory. The phenomenon of getting a portion of one's salary 'in an envelope' has been described in different places across the postsocialist area, and in some cases even the local terminology used to describe the practice is identical (see an analysis of a Latvian case in Sedlenieks 2003). Such income is usually interpreted in relation to practices of corruption or as a strategy for survival (Sedlenieks 2003). Taras described his economic situation as ordinary and perceives the combination of official and unofficial income as essential for making the ends meet. However, the perception of untaxed income 'in an envelope' as an ordinary part of everyday life reveals certain attitude towards the state: that the state has to provide its citizens with social security money, but that citizens do not have a duty to pay obligatory taxes. A study by Klavs Sedlenieks describes how informants in Riga tolerated tax avoidance and aimed to legitimise such practices by offering different rationales, including the belief that the government would not use the money in a rational way (Sedlenieks 2003, 45). Taras does not provide any arguments to legitimise the system of tax avoidance and depicts it as an ordinary, common practice and the sole way for economic survival.

Taras's unofficial income started declining with the onset of the world economic crisis in 2008: people did not need as many additional services since they were buying less; and the employer cut down Taras's official salary and unofficial payments. During the crisis Taras's income was reduced a few times and eventually he lost his job. At the time of the interview Taras had been unemployed for a few months and had been receiving a small social allowance from the local branch of the labour exchange. He was entitled to this support for half a year. He does not expect that the job exchange branch will help with employment, and intends to rely only on himself. He is even considering getting officially divorced, as his wife then would be a single mother and his son would receive more support from the state. Taras considers all available institutional/systemic resources in order to provide his family with income. In his view state support is not efficient, and he is ready to use any holes in the legal system in order to reach economic stability.

Taras has considered leaving for a more economically developed country in the EU and finding a job there. He estimates that the other more developed EU states take better care of their citizens. In this way he demonstrates the perception that the state is responsible for the social security of its citizens:

> You know, I was in Germany and I was told that if you worked there officially for a year and rented a flat, then if you lost your job or decided to quit, then the state of Germany would cover your costs for your apartment, kindergarten, education, medical services, and would even provide me with some allowance to cover everyday needs [...] And here [in Lithuania] what? Everybody leaves.

Taras relates the concept of homeland (Russian: *Родина*) to the idea of social security and support being provided by a state to its citizens. For him homeland and citizenship are related to state-guaranteed social protections and social provisions; i.e. the relationship between a state and its citizens is built around the idea of a state caring for its citizens.

> I do not know... I think that Lithuania or Ukraine, they are the same thing...I think that I do not have a homeland. I think that homeland has to be like a... for example if you ask a German person in Germany where his homeland is. Everybody would say that their homeland is Germany. Because they have laws, a government that does many things for the people. And here [in Lithuania] they just cut everything [social allowances] off.

Taras's case reveals that the social protection provided by a state for its vulnerable groups in the form of social security and unemployment paycheques is of crucial importance in building citizens' attachment to the state and a sense of belonging. Anthropologist Katherine Verdery has used the term 'socialist paternalism' (1996, 63) to describe the relationship between the state and its citizens under the socialist regime. The transformation of the Soviet state in the post-Soviet period is often described as a 'state retraction' (Pine 2002, 99) or 'state withdrawal' (Read and Thelen 2007) to show that citizens are left socially and economically unprotected by state institutions and have to survive by their own means. On the other hand, the notion of state withdrawal, which was broadly used by researchers to interpret sociopolitical processes in the early post-Soviet period, has been assessed critically in later academic discussions (Read and Thelen 2007; Thelen, Cartwright and Sikor 2008). Mataradze has related Georgian citizens' perceptions of the state as social provider to the paternalism of socialist state (2011, 482). Taras was born at the end of the Soviet period and has lived through socioeconomic transformations, so it would be too simplistic to attribute his perspective to the socialist legacy. Rather, in his case expectations of state protection are formed through processes of globalisation and migration when experiences of the social politics of wealthy countries are compared with domestic practices. Issues of identity or the distinction between we/they in a cultural sense lose their importance; access to certain socioeconomic benefits becomes the most important factor in building an individual's attachment to a state (for comparison see Yalçın-Heckmann 2012).

Concluding Notes

These two stories reveal how informants build their relation to the state such that it can be described as a grey zone. By this I mean that the relationship contains aspects of ambiguity and situationality. At the level of the individual, the ambiguity of one's national and civic belonging can be productive in opening up new possibilities to answer economic and social questions. However, in such cases the borders between we/they are seen as transgressible, situational and ambiguous. Secondly, the state is expected to provide full social security with minimal investment from citizens in the form of taxes. The need for state protection is related to certain expectations of state paternalism formed during the Soviet socialist period (Verdery 1996; Nielsen 2006 [1986]; Mataradze 2011) and fostered by recent processes of migration, which result in social support provided by economically more successful states being perceived as normal and ordinary.

These stories point to how notions of citizenship change when identity and cultural commonality are no longer perceived as the basis of citizenship (see also Soysal 2010). Citizenship was conceptualised pragmatically by both informants as they considered the advantages it can provide under certain circumstances, e.g. as a 'gate keeper' through which they can access government-predicated advantages and possibilities (Shachar 2009). These stories also support the arguments of those researchers who emphasise the need to analyse citizenship in light of issues of social inequality (Kipnis 2004). From the perspective of the state institutions, my informants would be seen as exploiting the state for their own benefit. In their own view, they are exploring the resources available to them in order to survive a situation of chronic socioeconomic uncertainty. As it has been pointed by Steven Robins, Andrea Cornwall and Bettina von Lieres, 'in the scramble for livelihoods and security, poor people tend to adopt plural strategies; they occupy multiple spaces and draw on multiple political identities, discourses and social relationships, often simultaneously' (Robins, Cornwall and Lieres 2008, 1079).

Additionally, I would like to point out that the above-mentioned dimensions of what I (and others) have referred to as a grey zone in the sphere of citizen–state relations must not be perceived as specific to the post-Soviet state or to post-Soviet citizens. I suggest that similar state–citizen relationship manifestations can be found in different societies (see for example Robins, Cornwall and Lieres 2008; Mataradze 2011) and should be examined with regard to processes of globalisation, migration, the demise of the nation-state ideology, and global economic processes.

Acknowledgements

I am very grateful to Victor C. de Munck and Janina de Munck, my colleague Monika Frėjutė-Rakauskienė and the editors of this volume for their insightful comments and suggestions, which helped me to improve this chapter significantly. The qualitative research in 2011–12 was conducted within the framework of the research project 'Social Challenges for Ethnic Minorities and New Immigrant Groups in Lithuania after Joining the EU' which was funded by a grant (No. MIP-029/2011) from the Research Council of Lithuania.

Notes

1 Information provided by email by Ignalina Nuclear Power Plant, requested by the Lithuanian Social Research Centre in December 2011.
2 Lietuvos Statistikos Departamentas. 'Registruotų bedarbių ir darbingo amžiaus gyventojų santykis: registruoti bedarbiai'. Available at: http://osp.stat.gov.lt/web/guest/ viesos-duomenu-rinkmenos (accessed on 10 September 2014)
3 The names of all informants have been changed to guarantee their anonymity.
4 All interviews were conducted in Russian and all translations of informants' words into English were done by the author of the chapter.

References

Bloch, A. 2013. 'Citizenship, belonging, and Moldovan migrants in post-Soviet Russia'. *Ethnos: Journal of Anthropology* 79(4): 445–72.
Dagnino, E. 2006. 'Meanings of citizenship in Latin America'. *Canadian Journal of Latin America and Caribbean Studies* 31(62): 15–52.
_____. 2007. 'Citizenship: A perverse confluence'. *Development in Practice* 17(4–5): 549–56.
European Commission. 2008. 'Dažnai užduodami klausimai apie Ignalinos atominę elektrinę ir jos uždarymą' (FAQ on Ignalina Nuclear Power Plant for public affairs). Available at: http://ec.europa.eu/lietuva/news_hp/hot_topics/ignalina_nuclear_power_ plant/index_lt.htm (accessed 30 December 2013).
Kavaliauskas, A. 1999. *Visaginas (1975–1999)*. Vilnius: Jandrija.
_____. 2002. 'Visagino miesto demografiniai pokyčiai ir kai kurios jų priežastys' (The demographical changes in Visaginas city and some of their reasons). In A. Čiužas (ed.), *Rytų Lietuva: Visuomenės ir socialinių grupių raiška bei sąveika* (Eastern Lithuania: The expression and interaction of society and social groups), 121–31. Vilnius: Socialinių tyrimų institutas, Tautinių mažumų ir išeivijos departamentas prie Lietuvos Respublikos Vyriausybės.
_____. 2003. *Visaginas: Istorijos fragmentai (1972–2002)* (Visaginas: Fragments of history [1972–2002]). Vilnius: Jandrija.
Kipnis, A. 2004. 'Anthropology and the theorisation of citizenship'. *Asia Pacific Journal of Anthropology* 5(3): 257–78.
Kymlica W. and W. Norman. 2010 [2000]. 'Citizenship in culturally diverse societies: Issues, contexts, concepts'. In W. Kymlica and W. Norman (eds), *Citizenship in Diverse Societies*, 1–44. Oxford: Oxford University Press.
Lietuvos Respublikos Seimas (Parliament of the Republic of Lithuania). 2010. Lietuvos Respublikos pilietybės įstatymas (Republic of Lithuania citizenship law), no. XI-1196. *Valstybės žinios* no. 144-7361. Available at: http://www3.lrs.lt/ pls/inter3/dokpaieska.showdoc_l?p_id=387811&p_query=&p_tr2= (accessed 11 November 2014).
Lietuvos Statistikos Departamentas (Lithuanian Statistics Department). 2002. *Gyventojai pagal lytį, amžių, tautybę ir tikybą* (Population by sex, age, ethnicity and religion). Vilnius: Lietuvos Statistikos Departamentas.
_____. 2011. 'Pranešimas spaudai nr. 18/287: Išankstiniai 2011 metų gyventojų surašymo rezultatai pagal apskritis ir savivaldybes' (Press release no. 18/287: Preliminary results of the 2011 census by counties and municipalities). Available at:

http://193.219.12.232/uploads/docs/gyv_sk_surasymas.pdf?PHPSESSID=5ca09f57e2 262fb54503e473c26cb48a (accessed 15 September 2014).

_____. n.d. 'Registruotų bedarbių ir darbingo amžiaus gyventojų santykis, Registruoti bedarbiai' (The ratio of registered unemployed persons and inhabitants of working age: Registered unemployed persons). Available at: http://osp.stat.gov.lt/web/guest/viesos-duomenu-rinkmenos (accessed 15 September 2014).

Mataradze, T. 2011. 'Is the state social or the computer inhuman? Claims for state support and citizenship in post-socialist Georgia'. *Citizenship Studies* 15(3–4): 471–84.

Nimmerfeldt, G. 2011. 'Sense of belonging to Estonia'. In R. Vetik and J. Helemäe (eds), *The Russian Second Generation in Tallinn and Kohtla-Järve: The TIES Study in Estonia*, 203–28. Amsterdam: Amsterdam University Press.

Nielsen, F. S. (2006 [1986]). *The Eye of the Whirlwind: Russian Identity and Soviet Nation-Building. Quests for Meaning in a Soviet Metropolis*. Available at: http://www.anthrobase.com/Browse/Aut/index.html (accessed on 19 January 2014).

O'Byrne, D. J. 2005. *The Dimensions of Global Citizenship: Political Identity Beyond the Nation-State*. London and Portland: Frank Cass.

Ong, A. 2000. *Flexible Citizenship: The Cultural Logics of Transnationality*. Durham, NC: Duke University Press.

Ortner, S. B. 2006 *Anthropology and Social Theory: Culture, Power, and the Acting Subject.* Durham, NC: Duke University Press

Pilkington, H. 1998. *Migration, Displacement and Identity in Post-Soviet Russia*. London and New York: Routledge.

Pine, F. 2002. 'Retreat to the household? Gendered domains in postsocialist Poland'. In C. M. Hann (ed.), *Postsocialism: Ideals, Ideologies and Practices in Eurasia*, 95–113. London and New York: Routledge.

Read, R. and T. Thelen. 2007. 'Introduction: Social security and care after socialism: Reconfigurations of public and private'. *Focaal – European Journal of Anthropology* 50: 3–18.

Robins S., A. Cornwall and B. von Lieres. 2008. 'Rethinking "citizenship" in the postcolony'. *Third World Quarterly* 29(6): 1069–86.

Sedlenieks, K. 2003. 'Cash in an envelope: Corruption and tax avoidance as an economic strategy in contemporary Riga'. In K.-O. Arnsberg and T. Borén (eds), *Everyday Economy in Russia, Poland and Latvia*, 37–52. Flemingsberg: Södertörns högskola.

Shachar, A. 2009. *The Birthright Lottery: Citizenship and Global Inequality*. Cambridge, MA: Harvard University Press.

Soysal, Y. N. 2000. 'Citizenship and identity: Living in diasporas in post-war Europe?' *Ethnic and Racial Studies* 23(1): 1–15.

Stack, T. 2012. 'Beyond the state? Civil sociality and other notions of citizenship'. *Citizenship Studies* 16(7): 871–85.

Stankūnienė, V. 2011. 'Bendrosios Lietuvos gimstamumo kitimo tendencijos: 1990–2010' (The general tendencies of birth rate changes in Lithuania: 1990–2010). *Demografija ir mes: Informacinis biuletenis* (Demography and us: Informational bulletin) 4: 6–7.

Šliavaitė, K. 2005. *From Pioneers to Target Group: Social Change, Ethnicity and Memory in a Lithuanian Nuclear Power Plant Community*. Lund: Department of Sociology, Lund University.

Thelen, T., A. Cartwright and T. Sikor. 2008. 'Local State and Social Security in Rural Communities: A New Research Agenda and the Example of Postsocialist Europe'. Max Planck Institute for Social Anthropology Working Paper no. 105.

Utenos Teritorinė Darbo Birža (Utena Territorial Labour Exchange). 2012. 'Utenos teritorinės darbo biržos 2012 m: I pusmečio situacijos darbo rinkoje apžvalga' (Utena Territorial Labour Exchange branches in 2012: The overview of the labour market situation for the first half-year). Available at: http://www.ldb.lt/TDB/Utena/ DarboRinka/Puslapiai/Darbo_rinkos_tendencijos.aspx (accessed 27 July 2012).

Verdery, K. 1996. *What Was Socialism, and What Comes Next?* Princeton: Princeton University Press.

Yalçın-Heckmann, L. 2012. 'Re-thinking citizenship in the South Caucasus'. *Europe-Asia Studies* 64(9): 1724–38.

Part III

INVISIBILITIES

Chapter 8

INVISIBLE CONNECTIONS:
ON UNCERTAINTY AND THE
(RE)PRODUCTION OF OPAQUE POLITICS
IN THE REPUBLIC OF GEORGIA

Katrine Bendtsen Gotfredsen

Every citizen of Georgia, no matter where he or she lives, has the same opportunities [...] Georgia is moving forward [...] Our students are accepted to the universities without bribes today... You probably remember how much it cost to apply for the law faculty, or the medical institute. How much it cost to apply for the agricultural university. We all have experienced that... Everyone knows that the government will do everything for people to come for treatment in these hospitals. If the government were only to care about its family members then a small clinic would be enough.

—President Saakashvili at the opening of a hospital in Gori, January 2012

The opening quote from 2012 illustrates how, according to then president Mikheil Saakashvili, the Georgian government had consolidated democracy and eradicated corruption over the previous decade (Saakashvili 2012). From this perspective Georgia was rapidly moving towards a bright future, increasingly distancing itself from its dark and corrupt past. Officially corruption did decline dramatically after the Rose Revolution that brought Saakashvili and his United National Movement (UNM) to power (Jones 2013, 195–98). Hence, in the years following the revolution Georgia was in many ways considered a textbook example of the rapid development of good governance and transparency in public institutions (see Kbiltsetskhlashvili 2008; Companjen 2010).

Commencing fieldwork in the provincial town of Gori in 2010, I was initially determined to get in contact with the local municipality to obtain official statistics and figures about the town I would be studying.[1] I asked around. Most of the people I addressed seemed puzzled, such as Olga, a middle-aged woman:

KATRINE: I will need some statistics from the municipality. Just the basic facts and figures about Gori – population, unemployment and so on. Maybe you can give me advice on how to get a hold of that?

OLGA: I don't know... I think it will be very difficult to get that information... I am not sure I understand. You are an anthropologist right? Why would you need this?

KATRINE: Well, as background material. I am trying to understand what people in Gori think about the political situation in Georgia today, and why...

OLGA: And you think people will tell you the truth?[2]

Olga seemed to suggest that I would get no useful or truthful information from public servants at the municipality. So why bother? As it turned out, Olga's puzzlement at my plans was illustrative of a general perception among my Georgian friends and interlocutors. In contrast to the image put forth by Saakashvili in his speech, they would incessantly insist that services, information and political processes that should ideally be transparent and accessible were in reality kept secret and, if revealed, would become distorted and flawed. Well into my fieldwork I managed to arrange a few meetings with officials through informal contacts – that is, through my friends' acquaintances, former schoolmates, family members and neighbours. Still, however, I would continuously be warned that I should not feel certain that these contacts would not have interests and obligations invisible to me that would prevent them from answering my questions truthfully.

My conversation with Olga and the initial challenges to my fieldwork plans illustrate two features of Georgian politics that I shall suggest are intimately connected. The first is the powerful idea among the population that politics is morally dubious and opaque, and that formal political institutions and personae are largely out of reach for ordinary people. The second is the belief that if one is to access such institutions and personae, and in general secure one's everyday livelihood in a murky and uncertain sociopolitical environment, personal links and networks are essential.

Against this background, this chapter will explore how, in Georgia, phenomena ranging from national politics to local-level government and immediate social relations are infused with an atmosphere of uncertainty and a feeling that nothing is really as it seems. More specifically, I will describe and analyse public ideas with regard to the nature of 'politics' and unfold how these ideas feed into the practical means by which ordinary people seek to manage the challenges of daily life. In short, I will discuss different aspects of public perceptions of the political as opaque and inaccessible, and the consequences such perceptions had on my interlocutors' engagement and disengagement with their sociopolitical surroundings. 'Invisible connections', then, refer to two interrelated aspects, one empirical and the other analytical. I ask: What are the kinds of accounts and rationales within which people address their immediate political surroundings at the macro- as well as micro-level? How can we analytically address the links between such everyday characterisations and the production and reproduction of a particular mode of politics? And, finally, what can be gained from conceptualising such everyday ideas and practices as grey zones of fluctuating visibility and invisibility, clarity and opacity?

I will develop an argument which suggests that responses to perceived political opacity and uncertainty, in the end, contribute to their reproduction in perception and experience. That is, I propose that a particular idea of 'politics', and the ways in which my interlocutors appropriate and act towards this idea, in the end produce and reproduce political practice as such. Micropolitics – maintaining and relying on informal networks and connections, and speculating about the nature of the connections of others – is simultaneously a response to an uncertain macropolitical reality and the continuing production and confirmation of this reality across the sociopolitical scale. My interest, then, is not in assessing the 'real' nature of formal politics *vis-à-vis* public ideas, or in passing judgements on the extent to which post–Rose Revolution good governance policies, as described by Saakashvili above, have failed. Rather than investigating the concrete relationship between 'formal' and 'informal' politics, or the ways in which large-scale political processes are dependent on patronage and other informal practices and vice versa (see Isaacs 2011), I will depart from the public commonsensical perception that there is no such thing as 'pure' formal politics or disinterested state structures or services. I will outline the processes by which uncertainty and mistrust have become primary emic markers of 'politics', a 'sort of theory of social order' that people attempt to live by (Greenhouse 2002, 10), and, consequently, how this 'theory', or imaginary, feeds into concrete everyday interactions and experience. Before addressing these issues further, however, a few contextual notes on Gori are in order.

Notes on Gori

Gori, located approximately 70 kilometres west of the capital Tbilisi, is the administrative centre of the Shida Kartli region. Heading into town by one of the bumpy roads leading from the main highway crossing Georgia from east to west, one is met by a patchy combination of Soviet-style five-storey apartment blocks, family houses, small kiosks and grocery shops, restaurants, and a newly built shopping centre with large glass facades. The streets appear rather quiet and empty apart from the area around the central market and bus station, which is no doubt the busiest, noisiest and most hectic place in town. In Soviet times Gori was an important industrial centre, but the economic crisis of the 1990s caused a shutdown of the majority of the former industries and factories and a general exodus among the population. In 2012 the town had an official population of 54,900 inhabitants – around 13,000 less than in the late 1980s.[3] This number, however, was disputed among the residents, most of whom insisted that the figures are too high and do not reflect the large number of people who have actually left in search of work in Tbilisi or abroad. Walking around, it was indeed hard to imagine more than 50,000 people living in the town.

According to official statistics from 2011, the Shida Kartli region has an unemployment rate of 8.9 per cent, with urban areas such as Gori having a higher rate than the rural areas. In contrast, Jones (2013, 194) points out that the design of unemployment statistics in Georgia masks radically different numbers, and he thus estimates the real unemployment rate across the country in 2010 to be as high as 60 per cent – a number intuitively much more fitting judging by my experience and the characterisations given by my interlocutors, many of whom were either unemployed or underemployed.[4] In short, whereas Tbilisi and the Black Sea city of Batumi have, at least on the surface, developed into vibrant economic and cultural centres over the last decade, Gori is an example of a provincial town that still struggles with economic development and prioritisation in national politics (Jones 2013, 144, 213).

Ideas, Detachments and Performance

Behind my argument lie a number of presumptions concerning the nature of politics. The first one is an empirical observation and builds on emic characterisations of politics, leading, as it were, to some more overall suppositions concerning useful ethnographic and analytical approaches to the political as a field of inquiry. I will briefly outline these below.

The Georgian state is 'semipresidential', with the president being head of state, and the prime minister, appointed by the president, head of government. Legislative authority is vested in the parliament. Between the 2003 Rose Revolution and the 2012 parliamentary elections, Saakashvili's UNM held a majority in the parliament and hence, in reality, both executive and legislative power. Quite possibly reflecting this macropolitical reality, there was frequently a popular conflation of the state and government. People working within state institutions were seen as adhering to, and performing, government politics – or, at least, they were perceived as people who could not afford to oppose the UNM political line in public. It was a relatively accepted fact among my friends and interlocutors that people relying on employment in public institutions necessarily have to, or at least must *pretend* to, adhere to government policies when outside of private settings. Adding to this, politicians and people involved in political structures were characterised as selfish and thus acting to preserve their own positions and privileges rather than in the interests of the people they were supposedly representing. These factors contributed to a particular understanding of politics as essentially dirty, insincere and opaque – a field rife with invisible connections and secret agendas. In short, politics was considered an immoral and flawed business that one was reluctant to admit practising or showing any interest in. People would repeatedly fiercely deny having anything to do with it. According to their statements, it was nowhere to be found in their daily lives – except as something imposing itself on them from the outside: *out there* or *up there* (see Gotfredsen 2013). However, as we shall see, practices that are not necessarily explicitly aimed at being political may be interpreted as such by others and, in the end, produce political outcomes and effects. Hence, it becomes relevant to ask the question: How can we analytically grasp the fact that ordinary people take part in producing the political even when they themselves claim not to?

First of all, answering this question requires that we adopt a rather wide perspective of what constitutes 'the political' as a field of inquiry – a perspective that is not, as such, foreign to anthropology (see Vincent 2002). I propose an analysis including both the practices undertaken by ordinary people in the 'pursuit of their daily lives' (Wedeen 2008, 3) and the social and cultural meanings and expressions giving form to these practices (Verdery 1999, 25–26). When referring to the everyday production of 'the political' then, I refer to this level of analysis: to the acts and utterings of ordinary people in their pursuits of security and certainty in their everyday lives, and to the social rationales and perceptions within which these occur. In doing so, I follow Carol Greenhouse in her call to ethnographically investigate the state, and political structure in general, as it comes forth in everyday social practice, 'treating it only and wholly in relation to its social reality – or irreality – "on the ground"' (Greenhouse 2002, 7; see also Navaro-Yashin 2002, 135).

Part of this social reality 'on the ground' are the derived effects of an emic perception of politics as being essentially dirty and opaque. Hence, just as we can see the state as both a set of tangible governing practices and institutions *and* a powerful idea or imaginary (Navaro-Yashin 2012), I suggest that we may see the political – in the Georgian setting at least – as both a set of concrete daily practices and an idea, or imaginary, that feeds into these concrete practices and their effects. In other words, similar to studies emphasising the state as an 'idea' (Abrams 1988), 'fetish' (Taussig 1992) or 'fantasy' (Navaro-Yashin 2002, 2012), I propose that *ideas* of politics among my interlocutors and the ways in which they appropriate and act towards these ideas produce the political in a particular fashion.

In her study of Yemeni politics, Lisa Wedeen argues for a performative perspective on political practice that accounts for the ways in which democratic or national persons are constituted through speech-acts and deeds associated with nationalism and democracy, without necessarily committing to their underlying ideals (2008, 16–17). Analogously, I propose that political statements may be produced through performative practices that are not necessarily aimed at being political in any such explicit sense (see Yurchak 2008, 732). By introducing what he terms a 'heteronymous shift' into discussions of late Soviet ideological discourse, Alexei Yurchak proposes an understanding of the relationship between performance and underlying meaning which is slightly different to Wedeen's. He argues that the replication of ideological form (reproducing the written form of ideological texts, raising your hand in favour at a party meeting, etc.) was increasingly decoupled from the level of meaning (values, ideals, ethics, etc.) in late Soviet discourse, ultimately leaving the literal meaning for which the form supposedly stood unpredictable and open to interpretation (Yurchak 2006, 51–54). I suggest that a similar dual potential for the interpretation of practice and performance is a defining characteristic of the production of Georgian politics. Thus, whereas I concur with Wedeen that we should focus our study of the political on what people *do*, I want to stress that this *doing* is still, in social practice, left to be interpreted and perceived in terms of its underlying meanings and values. These meanings and values, I argue, may be perceived as dual and unpredictable, and this duality, ultimately, produces the political as a grey zone that has, paradoxically perhaps, become relatively ordinary and predictable in its very opacity and unpredictability.

The Micropolitics of Everyday (In)security

$10,000

> It is a Monday morning in June, and Mari and I are sitting in the kitchen having breakfast. As often before, Mari is telling me about what she sees as her hopeless job situation. She graduated from university with high marks in financial management five years ago but has not yet managed to get a job.

She dreams about working in a bank. When she graduated, she applied for vacancies and went to Tbilisi to take test exams and participate in training courses, but without success. 'If you don't have contacts you will never find a job,' she concludes. 'You know, if you want a job in a bank, you need to pay the director of that bank…maybe $10,000. But then after six months a new director will come, and you have to start all over again. The people working there don't know what they are doing – they have no education. But their family or others know someone. Sopo [her sister] knows the school director where she works. That is why she has a job.'

Analyses describing everyday life in the context of state socialism have noted how an economy of shortage made social networks and connections an essential resource in terms of exchanges of goods and favours. This created a vibrant 'second economy', running parallel to the official state economy and involving a moral economy of its own (Sampson 1987; Humphrey and Hugh-Jones 1992; Verdery 1996). In many of the former socialist countries the importance of social networks and an everyday reliance on well-connected patrons still exist (Ledeneva 2006; Morris and Polese 2014). Even if the introduction of market economies has made consumer goods available for purchase (for those who can afford them) and the introduction of liberal democracies should ideally have limited informality and corruption within formal political structures, on neither count have the expectations of the political analysts of the early 1990s been met (Sztompka 1993; Nodia 1996; Wilson 2005; Isaacs 2011). This is also true in the Georgian case. Just as social networks, friends and kin were considered essential and often drew more loyalty and attention than society as a whole in Soviet times (Mars and Altman 1983; Dragadze 1988), several analysts indicate that this is no less true today (Dudwick 2003, 256; Jones 2013, 11). My conversation with Mari above illustrates that this perspective is not confined to academic analysis. Her characterisation of her personal situation drew heavily on a commonsensical notion that networks and connections are essential to social and economic security.

In arguing for an analytical distinction between the closely related terms 'uncertainty', 'insecurity' and 'contingency', Susan Whyte proposes that we understand uncertainty as a state of mind, whereas insecurity is to be understood as a social condition reflecting a 'lack of protection from danger, weakness in the social arrangements which provide some kind of safety net when adversity strikes […] a state of limited resources for action' (2009, 213). When dealing with uncertainty, she argues, we are trying to make things more secure. It is this process of 'making secure' that I suggest simultaneously feeds on and reproduces the opaque and invisible (or uncertain) nature of Georgian politics.

Among my interlocutors it was a generally accepted fact that the best insurance against the unforeseen outcomes of political opacity, and the socioeconomic hardships that come with unemployment, is a tight personal network that can be activated and depended on for resources (material or personal) when needed. This was illustrated in Mari's account of her job situation *vis-à-vis* that of her sister. She herself had no connections within the financial sector she wished to work in, whereas Sopo knew the director in the village school where she got a job as an English teacher after finishing university. The point here is not so much whether Mari's story about jobs 'costing' $10,000 is true, but rather her statement that having no connections means having no opportunities – and vice versa: connections yield opportunity. Shortly after I had had the above conversation with Mari, another friend of mine, Davit (who has no education in finance), was offered a job in one of the local bank offices, because, as he admitted with a shy smile, his cousin was the local branch director.

The widespread reliance on personal connections entails a social stratification among 'ordinary' people in terms of who has such connections and who has not. Davit told me about his cousin's influence on the job offer, but Mari and others like her are most often left to speculate about the real nature of the – to them invisible – connections that provide others with their relative successes. In the end, this causes not only large-scale politics but also the micropolitics of everyday security and opportunity to be covered in suspicion for the perceived outsider. Or said otherwise, the pursuit of micropolitical goals comes to mirror perceptions of macropolitics – and vice versa. This link will become more explicit below.

Everyday Suspicion

Neighbours and agents

One Sunday afternoon we are sitting in Manana's kitchen facing the common courtyard. The yard is laid out between staircases and landings leading to the surrounding flats – some of these, such as Manana's, being shared by several families. One of the neighbouring women, Nino, is visiting. She and Manana are in heated discussion. Another neighbour has claimed ownership of the common areas of the courtyard. She has obtained a document from the municipality, apparently proving that she has sole ownership of several of the – previously common – areas of the yard, including the landing leading to Manana's kitchen. The legal decision seems absurd, we agree. In reality, Manana now does not have passage from the courtyard to her flat, and Nino, in principle, cannot access her toilet, which is situated in the yard. I ask how this is possible, and Manana explains: 'I think she is a secret agent for the government. Every day she goes to the municipality – it is very interesting…like Soviet times,' she adds. She chuckles, as if pointing to the irony of nothing having changed. 'And what do you think she is supposed to find out?' I ask. 'Yes, it is very hard to understand what would be interesting about our lives, isn't it?' Manana replies, with a dry smile. I shrug, thinking that it is indeed hard to imagine. Still, the women agree, the only plausible explanation for the municipality's decision is that the neighbour has exchanged information about the residents of the house for her new privileges.

Manana's irony reflected the seeming silliness of a neighbour informing on her to the local municipality. In the end, as she implied, there was hardly anything about her life that was worthy of such attention. Her reasoning, then, was not so much connected to fear of what the neighbour might find out and tell. What is of interest here, and what I shall further elaborate on below, is the swift conclusion that the neighbour must have a secret deal, a hidden connection, with someone at the municipality in order to have obtained the paperwork. It draws on the same general atmosphere surrounding the topic of national politics that I discussed above: that nothing is as it seems.

The cases of Mari and Manana illustrate the relationship between macro- and micropolitics. That is, how ideas regarding the nature of large-scale politics both feed on, and feed into, everyday perceptions and experiences encountered when pursuing daily life. Power, and the real sources of influence, it seems, always try to keep themselves masked and rarely come forward with true intentions or truthful information. The very diverse situations and events these examples address could call into question the extent to which they reveal anything general or at all comparable. What I wish to argue, however, is precisely that the general idea of politics is informed by an atmosphere of fragments such as these – of bits and pieces of information received from politicians, media, friends, family and people gossiping in the neighbouring yard (see Navaro-Yashin 2002). The multiple fragments of knowledge and accounts that people are confronted with may or may not be true. Actually it seems that the very foundation for assessing such information is an acknowledgement that one cannot really trust what was being said – as Manana's account illustrates there might well be ulterior motives at play. In other words, everyday interactions often build on the premise that what people *really* think and contemplate is not necessarily reflected in what they say or do. This awareness will become more evident below.

Dualities of Cynicism

Hospital openings

My former landlady, Tamuna, and I are watching the evening news in her flat in Tbilisi. The president appears on screen speaking to a crowd of people gathered in front of a newly constructed building. 'Ah, you see? Every day our Misha is opening a new hospital somewhere,' says Tamuna. 'It is something very interesting...' she adds – giggling as she often does when commenting on politics. A giggling that I have come to know as a sign of her pointing to a profound irony of events, or, as is often the case, life in general. 'Look he is in your town, in Gori!'

In his speech, Saakashvili talks about the continuous and seemingly unstoppable development of modern infrastructure initiated by the government – exemplified by this hospital. Georgia is on a track moving forward, and there is no going back. Corruption, bribes, and politicians caring only for themselves and their families are history. Now all Georgians have the same opportunities, he optimistically states.[5]

A few days later I am watching the news with Lali, my landlady in Gori. Another hospital is being opened. 'I saw on the news a couple of days ago that Misha had opened a new hospital in Gori,' I say. Lali nods and smiles. 'I was surprised that so many people were there...' I add. 'I was there too,' Lali laughs. 'Really?' I say sceptically – knowing that Lali is anything but a fan of the president. 'They had lists with our names at the school, and we were told to go... And, so we went.'

What informed the irony and laughter at play when I talked to Tamuna and Lali about the hospital openings? To Tamuna, events like this, and similar ones daily reaching the evening news, were ironic because of their unrecognisable relationship to the reality she saw herself as being a part of. When her mother suffered a stroke the previous summer, Tamuna's only perceived access to a proper doctor was through a childhood friend and not the public hospitals. She would not have been able to pay the 'fees' needed for a stranger to give her mother the proper treatment and care, she told me. The point here is not to discuss whether hospital staff generally demand extra 'fees' to care for patients or not. The point is rather that to Tamuna's best knowledge, this was definitely the case. This awareness rendered public channels of hospitalisation and care out of her reach, and left her to use her personal network for healthcare.

The funny thing to Lali was that I was surprised to have seen so many people and did not realise the 'fakeness' of the event. In that sense Lali's laughter represented a cynical assertion that the number of people present at an event like that was not an expression of the number of supporters of the president. It was simply a part of what people now and then have to do, in Yurchak's (2006, 23–24) pragmatic and performative sense of the word, in order to satisfy the expectations of being a public employee: that you, at least in public, support the government that is employing you. In the end, who wants to risk losing one's job over something as silly and ordinary as this?

Lali and Tamuna's laughter, in short, played on irony and cynicism rather than joy. I was somewhat surprised when I first realised that many public political events, such as the opening of the hospital in Gori, were staged; that people were either paid to go or indirectly threatened to. Intuitively, to me, this was a reproduction of Soviet political practices and forms of oppression that I had not anticipated. Lali's laughter, on the other hand, cynically suggested that this was only what was to be expected. Everyone knows that, she seemed to imply. Knowing to what extent this is actually happening is of course difficult, as are the real consequences of not going if told to. But rumours were plenty. Several friends would tell me that they – being teachers, employed at the local hospital or at a state museum – of course had to support the government in office if they wanted to be sure of keeping their jobs.

The cynicism of Lali and Tamuna, then, mirrors the type of binary thinking that Yurchak critiques in academic analyses of Soviet authoritative discourse. That is, the immediate conclusion that people act in public 'as if' they comply with the authorities while privately believing something different. This, he argues, diverts attention from the continuing production and reinterpretation of discourse and knowledge (Yurchak 2006, 16–18). I believe, however, that we must make a distinction here between Lali's reasoning, which reflected *her* interpretation of situations such as the hospital opening, and a more abstract analytical level reflecting Yurchak's point. Showing up at a hospital opening may either, by spectators, be interpreted as a statement that one supports the government and its initiatives or, within the commonsensical understanding expressed by Lali and Tamuna, that there is not necessarily a connection between the number of people and the level of public support. In other words, there is an acute awareness that you cannot assume that there is a one-to-one relation between what people think and intend, and what they actually say or do. From a strictly performative perspective, we can argue that the very act of showing up at a hospital opening produces support. My suggestion, however, is that we see it as an ambiguous act enabling a dual interpretation and hence, in effect, as contributing to the production and reproduction of public politics as being *potentially* 'not as it seems'. We are faced, then, with what seems a paradoxical practice of critiquing the fake and opaque nature of politics and simultaneously potentially contributing to its reproduction.[6]

The Grey Zones of Georgian Politics

Johnson-Hanks observes how, in Cameroon, *la crise* and the uncertainty that it has brought about 'has become available as a trope that serves to legitimate and reinforce both the interpretation of the world as uncertain and behavior that contributes to that uncertainty' (2005, 366). In the previous sections

I have shown that the uncertainty resulting from the (perceived) opaque and suspicious nature of political institutions and social agents with successful connections in the Georgian context has a similar dual effect. The widespread perception of large-scale politics as being opaque, double-faced and dirty trickles down and serves as a trope both explaining and reproducing this opacity as an experience and reality in more micropolitical contexts.

The cases above have served to illustrate exactly this process of addressing politics as opaque and simultaneously confirming and reproducing it as such. In other words, the sense of being caught up in an uncertain political reality that is merely *out there*, impossible to engage with and grasp, is reinforced by the very practices engaged in to limit this experience of uncertainty. When 'making secure' by means of upholding and nurturing social networks through favours and their expected returns, or by faking support at certain public events, one is simultaneously confirming and enacting the perception that invisible connections and secrecy are the basis of political action. The widespread proclaimed detachment from the morally dubious and opaque realms of formal politics and institutions, the favouring of nurturing personal connections, and the insistence that if one *does* act in a explicitly political manner this is merely pretence, serve as examples of how ideas and perceptions of large-scale politics feed into micro-practices that, in the end, produce the political in an image of these ideas and perceptions.

As I suggested earlier in this chapter, even if we look for politics in what people *do* rather than in the intentions informing this doing, people's acts are still, in social practice, left to be interpreted (and perceived) for their underlying meanings and values. Even if we take seriously people's claims that they are not engaging in politics, acts and accounts such as those we have encountered above are still left *out there* for others to interpret and make sense of. In this continuous effort of making sense of one's personal position *vis-à-vis* others' positions as reflected in their acts and utterings, I argue that uncertainty and opacity are dominant tropes. In the cases analysed here, explanations for a seemingly absurd situation are found in other people masking the real motives for their actions and decisions. Circumstances and personal positions have been explained by reference to a commonsensical understanding that power and influence operate in the murky and invisible corners of social and political life. However, in that sense, the three stories also share an inherent paradox: on the one hand the people we have met above would stress the opaque nature of power and influence, and yet, immediately, they would also add quite precise characterisations of what was *actually* going on. From one analytical angle we could interpret this as a series of examples of how the articulation of certainty actively works to eliminate doubts and uncertainty (Vigh 2011; Pelkmans 2013). My point is, however, that while the accounts may work at some level to clarify matters – to render them visible, as it were – they simultaneously disclose the overall idea that you cannot necessarily trust what people around you say or do, thus leaving even the clarifying stories themselves up for interpretation and speculation.

Such fluctuations of opacity and clarity, visibility and invisibility, direct our attention to a characterising aspect of political practice in contemporary Georgia. The seeming paradox of opacity and clarity that we have seen in Manana, Mari and Lali's stories may not be an anomaly but rather a defining, and on its own terms reasonable, feature of a widespread practice of engaging with uncertainty in the pursuit of everyday security and certainty; a practice in which opacity and clarity may not be mutually exclusive but, rather, run parallel (see West and Sanders 2003; Larson 2008). The effort of making sense of the inequalities of influence, then, simultaneously reproduces the widespread perception that things are – potentially – not as they seem. Besides large-scale political structures, formal political institutions, and government imaginaries and practices, the political as a field of experience and inquiry is shaped by the duality of people's engagements with the connections, influences and motives informing the everyday micropolitics of their lives. This is a duality of engagement that, as we saw most evidently illustrated in the case of Lali above, feeds into the wider political landscape and reproduces it as a predictably ambiguous formation fluctuating between clarity and opacity, visibility and invisibility – a grey zone that is continuously (re)produced by the very efforts pursued to control it and render it legible.

Notes

1   Data for this chapter stem from ethnographic fieldwork carried out between 2006 and 2012 in Georgia, notably over the course a 10-month period in 2010 and 2011 in Gori.
2   This initial conversation with Olga was conducted in English. The majority of the conversations cited in this chapter, however, have been translated from Georgian by the author.
3   Statistics from www.geostat.ge (accessed 18 November 2014).
4   Of the population listed as employed in the entire region of Shida Kartli, approximately 70 per cent are self-employed. This partly reflects the fact that it is predominantly an agricultural region. However, this simultaneously constitutes a statistical masking of the many households living mainly from subsistence farming on small plots of land and now and then selling off surplus produce at local markets. Also, these statistics do not count the unregistered unemployed and women who have stopped seeking work (Jones 2013, 194, 202).
5   The optimism displayed by Saakashvili in his speech bears remarkable resemblance to Soviet modernist optimism. In other words, even if the political project of the UNM was 'effectively neoliberal' (Manning 2007, 176), the tone and communicative form displayed a marked continuity with Soviet political discourse, and, as we shall see

below, so did popular responses. For an analysis of the similarities of the discursive practices of late liberalism and late socialism, see Boyer and Yurchak (2010).

6   In comparison, Navaro-Yashin proposes that cynicism is a feeling of political existence that reproduces the political by default. Cynicism, she argues, 'encapsulates both state fetishism and everyday public critiques of the state' (Navaro-Yashin 2002, 159). Along similar lines I suggest that the cynicism expressed by Lali was equally critiquing, essentialising and reproducing the political.

References

Abrams, P. 1988. 'Notes on the difficulty of studying the state'. *Journal of Historical Sociology* 1(1): 58–89.

Boyer, D. and A. Yurchak. 2010. 'American *stiob*: Or, what late-socialist aesthetics of parody reveal about contemporary political culture in the West'. *Cultural Anthropology* 25(2): 179–221.

Companjen, F. J. 2010. 'Georgia'. In D. Ó Beacháin and A. Polese (eds), *The Colour Revolutions in the Former Soviet Republics: Successes and Failures*, 13–29. London and New York: Routledge.

Dragadze, T. 1988. *Rural Families in Soviet Georgia: A Case Study in Ratcha Province*. London and New York: Routledge.

Dudwick, N. 2003. 'No guests at our table: Social fragmentation in Georgia'. In Nora Dudwick, Elizabeth Gomart and Alexandre Marc (eds), *When Things Fall Apart: Qualitative Studies of Poverty in the Former Soviet Union*, 213–57. Washington DC: World Bank.

Gotfredsen, K. B. 2013. 'Evasive Politics: Paradoxes of History, Nation and Everyday Communication in the Republic of Georgia'. PhD dissertation, University of Copenhagen.

Greenhouse, C. J. 2002. 'Introduction: Altered states, altered lives'. In C. J. Greenhouse, E. Mertz and K. B. Warren (eds), *Ethnography in Unstable Places, Everyday Lives in Contexts of Dramatic Political Change*, 1–31. Durham, NC: Duke University Press.

Humphrey, C. and S. Hugh-Jones. 1992. *Barter, Exchange and Value: An Anthropological Approach*. Cambridge and New York: Cambridge University Press.

Isaacs, R. 2011. *Party System Formation in Kazakhstan: Between Formal and Informal Politics*. London: Routledge.

Johnson-Hanks, J. 2005. 'When the future decides: Uncertainty and intentional action in contemporary Cameroon'. *Current Anthropology* 46(3): 363–85.

Jones, S. F. 2013. *Georgia: A Political History since Independence*. London: I.B. Tauris.

Kbiltsetskhlashvili, T. 2008. 'Investment climate of Georgia after "Rose Revolution": Recent improvements and new challenges'. *IBSU Scientific Journal* 2(2): 47–86.

Larson, J. L. 2008. 'Ambiguous transparency: Resumé fetishism in a Slovak workshop'. *Ethnos: Journal of Anthropology* 73(2): 189–216.

Ledeneva, A. V. 2006. *How Russia Really Works: The Informal Practices that Shaped Post-Soviet Politics and Business*. Ithaca, NY: Cornell University Press.

Manning, P. 2007. 'Rose-colored glasses? Color revolutions and cartoon chaos in postsocialist Georgia'. *Cultural Anthropology* 22(2): 171–213.

Mars, G. and Y. Altman. 1983. 'The cultural basis of Soviet Georgia's second economy'. *Soviet Studies* 35(4): 546–60.

Morris, J. and A. Polese (eds). 2014. *The Informal Post-socialist Economy: Embedded Practices and Livelihoods*. London: Routledge.

Navaro-Yashin, Y. 2002. *Faces of the State: Secularism and Public Life in Turkey*. Princeton: Princeton University Press.

———. 2012. *The Make-Believe Space. Affective Geography in a Postwar Polity*. Durham, NC: Duke University Press.

Nodia, G. 1996. 'How different are postcommunist transitions?' *Journal of Democracy* 7(4): 15–29.

Pelkmans, M. 2013. 'Outline for an ethnography of doubt'. In M. Pelkmans (ed.), *Ethnographies of Doubt: Uncertainty and Faith in Contemporary Societies*, 1–42. London: I.B. Tauris.

Sampson, S. L. 1987. 'The second economy of the Soviet Union and Eastern Europe'. *Annals of the American Academy of Political and Social Science* 493(1): 120–36.

Sztompka, P. 1993. 'Civilizational incompetence: The trap of post-communist societies'. *Zeitschrift für Soziologie* 22(2): 85–95.

Saakashvili, M. 2012. Presidential address to the population of Gori, 11 January.

Taussig, M. 1992. 'Maleficium: State fetishism'. In M. Taussig, *The Nervous System*, 111–40. New York: Routledge.

Verdery, K. 1996. *What Was Socialism, and What Comes Next?* Princeton: Princeton University Press.

———. 1999. *The Political Lives of Dead Bodies: Reburial and Postsocialist Change*. New York: Columbia University Press.

Vigh, H. E. 2011. 'Vigilance: On conflict, social invisibility, and negative potentiality'. *Social Analysis* 55(3): 93–114.

Vincent, J. (ed.). 2002. *The Anthropology of Politics: A Reader in Ethnography, Theory, and Critique*. Malden, MA: Blackwell.

Wedeen, L. 2008. *Peripheral Visions: Publics, Power, and Performance in Yemen*. Chicago: University of Chicago Press.

West, H. G. and T. Sanders. 2003. 'Power revealed and concealed in the new world order'. In H. G. West and T. Sanders (eds), *Transparency and Conspiracy: Ethnographies of Suspicion in the New World Order*, 1–37. Durham, NC: Duke University Press.

Whyte, S. R. 2009. 'Epilogue: Insecurity, contingency and uncertainty'. In L. Haram and B. Yamba (eds), *Situating Uncertainty in Contemporary Africa*, 213–16. Uppsala: Nordic Africa Institute.

Wilson, A. 2005. *Virtual Politics: Faking Democracy in the Post-Soviet World*. New Haven: Yale University Press.

Yurchak, A. 2006. *Everything Was Forever, Until It Was No More: The Last Soviet Generation*. Princeton: Princeton University Press.

———. 2008. 'Suspending the political: Late Soviet artistic experiments on the margins of the state'. *Poetics Today* 29(4): 713–33.

Chapter 9

THE LITHUANIAN 'UNEMPLOYMENT AGENCY': ON *BOMŽAI* AND INFORMAL WORKING PRACTICES

Ida Harboe Knudsen

A small group of men has gathered under the shadow of a tree close to the riverside in Lithuania's second largest city, Kaunas. They have weathered faces, are dressed in worn-out clothes and are talking loudly while smoking and drinking beer. They sit on some old blocks of cement on the ground. Around them garbage is carelessly scattered by people passing by. A wooden sign is hammered onto a nearby tree: 'DARBO BIRŽA' – 'Unemployment Agency'.[1] The sign shows that the men are looking for work. At the same time it serves as a sarcastic comment on the official unemployment agency (also called Darbo Birža), as the men both display their subaltern position and, in a counter-hegemonic approach, replicate the symbols of what they perceive to be an oppressive system (cf. Keesing 1992). They have created their own institution, one that aims to meet needs that the official system neglects. The principle behind the Darbo Birža[2] at the riverside is that people who need to get work done – such as cutting wood, painting, cleaning stables, simple construction work or other kinds of physical work – drive by in their cars and collect the men they need for the day. For a day of hard work the men earn about 50 litas (14.50 euros).

I came across the men at the riverside during a research project in which I was investigating 'invisible citizens'. By invisible citizens I mean people who opt to avoid formal and institutional relations with the state due to a general scepticism, mainly towards politicians, the police and public bureaucrats, who are perceived as showing little if any attention to the problems and concerns of the lower-middle-class, 'ordinary' people. The 'invisible' do not register their employment and therefore pay no tax. This is more than a little moonlighting on the side; it is a way of living. In Lithuania this means that they are deprived of any kind of state support – most importantly public health insurance and economical and social support in case of unemployment – just as they will not receive an adequate pension when they reach the age of retirement. Following the global financial crisis of 2008 – which, with a little delay, reached Lithuania in 2009 – the prevalence of informal work moved to the top of the political agenda, as the Lithuanian government was in need of the unpaid tax money.

The emergence of shadow work in contemporary Lithuania, I suggest, is based on previous experiences of instability, a lack of state security, and growing scepticism towards institutional arrangements, leading people to stray away from state institutions and formal employment. Some do so due to an active contempt for present-day Lithuania, while others, like the men at the Birža, find themselves in a position of exclusion and bewilderment. Anthropologist David Kideckel has interpreted such tendencies as new forms of subalternisation among workers in the post-Soviet states (2002). Based on his research among Romanian miners, he poses the argument that workers have been placed at or near the bottom in postsocialist societies. This hierarchical displacement has been radical in the sense that workers went from being the celebrated class during socialism to degraded supplicants during the period after the Soviet breakdown (Kideckel 2002). The men at the Birža are the visible expression of this. They have moved from being integrated in (Soviet) society as citizens and persons, with work, an income, a place to live and a family, to being what Lithuanians popularly refer to as *bomžai* (bums) and *pijokai* (drunkards), without stable work, residence or family, and with a highly irregular income based on undertaking a variety of tasks in the form of day labour.

In this chapter I provide a case study of how people experiencing social and economic marginalisation are turning to normative coping strategies to compensate for the security they are deprived of by the state. While dealing with their own ambiguous and contradicting feelings of identity, they try to negotiate a status of being more than just homeless, poor and alcoholic *bomžai*; they reclaim space and a certain state of personhood at the margin of society as day labourers searching for occupation. While the Birža in itself is a small place and hosts but a few people, its existence testifies to larger issues of instability and insecurity in present-day Lithuania. I treat it as a grey zone of personhood and practices, taking grey zones to be places and situations where uncertainty, ambiguity and unsettled identities have become part and parcel of everyday life, resulting in social and economic practices that straddle the border between legal and illegal. In line with the core argument of this volume, I propose that such normative solutions to everyday shortages should be seen as something in and of themselves, not as a transitory state of being before a 'functional' capitalist model kicks in. What once might have been perceived as a temporary period of hardship on the way to something better has taken the form of a permanent crisis.

Conducting Research

This chapter is based on fieldwork conducted first in 2011 and continued for part of the summer of 2012 and the summer of 2013. The research was part of a larger project in which I investigated informal working practices in present-day Lithuania. The Birža constituted an important part of my research. My fieldwork was conducted in Kaunas, a large former industrial city in the centre of Lithuania with more than 300,000 inhabitants. I carried out 17 interviews with the men at the riverside and regularly spent time there with them as they were waiting for work. In addition I carried out interviews about unregistered work with people from public institutions: the State Tax Inspectorate (Valstybinė Mokesčių Inspekcija), the Lithuanian Trade Union Confederation (Lietuvos Profesinių Sąjungų Konfederacija), the Lithuanian Labour Inspection (Lietuvos Respublikos Valstybinė Darbo Inspekcija) and the Lithuanian Unemployment Agency (Lietuvos Darbo Birža).

The fact that the men were in a precarious situation money-wise had an impact on my fieldwork. While I initially thought I could invite them to a café, such attempts were fruitless. None of the men felt comfortable being in a public café because of the stigma attached to their visible poverty, and often, to their distinct odours. They would not even cross the main street to carry out interviews on some comfortable benches instead of on the stones at the riverside, as the benches were not on 'their side of the street'.[3] Providing them with food did not go down well either, as they were struggling to uphold their identity as *workers* and *men*, not beggars for food. I thus decided to pay for interviews. This was a way to bridge our uneven positions and to compensate the men for the time they spent with me. Telling me their stories and showing me their lives was classified as them assisting me with my work, except on the days when they managed to get a day's work through the Birža. On these rare occasions our interactions were perceived as friendly chatting, and they took pleasure in buying alcohol, cigarettes, dried fish or some snacks and sharing these with all at the Birža – including me.

The money I paid always left me feeling slightly ambivalent, as I knew that the main part of it would be spent on alcohol. Drinking remained a central part of their everyday existence, and was something for which they had received plenty of punishment throughout their lives; it had resulted in them losing permanent jobs (after the declared independence, notably), experiencing imprisonment and social exclusion, and suffering domestic violence – something which they on one occasion eagerly demonstrated to me by showing and comparing the number and sizes of various scars received from beatings with pots and pans by wives or girlfriends. As James Spradley (2000 [1970]) remarks in his monograph about homeless men in the USA in the 1960s, alcohol becomes both a means and an end in an unsettled situation. While his informants – urban nomads, as he described them – had been arrested countless times for being drunk in public, it was at the same time society's approach and treatment of them that caused their continued drinking. As one of his informants expressed it: 'After 30 days in jail, you owe yourself a drunk' (Spradley 2000 [1970], 26). While I was perplexed about contributing to my interlocutors' alcohol consumption, I had also no desire to attempt to 'regulate' a presumed abnormal behaviour. What would have been 'ethical' or 'correct' behaviour on my side remains obscure to me to this very day. Thus bemused I have taken comfort in anthropologist Tova Höjdestrand's reflections on a similar situation she encountered studying homeless people in St Petersburg, Russia: 'Anything I gave to anybody [...] was potential currency in the great "booze exchange", so the only morally pure option would have been not to give away anything (which in itself is immoral) or to avoid studying alcoholics in the first place' (2009, 17).

In the post-Soviet context it is pertinent to take an additional dimension into consideration with regard to alcohol consumption: namely, that drinking was not a response to the unstable environment in the 1990s and the men's social and economic derailment after independence. Rather, the men had always been drinking. The main difference was that while drinking in the socialist context had been integrated at the workplace as a way of expressing social relations (Rogers 2005), drinking during working hours was no longer accepted in the post-Soviet context. As a result drinking had in many instances been moved to the public sphere. During my fieldwork I often overheard people expressing the opinion that alcoholism had increased in Lithuania after the declared independence. I tend to believe that it merely seemed so because it had become more *visible*. As Douglas Rogers argues (2005), in order to be acceptable drinking has to be incorporated into a legitimate social context, such as social drinking after a day of hard work – and I add: located inside people's homes. Drinking detached from legitimising circumstances positioned a person in a negative light both in the public's eyes and at home. The space used for drinking and the social setting surrounding it were both vital components in determining whether or not drinking was perceived as acceptable.

Contextualising the Birža

The story of the Birža at the riverside is intertwined with the disruptive period in Lithuania in the 1990s that followed the Soviet breakdown. For many citizens living standards decreased; many lost their jobs, while reforms for privatisation were introduced overnight, giving way to economic shock therapy and escalating inflation (Smith et al. 2002). As noted by anthropologists Morris and Polese (2014), Western international financial institutions engaged in an ideologically driven transition with the aim of finally doing away with the remnants of the socialist state, attempts which led to an increase in informal economic activities and relations throughout the 1990s. Indeed, as postsocialist scholars have documented, the breakup of the Soviet Union was for many not accompanied by success and greater wealth (Anderson and Pine 1995; Bridger and Pine 1998; Hann 1994, 2002, 2003; Kideckel 2002; Verdery 2003). On the contrary, increasing gaps between rich and poor led to a spiral of downward mobility for the previously privileged workers who were more or less left to their own coping devices (Kideckel 2002; Schröder 2008). Such tendencies were reinforced with the EU membership in 2004: while strong political forces led the country's way to the geopolitical remaking of the state, proclaiming Lithuania anew as a modern, self-conscious and liberal country, many promises were yet again unfulfilled for the poorer parts of the population, who were left dissatisfied with what was perceived as a political lack of attention to social and economic deficits (Vonderau 2007; Harboe Knudsen 2012).

The Birža emerged in the unstable environment of the 1990s. It was originally established by a young man who was unable to find a permanent job through official institutions. Thus frustrated, he decided to make his own unemployment agency in order to access jobs directly. The place attracted other people who were looking for work, and soon the Birža was a real draw. The place functioned according to certain rules. When people came in their cars, the men first enquired about the work, and then decided among themselves who would be most suitable for the job according to education and previous experience. The person or persons singled out would then take off to carry out the respective work. Rogers (2005) has documented similar practices in Russia in his article about labour and exchange in the post-Soviet context. Townspeople referred to it as 'collecting the bums' – driving out and picking up unemployed people from the nearby village to carry out work in their households. In the Russian context moonshine (Russian: *samagon*; Lithuanian: *samagon'as, naminukė, naminė degtinė*) was often used as a payment in itself if people could not afford to pay money. The men at the Birža , however, often received a meal as part of their salary, and sometimes alcohol to go with it, but *samagon'as* did not figure as a salary in itself.

As I inquired about the Birža among friends and acquaintances in Kaunas, I was told that it used to be a lively place where up to 20 men would gather each day, and that cars would pass by frequently. Yet the global financial crisis of 2008 had an impact: most Lithuanians stopped renovating their homes or spending money on extra help. Now the place is almost abandoned except for four to six regulars, who often wait in vain for work. I noticed up to 15 people visiting the Birža as workers during my stay, but except for the regulars they were inconsistent visitors at the riverside – their participation in the Birža depended mainly on their financial situation, whereas the regulars also used the space for social interaction.

The Men at the Birža

The three men I spent most time with at the Birža were Juozas, Mantas and Vytas. Juozas was a 55-year-old former construction worker. He always had a mild look on his face and a well-trimmed beard. He had been married – and divorced – twice, and had two children whom he hardly ever saw. During the Soviet regime he had first been employed according to his specialisation, but had later taken up work at a collective farm in the countryside. After independence, at the age of 34, he had lost his formal employment. Incapable of finding a new job, he had started working 'outside' the state. By taking up informal employment he had also lost his health insurance. Twice he had needed to go to hospital due to accidents at the workplace, and had had to bribe the doctors in order to get the help and attention he needed. For a while he had worked informally at construction sites, but losing this work too, he had turned to the Birža at the riverside. He could hardly make ends meet. At our first meeting he told me that he was renting a small flat in the city; however, as we get to know each other better, he revealed that he was homeless. His only income was what he got from the Birža, while he got his clothes from various waste containers around in the city.[4] He referred to himself as a 'victim of the political system' (*santvarkos auka*). He was mainly passing time until reaching retirement age (62.5 years), as he would then get a pension from the state. The pension paid by the Lithuanian state consists of two parts: a basic amount and an additional amount. The basic pension is 266 litas monthly (77 euros).[5] The additional part depends on a person's social security contributions and the number of years they have been employed. In order to receive more than the basic pension a person needs to have been working officially for at least 15 years.[6] The reason Juozas hoped for a pension was due to the years he worked legally during the Soviet system. His various unregistered employments after independence would not contribute to the official pension.

Mantas was 36 years old. He was a tall and handsome man with black curly hair – only his scarred and calloused hands bore witness to years of hard work. He had received no formal education. After some unruly teenage years he had decided to leave for Spain, where he worked on a grape farm for 11 years. This had ended with him being imprisoned for one year for failing to pay a range of fines for drunk driving. After his release he had been sent back home to Lithuania, where he turned up at the Birža. In Spain he had worked with his Lithuanian wife. She, however, had left him for a Spaniard while he was serving his time in prison. Back in Lithuania Mantas had met another woman and moved in with her on the rebound. At the beginning of our acquaintance he told me that he was only at the Birža for a few days, passing time before he would get 'real work' (*tikrą darbą*). Together with two other men, he narrated, he had formed an unofficial construction work company. They travelled around Lithuania and worked on people's houses and had just got a big job in northern Lithuania. In a few days they would be off again. Yet, days, weeks and months passed by without Mantas leaving the Birža for 'real work'. Based on a subtle understanding of the situation, I never inquired about this again.

Another regular was Vytas, a man of 49. In his scruffy clothes and with a face swollen from heavy alcohol consumption he looked older than he actually was. His parents had divorced when he still was a toddler and left him in the care of his grandmother. During Soviet times he had first worked at a radio factory, later a machine factory, and finally at a match factory, all in Kaunas. After Lithuania regained independence he had taken up work at a factory where they produced nails; he had lost his job there as a result of being found drunk during working hours. He had then taken up informal work, starting with a job at his father-in-law's, where he worked at a sand quarry. His next job had been collecting old pieces of metal that he sold to scrap dealers. Finally, after jumping from job to job, he had settled with work at the Birža. Vytas had two marriages and two divorces behind him, with a daughter from the first marriage. In both divorces he had lost the right to reside in the flats where he had lived with his respective wives. He had then moved in with his elderly mother, who still lived in Kaunas. After his second divorce he went to Tikėjimo Žodis (The Word of Faith), the Pentecostal community in Kaunas, where he, according to himself, spent half a year crying about his unfortunate destiny. Later he left the Pentecostal movement as he found them to be too intense in their worshipping of God. I often wondered if his dismissal of their worshipping also was related to the movement's strict non-alcohol policy. His attachment to God was still something he took with him to the Birža. He would, for example, start a sentence with 'God gave me these words...' (*Dievas davė man šiuos žodžius*) or refer to his drinking as 'a great sin' (*didelė nuodėmė*).

The men at the Birža were all struggling with quite similar problems: unemployment, poverty, personal tragedy and a steady disintegration from society. While Juozas and Vytas hoped for some minimal security in the future in the form of a pension, Mantas had no such future guarantee, as he had never held an official job. A concern that they all shared was their lack of health insurance. According to official law, any working citizen of Lithuania is guaranteed health insurance by the state. The same counts for children, school pupils, students and pensioners. An unemployed person is guaranteed health insurance as long as he or she is registered at the official unemployment agency. In addition, the unemployed person will get monetary support from the state for the first six months of his or her unemployment. The average sum paid a month is 530 litas (153.50 euros) and the maximum sum is 600 litas (174 euros). If the person is still unemployed after six months, this monetary contribution stops, although their unemployed status and provided health insurance continue. In such instances there are other options for support available through social services, who, depending on the case, will support the unemployed in different ways.[7] People who fail to fulfil any of the above-mentioned criteria have no health insurance. They are entitled to first aid at the hospital in case of an accident, but cannot receive any other treatment unless they pay for it themselves. The men at the Birža were left with their own unemployment agency and sometimes support from relatives and friends. Yet, the Birža remained key in their daily estimations. Even in periods without any work they kept showing up. 'Hope dies last,' Juozas explained to me (*viltis miršta paskutinė*).

On Bomžai: A Grey Zone of Personhood

In his work on urban nomads (2000 [1970]) Spradley describes how, primarily, alcoholics are the common reference point upon which his informants' identities are based. Drinking is not only something they do, it is also a disease they have become; they *are* alcoholics. By referring to them as *bums* and *common drunkards*, the average citizen and the lawman define them according to his or her own perception of norms and correct behaviour, and treat them accordingly as something sick or abnormal (Spradley (2000 [1970]). According to Bauman, the production of 'human waste' is an unavoidable consequence of any given society's pursuit to become 'modern', while these people at the same time remain a barrier to reaching this exact goal (Bauman 2012 [2004]). Here he draws a parallel to Michelangelo's philosophy as an artist, as he, once asked how he made so perfect sculptures replied: 'Simple. You just take a slab of marble and cut out all the superfluous bits' (Bauman 2012 [2004], 21). The present-day pursuit of getting rid of 'waste humans' follows the same logic, as they are the superfluous bits that should be done away with, or at the very least exposed as the unwanted other that disturbs 'normal' everyday life. The very location of the Birža coincided with the idea of waste, as rubbish was left everywhere on the riverbanks. As a British friend of mine working in traffic planning in Kaunas more than once noted in irritation, the riverside could have been a nice and tidy place to take a stroll, yet had turned into a most unpleasant area of the city with waste scattered all over the green banks. 'Human waste', in Bauman's sense, was thus placed side by side with concrete waste, establishing a visible parallel between the men's physical location and their position in society. My interlocutors at the riverside clearly experienced this societal degradation. As one of them expressed with reference to his status as an informal worker: 'This doesn't count at all. Say, it's like you don't even exist' (*Čia išvis nieko nesiskaito. Kaip va tave ir nėra, skaityk*). Outside the narrow boundaries of the Birža their marginal position was enforced on a daily basis. People in the street would turn away from them, while cashiers would treat them with disgust, demonstratively holding their breath or covering their noses as the men entered shops to buy their daily beer(s). Besides its practical function, the Birža thus also served as a legitimate space where the men could meet with others in similar situations without being harassed by others in their surroundings.

Their unsettled position took the form of a 'grey zone of personhood', where living on society's outskirts was both a constant feature, and, at the same time, an ambiguity that the men never seemed to come to terms with. This led to constant self-reflections on identity, which were influenced by others' perceptions of the men and their own perceptions of themselves. In emic terms the men at the Birža were referred to as 'bums' (*bomžai*, singular *bomžas*), a term they themselves occasionally used as a way of self-description, albeit with a certain degree of ambiguity. Once Vytas, contemplating his many losses, exclaimed: 'I am a *bomžas*, I am a *bomžas*, I am a *bomžas*...' each time repeating the phrase louder and louder. In the end Juozas got tired of listening to him and shouted: 'Of course you are a *bomžas*. We all are! Now shut up!' Yet, on at another occasion when Vytas again took up the theme of being a *bomžas*, an older man who came irregularly to the Birža interrupted him: 'But you are not. No, are you not a man, can you not work? We work. We are still men. Not like they think about us' – by 'they' referring to people integrated in society with work and housing. The emphasis on manhood and work as inseparable entities was also what gave the Birža its importance, as the men struggled with feelings of emasculation due to the fact that they no longer saw themselves able to support themselves, let alone a family (see also Frederiksen 2013; Harboe Knudsen 2012). Work was of crucial importance in these negotiations of identity, and how to get work, when to get work and where to get work occupied the daily thoughts of the men. Work not only meant money; it also meant that at least for a short period the men could shrug off the feeling of being *bomžai*. It appeared to me that much of their self-identification depended on the particular situation of the day. Mantas, for example, would on a good day (with work) buy cigarettes and put them into his nicely decorated cigarette case and invite all at the Birža to smoke, visibly enjoying his own generosity. On a less fortunate day, he would gather old cigarette butts, empty them carefully into a small piece of newspaper, roll the substance into a cigarette, light it and with a wry smile remark: 'But hey, I am a *bomžas*.'

The term *bomžas* is not originally Lithuanian, but origins from the Russian word *bomzh* (бомж), which consists of the first letters of *bez opredelionnogo mesta zhitelstva* (без определенного места жительства; in English: 'without a permanent place to live'). As explained by Höjdestrand (2009), this was the term originally used by state administrators to classify people without a home. Originating from the protocols of the Soviet Militsiya in the 1970s it was used in a purely administrative sense. However, after the Soviet breakdown the term spread into daily language and gained a specific humiliating and contemptuous meaning.[8] This development should be seen in the context of the increased number of homeless people in the post-Soviet era, as the previous system of social security fell apart and many were left without work and home. In contemporary Lithuania people use this term with reference to socially excluded people, without explicitly knowing whether they are homeless or not. In this sense the present use refers to what Wardhaugh calls 'bomzh-bums': people who are barred from spaces where social persons are created and maintained (2000).[9] The present-day use in Lithuania likewise tends to characterise representatives of the (Soviet) working class, who were not capable of upholding a 'normal' working life during independence. *Bomžai* exist in opposition to the politically promoted idea of the 'new Lithuanian': a modern cosmopolitan citizen who can easily navigate in Europe and succeed and gain from the 'Westernisation' of the society (de Munck 2008). Successful change in society is attached to the creation of particular *persons* who embody new values and skills, and thus the cultivation of a certain *personhood* (for comparison see Dunn 2005). The construction of new persons serves the political role of being the outward expression of progress and modernity, while people embodying a presumed Soviet heritage, notably poor villagers and former industrial workers, have become the new social outcasts in the post-Soviet state (Klumbytė 2006).

Normative Orders and Grey Zones of Practice

Despite my emphasis that the men's constructions of personhood in part resembles the socialist past, this is to be understood as a symbolic and political role that the men at the Birža play, not as an actual continuation of socialist practices. There is factually nothing Soviet about the Birža. Whereas the second economy during the Soviet regime was characterised by the circulation of goods and state resources as a necessary supplement to the household (Firlit and Chlopecki 1992; Ledeneva 1998; Verdery 1996; Wedel 1992), the men at the Birža are engaged in *employment* for cash wages, a fairly recent phenomenon built on exchanges between individuals that avoid state involvement altogether (see also Morris and Polese 2014). Thus, whereas the socialist informal economy depended on the state, the current practices avoid the state altogether. As emphasised by Burawoy and Verdery, an unstable environment acts as an impetus for innovations in practices as well as reversions (1999). Rather than 'restorations' of socialist patterns, practices of informal work should be seen as direct *responses* to the new neoliberal environment, not as a legacy of a certain culture or a specific 'Soviet mentality' (Burawoy and Verdery 1999).

The debate about informal shadow work in the post-Soviet period reappeared in the Lithuanian media in light of the global financial crisis of 2008. With a little delay the crisis reached Lithuania in 2009, severely impacting the country's economy; it led to several banks being bailed out, companies going bankrupt and a steady rise in unemployment. As a way of reviving the financial sector economic experts suggested that large sums could be recovered from Lithuania's 'shadow economy'. Indeed, the lack of control over informal work was singled out as one of the main problems in Lithuania's economy, and the issue frequently appeared in newspapers and on TV. New legal initiatives tightened the grip on shadow workers, just as campaigns against illegal work were initiated, attempting both to scare people into working in the formal sector and appeal to their feeling of solidarity with the state and their fellow citizens. Shadow workers had become a thorn in the side of the state – their sudden visibility undermined the proclaimed progress in the realm of law and order, as their working strategies increasingly challenged the hegemony of the state. While the men at the riverside were aware of the campaigns, these never interfered with their daily strategies for obtaining work. Actually, the men were left completely in peace by the bypassing police, despite their clear intention to break the law. Juozas explained that in principle the police would not intervene unless they caught them in the act. 'If they come now, what are they going to say to us? We just sit here and chat with you, don't we?' The police would not wait around for a car to show up and take the men to work, he explained. As long as the men did not disturb the public order, the police left them alone. The men seemed far more concerned about hiding their beers than hiding the fact that they were looking for work, as drinking in public spaces is illegal in Lithuania.

Their unsettled grey zone of personhood gave them the ability to find a way around formal law, and the limitations of their marginalisation likewise enabled them to make use of normative orders. The one thing the men strived to be, workers, was the one identity *not* associated with them by the lawmen, while the one thing they *were* recognised as – *bomžai* or *pijokai* – was a prescribed identity that they were not eager to embrace. Ironically, alcoholism and public drunkenness were the sole crimes they feared that the police would punish them for, despite recent massive campaigns against informal work. Here we must take into consideration how normative constellations of orders are capable of overruling formal law, even such normative rules that guide behaviour which is against official law (see also Benda-Beckmann 1997; Benda-Beckmann and Benda-Beckmann 2006). By treating the Birža as a 'grey zone of practices' we see how the men managed to create space for manoeuvre through their ironic circumvention of hegemonic symbols. They created a hideout for otherwise excluded citizens, which became their domain in the sense of what F. and K. von Benda-Beckmann and Griffiths have referred to as 'spatial idiom-shopping' (2009). Through this term they interpret law and its (spatial) limitations as providing resources for people, allowing them to pursue their own interests within a given space. While they visibly ignored the working regulations, the regulars at the Birža remained largely uninteresting to the police, which again testified to their profound marginalisation in terms of personhood.

As F. von Benda-Beckmann (1992) argues, it is unhelpful to classify some legal orders as superior to others because it prevents us from understanding the influence of complex normative orders in a given setting. Indeed, my original interest in the Birža had been stimulated by my search for people working 'in the shadows'. Now that I had found a place designed especially for informal work, I realised that concerns about tax, campaigns and police were the least of their considerations. While they successfully circumvented official law, there were other forms of normative orders that caused daily struggles. Everyday concern was thus centred on the actual agreements made with employers. Three times during my fieldwork Juozas was paid less than originally agreed, while an irregular worker at the Birža said that he had lost count of the times he had been cheated. Another frequent disturbance was whether or not people showed up as agreed. Sometimes an employer would come and make an agreement about work the following day, yet never show up as promised. Often the men were thus waiting in vain for a specific person to appear. Contrary to the case of moonlighting Douglas describes (2005), there were no social relations involved in the labour exchange at the Birža. The men did not come from a single village, and as Kaunas is a big industrial city they did not know their employers personally. Labour was conducted outside of houses (they were never allowed inside), and both the men and their employers kept the labour as an impersonal exchange with money as the mediator. The fact that the work they carried out was both without a contract and not imbedded in any social relations made them the more vulnerable in the exchange relation. Paying less than agreed, demanding more work than agreed or finding other similar ways of getting around an agreement was not difficult for employers, as the men had no legal and social rights when working for strangers at the Birža.

Among the older workers this unfair treatment resulted in narratives about the better Soviet times: 'What we do here does not challenge the official system,' an older construction worker once explained to me while we were waiting for potential employers at the Birža, 'it is an *improvement* of the system [*pagerinimas*].' He made a small pause and continued: 'It was better during the Russians. If we had stayed with the Russians, we would have work. I did not even want this independence. Those politicians destroyed the entire life, especially Landsbergis' (*Sugadino tie politikai visą gyvenimą, ypač Landsbergis*).[10] I often overheard similar comments at the Birža, where expressions of loss, sorrow and even cynical devaluations of the political system were imbedded in the men's discussions about their current situations. According to anthropologist Neringa Klumbytė, such expressions of longing for a Soviet past are too often dismissed as 'a disease' of Soviet nostalgia in current political discourse, which is used as a way of discrediting such voices altogether. However, she elaborates, expressions of nostalgia are a way of coming to terms with the experiences of loss (of work, savings, security, stability) in the current Lithuanian society (Klumbytė 2008).

Concluding Remarks

In this chapter I have provided a case study of people living on the margins of society and have shown how their unsettled grey zones of personhood and practices have become constant features of their daily lives, with no hope of better times in sight. The Birža is a normative solution to everyday shortcomings in a situation defined by uncertainty and scarcity. At the same time the Birža takes up an unsettled position in current Lithuania, as it on the one hand works against the government's goal of eliminating shadow work, and visibly so, yet on the other escapes police control due to the fact that the men are not even perceived as workers. They remain classified as society's outcasts, *bomžai* and *pijokai*. This grey zone of personhood emerges at a crossroads between the men's own perception of who they are, their surroundings' perception of who they are and the role they play in the current geopolitical climate. They have become the new poor, people who in the words of Bauman are 'fully and truly useless and redundant, and thus become burdensome "others" who have outstayed their welcome' (1997, 5). Despite the fact that their Birža nowadays seldom fulfils its original purpose of getting the men a day's work, the symbolic power of the place remains. It becomes a place to signal new subalternisations in society, a place to uphold an identity as a worker, a place to socialise, just as the wooden sign in itself justifies the men's existence in society – when they confine themselves to the narrow boundaries of the Birža.

Notes

1 *Darbo birža* literally translates as 'labour market', yet it has the practical meaning and function of an unemployment agency.
2 Henceforth I will refer to the unofficial unemployment agency at the riverside as the 'Birža'.
3 All quotations are taken from my fieldnotes and have been translated from English to Lithuanian by the author.
4 In the cities some people leave bags with used clothes in front of the containers for poor people to find.
5 Numbers from January 2012. Data available at: http://www.pensionfundsonline.co.uk/content/country-profiles/lithuania/87 (accessed 26 November 2014).
6 A person will need to have worked 30–35 years in order to receive a normal state pension (the basic pension plus the additional amount), which is approximately 766 Lithuanian litas (222 euros) per month. This comes third on the list of lowest pensions in the EU, with Romania having the second lowest average monthly pension (762 Romanian lei [175 euros]) and Bulgaria the lowest (225 Bulgarian lev [125 euros]). Data available at: http://bnn-news.com/smallest-pensions-eu-%E2%80%93-bulgaria-romania-lithuania-14778 (accessed 2 April 2014). Lithuanians who have not worked a sufficient number of years are left with the basic monthly pension of 266 litas (77 euros), which is difficult, if not impossible, to survive on.
7 All information obtained from Lietuvos Darbo Birža in Vilnius. See also http://www.ldb.lt/Informacija/Puslapiai/default.aspx (accessed 11 January 2015). Other forms of help from social services can include small one-time payments, discounts for firewood and help with other daily basic needs.
8 See http://ru.wikipedia.org/wiki/Бомж (accessed 20 January 2014).
9 The English 'bum' and the Russian *bomzh* appear quite similar by sound. However, the origins of the words differ. Whereas *bomzh* is an abbreviation originating from the Soviet Militsiya, the English 'bum' is believed to originate from the German word *Bummler*, which translates as '*loafer*'.
10 Professor Vytautas Landsbergis (born 18 October 1932) was the first head of state of Lithuania after the declared independence and served as the head of the Lithuanian parliament, the Seimas. Landsbergis worked actively towards Lithuanian independence from the Soviet Union.

References

Anderson, D. G. and F. Pine (eds). 1995. *Surviving the Transition: Development Concerns in the Post-socialist World*. Cambridge: University of Cambridge, Department of Anthropology.
Bauman, Z. 1997. *Postmodernity and Its Discontents*. Oxford: Polity Press.
_____. 2012 [2004]. *Wasted Lives: Modernity and Its Outcasts*. Cambridge: Polity Press.

Benda-Beckmann, F. von. 1992. 'Introduction: Understanding agrarian law in society'. In F. von Benda-Beckmann and M. Van der Velde (eds), *Law as a Resource in Agrarian Struggles*, 1–22. Wageningen: Pudoc.

————. 1997. 'Citizens, strangers and indigenous people: Conceptual politics and legal pluralism'. In R. Kuppe, R. Potz, F. and Keebet von Benda-Beckmann and A. Hoekema (eds), *International Yearbook for Legal Anthropology, Volume 9*, 1–43. Leiden: Brill.

Benda-Beckmann, F. von and K. von Benda-Beckmann. 2006. 'The dynamics of change and continuity in plural legal orders.' *Journal of Legal Pluralism and Unofficial Law* 38(53–54): 1–44.

Benda-Beckmann, F. von, K. von Benda-Beckmann and A. Griffiths. 2009. 'Introduction'. In F. von Benda-Beckmann, K. von Benda-Beckmann and A. Griffiths (eds), *Spatializing Law: An Anthropological Geography of Law in Society*, 1–29. Farnham: Ashgate.

Bridger, S. and F. Pine. 1998. 'Introduction: Transitions to post-socialism and cultures of survival'. In S. Bridger and F. Pine (eds), *Surviving Post-socialism: Local Strategies and Regional Responses in Eastern Europe and the Former Soviet Union*, 1–15. London: Routledge.

Burawoy, M. and K. Verdery (eds). 1999. *Uncertain Transition: Ethnographies of Change in the Postsocialist World*. Lanham, MD: Rowman & Littlefield.

de Munck, Victor. 2008. 'Millenarian dreams: The objects and subjects of money in new Lithuania'. In I. W. Schröder and A. Vonderau (eds), *Changing Economies and Changing Identities in Postsocialist Eastern Europe*, 171–91. Münster: LIT Verlag.

Dunn, E. C. 2005. 'Standards and person-making in East Central Europe'. In A. Ong and S. J. Collier (eds), *Global Assemblages: Technology, Politics and Ethics as Anthropological Problems*, 173–93. Malden, MA: Blackwell.

Firlit, E. and J. Chlopecki. 1992. 'When theft is not theft'. In J. R. Wedel (ed.), *The Unplanned Society: Poland During and After Communism*, 95–109. New York: Columbia University Press.

Frederiksen, M. D. 2013. *Young Men, Time and Boredom in the Republic of Georgia*. Philadelphia: Temple University Press.

Hann, C. M. 1994. 'After communism: Reflections on East European anthropology and the "transition"'. *Social Anthropology* 2(3): 229–49.

————. 2002. 'Farewell to the socialist 'other'. In C. M. Hann (ed.), *Postsocialism: Ideals, Ideologies and Practices in* Eurasia, 1–11. London: Routledge.

————. 2003. 'Introduction: Decollectivization and the moral economy'. In C. M. Hann (ed.), *The Postsocialist Agrarian Question: Property Relations and the Rural Condition*, 1–47. Münster: LIT Verlag.

Harboe Knudsen, I. 2012. *New Lithuania in Old Hands: Effects and Outcomes of EUropeanization in Rural Lithuania*. London. Anthem Press.

Höjdestrand, T. 2009. *Needed by Nobody: Homelessness and Humanness in Post-socialist Russia*. Ithaca, NY: Cornell University Press.

Humphrey, C. 1995. 'Introduction'. In D. G. Anderson and F. Pine (eds), 'Surviving the Transition: Development Concerns in the Post-socialist World', *Cambridge Anthropology* (special issue) 18(2): 1–12.

Keesing, R. M. 1992. *Custom and Confrontation: The Kwaio Struggle for Cultural Autonomy*. Chicago: University of Chicago Press.

Kideckel, D. A. 2002. 'The unmaking of an East-Central European working class'. In C. M. Hann (ed.), *Postsocialism: Ideals, Ideologies and Practices in Eurasia*, 115–33. London: Routledge.

Klumbytė N. 2006. 'Biographic Citizenship: Memory, Subjectivity, and Politics in Post-Soviet Lithuania'. PhD dissertation. University of Pittsburgh.

_____. 2008. 'Post-Soviet publics and nostalgia for Soviet times'. In I. W. Schröder and A. Vonderau (eds), *Changing Economies and Changing Identities in Postsocialist Eastern Europe*, 27–47. Münster: LIT Verlag.

Ledeneva, A. V. 1998. *Russia's Economy of Favours: Blat, Networking and Informal Exchange*. Cambridge: Cambridge University Press.

Morris, J. and A. Polese (eds). 2014. *The Informal Post-socialist Economy: Embedded Practices and Livelihoods*. New York: Routledge.

Rogers, D. 2005. 'Moonshine, money and the politics of liquidity in rural Russia'. *American Ethnologist* 32(1): 63–81.

Schröder, I. W. 2008. 'The classes of '89: Anthropological Approaches to capitalism and class in Eastern Europe'. In I. W. Schröder and A. Vonderau (eds), *Changing Economies and Changing Identities in Postsocialist Eastern Europe*, 3–27. Münster: LIT Verlag.

Smith, D. J., A. Pabriks, A. Purs and T. Lane. 2002. *The Baltic States: Estonia, Latvia and Lithuania*. London: Routledge.

Spradley, J. P. 2000 [1970]. *You Owe Yourself a Drunk: An Ethnography of Urban Nomads*. Long Grove, IL: Waveland Press.

Verdery, K. 1996. *What Was Socialism, and What Comes Next?* Princeton: Princeton University Press.

_____. 2003. *The Vanishing Hectare: Property and Value in Postsocialist Transylvania*. Ithaca, NY and London: Cornell University Press.

Vonderau, A. 2007. 'Yet another Europe? Constructing and representing identities in Lithuania two years after EU accession'. In T. Darieva and W. Kaschuba (eds), *Representations on the Margins of Europe: Politics and Identities in the Baltic and South Caucasian States*, 220–42. Frankfurt and New York: Campus Verlag.

Wardhaugh, J. 2000. *Sub City: Young People, Homelessness and Crime*. Aldershot: Ashgate.

Wedel, J. R. (ed.). 1992. *The Unplanned Society: Poland During and After Communism*. New York: Columbia University Press.

Chapter 10

THE LAST HONEST BANDIT: TRANSPARENCY AND SPECTRES OF ILLEGALITY IN THE REPUBLIC OF GEORGIA

Martin Demant Frederiksen

In the wake of the Cold War the notion of 'transparency' became almost synonymous with that of 'good governance'. Emerging as a keyword in programmes seeking to establish solid democracies in former authoritarian states, it was celebrated by international organisations, Western bilateral donors and the UN alike as a precondition for aid (West and Sanders 2003, 1). It became a 'globalized governance ethos' promoting formalised types of accountability (Ballestero 2012, 161; see also F. von Benda-Beckman, K. von Benda-Beckmann and Eckert 2009, Larson 2008). However, as Harry West and Todd Sanders have argued, there is reason to believe that despite the best efforts of such organisations and institutions, the operations of power and politics in the contemporary world are not necessarily becoming more transparent. As they note, 'amid all this talk of transparency, many people have the sense that something is not as it is said to be – that power remains, notwithstanding official pronouncement, at least somewhat opaque' (West and Sanders 2003, 2; see also Gotfredsen, this volume). Others have, in a similar vein, argued that political quests for order and clarity are fickle projects that may in the end create areas of absence in which life is anything but clear cut (Dunn and Frederiksen 2014; Hetherington 2012); spheres of invisibility and greyness that come to signify an ambiguous or even demonic place where certainty gives way to doubt and insecurity (Coombe 1997; see also Taussig 1980). This chapter departs from these considerations in exploring how and why, after the political introduction of 'transparency' and reforms seeking to diminish the role of informality and corruption, society in Georgia became so transparent that some phenomena (or figures) resided out of view. Empirically

I focus on organised crime, informal practices and corruption. I argue that whereas crime and corruption before had been something that was plain to see, with the introduction of transparency such phenomena paradoxically became more hidden and inconspicuous.

Informal, hidden, shadow or parallel economies in terms of networking, bribes, favours, loans or corruption are widely held to be phenomena with long histories in Georgia, preceding the Soviet period, thriving during it, and being a significant part of keeping life together in the years following it (e.g. Dudwick 2003; Jones 2013; Mars and Altman 1983, 2008). The degree (or kind) of illegality connected to them, however, has not always been clearly discernible. As this chapter aims to show, this particularly became the case following the revolution in Georgia in 2003, after which quests for transparency and good governance, and the eradication of corruption, became part of the political agenda. My interest in what followed is connected to a sphere of the informal economy that, at least politically, was seen as inherently illegal – namely that connected to organised crime. With roots in both tsarist and Soviet prisons, organised crime gained prominence in Georgia during the 1990s, and the Georgian mafia was politically targeted as a major societal problem after the revolution (Di Puppo 2012; Frederiksen 2013; Slade 2013). Although being politically unwelcome, elements of organised crime and the informal economy have, however, paradoxically come to be seen by large parts of the population as inherent within, and increasingly connected to, politics.

I take as my point of departure Alena Ledeneva's definition of informal practices as being enactments of know-how used to compensate for things that are defunct within society (such as weak state institutions) and the networks of favours connected to such practices (Ledeneva 2006, 1). Informality in this view is an inherently ambiguous aspect of daily life, one that is 'condoned by some and condemned by others, and just as often, condoned and condemned by the same people' (Ledeneva 2006, 190). What I pursue is the question of how, in a context of transparency, such commendation and condemnation have existed in Georgia in recent years both within criminal networks and within the political sphere – with each sphere accusing the other of deploying informality in an illicit manner. In doing so, I recount the story of a member of the Georgian mafia, an 'honest bandit' in his own understanding, as well as the political reforms that were undertaken by the now-previous Georgian government which sought to eradicate the influence of such criminals and declare them not only unequivocally dishonest but also a thing of the past. I argue that rather than creating clarity, the political introduction of 'transparency' created a societal grey zone in which illegality came to have a spectral presence – both in the form of officially invisible or eradicated criminal figures, but also within politics itself.

An 'Honest Bandit' Recounts His Life

To say that Levan[1] was retired would be to go against one of the main principles of his life: to never have a proper job. It would be more accurate to say of Levan that his level of activity was not as high as it had been before. In his own words he was an elderly man, approaching 60, and his 'business' was no longer what it once had been. This did not, however, mean that nothing ever happened in Levan's house. For instance, a man was shot the first time I visited there. The man was only shot in the hand, 'nothing serious', I was later told, although the exact reasons for why it had happened always remained somewhat unclear. There were generally many things that remained unexplained regarding Levan's life, either because I was never given an answer when I asked, or because I never managed to ask him before his death in 2011. Levan was a thief, a former long-term inmate in various Soviet prisons and a prominent member of the organised criminal fraternity *vory-v-zakone* ('thieves-in-law'). My first meeting with Levan took place in early 2009. The meeting was arranged by Shota – a local young man I had come to know. At this time, Levan, Shota and I were all residents of Batumi, the regional centre of the Autonomous Republic of Ajara in western Georgia, where I was conducting long-term fieldwork in relation to a project about youth and marginality.[2] The backyard where Levan lived looked like many others did in the old part of Batumi during this period: wooden balconies, stairways and vines intermingling; dereliction, dilapidation, and minor amendments here and there; wood partly rotted behind scraped paint. His apartment was located on the second floor, and before venturing up the steep metal stairway leading to the entrance Shota gave a subtle whistle to let Levan know that we had arrived. The aim of our visit, and more that were later to follow, was for me to interview Levan about his past experiences of incarceration and the world of organised crime in general. This was a world that fascinated many of the young men among whom I conducted my fieldwork, and Shota believed it best if I learned about it from an expert. This, Shota told me, was exactly what Levan was, and furthermore he was always happy to talk about his life and experiences. We were thus rarely alone during the interview sessions at Levan's apartment. A series of younger men casually came and went, some to sit and listen to Levan's stories for while, others to ask him questions or favours.

Levan was born in Batumi in 1951 and had been a bright young man doing well in school. At the age of 19 he had begun a university education in aviation construction. It was during his first semester here that things began to go awry, when an acquaintance at the university had presented him with a joint. He had no prior experience with drugs and decided to try it just once.

They were caught and Levan was subsequently sentenced to 18 months in a Ukrainian prison. 'The place was like a concentration camp,' he recalled in one of our interviews. 'And after I got out I was treated like trash – I couldn't get a job, I couldn't study, nothing. All I could do was stay in the crime circle I had come to know – when you're in prison you automatically find bad company.' Prison life had been harsh, he noted. 'In the first period it was very bad. There was no food and no cigarettes, and every day, four or five times each day, I was beaten by the police because they wanted to turn me into an informer, a spy. But I knew that if I became a spy for them, other prisoners would know and not help me. So, I kept fighting the police and they would throw me into a room underneath the prison, in isolation. There was no light, it was damp. After some weeks they would try to make me a spy again – I said no, and they threw me back in isolation. I spent almost all of my time in there.' He pauses to smoke a cigarette, after which he continues. 'But when you spent time in isolation other prisoners started to respect you – they knew that the police couldn't break me. Everyone knew their place in prison, there were servants and there were masters. Out of the 2,000 men in this prison only 10 or 11 had not been broken by the police and I was one of them.'

His second sentence was for a period of three years. In principle his third would have been even longer but he managed to bribe someone into reducing it to only one year. But his imprisonments generally became longer and longer. He met, he explained, 'interesting people' in prison, and during his relatively short periods of freedom they were the only ones he could rely on, and the ones who made sure he had something to do on the outside. During his various periods of imprisonment Levan learned to live by the laws of the *vory-v-zakone*: a regulatory fraternity and system standing in opposition to the official laws of the Soviet system. These fraternity rules were based on codes of honour and respect, on not being afraid, on not betraying anyone within the fraternity, on keeping crime organised rather than random. He recalls how the youth camps were the worst. Here, inmates 'acted like dogs', carried knives, fought. Daily someone was killed. However, as he grew older and closer to the *vory-v-zakone* things became (relatively speaking) more peaceful, as older inmates adhered to the code and knew their place within the system.

The Relative Comfort of Clear-Cut Crime

With the fall of the Soviet Union the influence of the *vory-v-zakone* spread beyond prison. Members of the fraternity became influential parts of economic life in many former Soviet republics. The anthropologist Nancy Ries recounts how an encounter with bandits in the mid-1990s in Russia made her realise how the mafia had become a comforting presence in everyday life. While in the early 1990s the mafia had been seen as 'the supreme symbol of evil and terror', only a few years later it had come to represent 'the means by which avarice and corruption might be reined in' (Ries 2002, 305; see also Borenstein 2007, Humphrey 2002). In this sense, Ries writes, members of the mafia came to be seen as honest bandits. With the formal economy in ruins, the informal economy upheld by the mafia came to provide a form of safety net for many citizens. And although the activities of the mafia were generally acknowledged as being illegal, they could at least be counted on by virtue of them being organised. Unlike the state, the mafia could provide both work and protection.

There are striking parallels between Ries's depiction of Russia in the mid-1990s and the same period in Batumi (cf. Frederiksen 2012b, 2013). A person like Levan equally considered himself an honest bandit as his crime had been well organised and not random or petty. Furthermore, his stories of his life as a criminal resonated with the young men who came to his apartment to listen to them. Many of them were unemployed and engaged in various forms of criminal activity. Largely disinterested in the Soviet period, the particular aspect of *vory-v-zakone* fascinated them – not least its prevalence during the 1990s when they had been children. At this time, the Ajara region was ruled by the local politician Aslan Abashidze semi-independently from the rest of Georgia. Outside Ajara, Abashidze was widely held to be closely connected to organised crime, but for many residents in Batumi this did not pose a problem. For many of the young men who came to Levan's apartment, illegality and informality had thus not necessarily been seen as a problem during their childhoods. Rather, they had been an obvious part of everyday life. If one wanted a job it was a necessity to be well connected, and being well connected most often meant knowing someone within the political or criminal system – two systems that were almost conflated. This did not, however, entail that they did not see any form of crime as being problematic. Rather, the perception was that there were important differences between *organised* and *random* crime. While the former, in the shape of people like Levan, represented a form of honest banditry in which respect and honour were part of the organisation of daily life and economic activity, the latter was seen as a malice that should not be engaged with. The principle of being an honest bandit rested on at least two things. Firstly, it was a question of not being engaged in petty crime or meaningless violence – crime had to serve a point and be respectable within its own logic. Secondly, it was a question of one never being ashamed or secretive about one's activities. That meant distancing oneself from what Katherine Verdery (1996) has termed 'the conceptual mafia': individuals or groups who acted as if they were part of the mafia without actually being so, and who did not adhere to the internal codes of honour but simply did 'biznes' or sought to gain profit no matter the cost to others.

Breaking the Backbone of Crime and Corruption

Although some saw a virtue in certain aspects of organised crime, and particularly the aspects connected to economic activity, others did not. Up to 33 per cent of thieves-in-law operating in the former Soviet republics in the 1990s were of Georgian descent (Slade 2012b, 38), and as thieves in Georgia were often protected by high-ranking policemen, crime thrived in the country in the 1990s (Shelley, Scott and Latta 2007). This increasingly rendered it an issue that international observers looked upon with concern, and it also became a concern on the local political level following the revolution in Georgia in 2003. The revolution itself entailed a regime change. Due to accusations of fraud and corruption, the government of Eduard Shevardnadze, who had been president of Georgia since 1995, was overthrown. Immediately afterwards the new president Mikheil Saakashvili embarked on a crusade against corruption and organised crime – the aspects of society that he held to be the roots of the socioeconomic problems that had tormented the country throughout the 1990s (Di Puppo 2012) – and a series of reforms were implemented to suppress the influence of groups such as *vory-v-zakone* (Georgian: *k'anonieri kurdi*) and create a transparent society. The latter was materially symbolised in the construction of new police stations with large glass facades. Corruption had previously thrived within the police itself, something the new government aimed to change, and the building of 'transparent' police stations was to signify this being done.

As Stephen Jones has noted, the new government's anticorruption and anticrime campaign was in some senses successful in its 'netting of corrupt ministers, MPs, Tax and Customs Department heads, judges, and millionaires' (Jones 2013, 197). However, as he further notes, several factors also undermined the campaign: 'Raids by masked tax policemen, arrests of businessmen without proper process, confiscation of business assets that [were] funnelled into the coffers of the ruling party, sackings of whole departments, and favouritism in appointments and privatization tenders' (Jones 2013, 198). Such side-effects of the campaign generated an increasing public distrust. Albeit dramatic, many of the reforms and actions of the campaign were needed, but the process was rushed and itself not always completely transparent.

One of the reforms of the campaign was the introduction of a zero-tolerance policy, which was designed to reduce cases of criminal activity from the smallest level upwards. This corresponded well with President Saakashvili's visions of reforming civil society, eliminating corruption and strengthening the economy. The idea of the zero-tolerance policy was copied from a US-run programme in New York City that came with excellent references; between 1990 and 1998 there was a 70 per cent reduction in murders and a 50 per cent drop in violent offences in New York City due to the implementation of a zero-tolerance crime-fighting stance. Due to the rise in criminal offences in Georgia similar statistics were sought after, and so the policy was put forward by the president in his annual speech, in which he stated that 'there will be no probation sentences [...] everyone who commits these [petty] crimes will go to prison' (quoted in Slade 2006). Besides the zero-tolerance policy, the government also approved another piece of legislation giving the police the right to shoot if threatened or faced with resistance by persons caught committing a crime. As to implementing the visions of the government, it all seemed fine: crime was high in Georgia, something needed to be done, and something was now being done. However, one factor that was central to the New York City model was not taken into account in the Georgian version: that punishment does not work as a form of prevention without there simultaneously being a strategy of problem-orientated community-based policing (Slade 2006). In New York City the policy was implemented in combination with localised policing that demanded close proximity to the community, which provided a information base and knowledge *of* the community as well as a relationship *with* the community. This ensured that the public had an increased sense of confidence in the police and regarded them as being trustworthy, which meant that people actually testified and reported cases of crime. There was no such implementation in the Georgian model. Rather than reducing crime, creating awareness and creating a relationship between the public and the police, cases of police violence instead rapidly increased during the spring of 2006, while cases of petty crime only decreased very little. A total of 21 suspects were killed by the police in 2005, and a further 17 suspects were killed just in the first four months of 2006 (Basilaia 2006).

Janine Wedel has argued, in relation to the import of Western models for fighting crime and corruption into Eastern Europe, that 'anticorruption programs conducted by the World Bank and other international organizations are grounded in a widely employed definition of corruption [...] and are often based on idealized notions of state–private relations that may not apply even in the West' (Wedel 2003, 222). This certainly held true for the process that was taking place in Georgia, where the import of Western models to fight crime and corruption looked good on paper but was not always successful in practice. Still, regardless of the defects in the implementation of various reforms, a few years into the process the president declared that system of organised crime in the country had been broken (Frederiksen 2013). This did not, however, mean that people such as Levan no longer had a function to serve. Although he withdrew from criminal activity himself, he could still assist when trouble arose for young men in the neighbourhood – he could mediate in conflicts and give advice on most aspects of criminal activity, whether it being how to avoid it or how to do it properly. But he no longer had the connections that could secure anyone a job, despite this being one of the main problems faced by many youths in the city of Batumi. At the time of our interviews in his apartment in Batumi, five years into the reform process, this ability had been taken over by others who were closer to the sociopolitical power-elites in the country's vast network of businesspeople, companies and politicians. One man in particular was often mentioned as 'someone to go to' if one desperately needed work: Mr Ruslan. He was a businessman living in Batumi and the owner of several hotels and complexes in the city. Everyone was cautious not to openly associate him with anything other than 'proper business', as it would be potentially dangerous to call him what most people believed him to be: a person deeply entangled in the shadow economy, and possibly also political corruption. This was paradoxical in that Mr Ruslan was in fact part of the new economic and political elite promoting transparency. There were many stories about Mr Ruslan, and the only common trait among these was that there was nobody who could place him with certainty in a sphere of either complete legality or complete illegality, and in this sense he was an archetype of a new form of grey zone. The problem in calling Mr Ruslan a criminal was that this might deny one his help. Shota, the young man who had introduced me to Levan, had gained most of his jobs through Mr Ruslan, as one of Shota's family members was acquainted with Mr Ruslan's family. These jobs usually consisted of working in one of the bars, cafés or restaurants that Mr Ruslan owned. The salary of such work was nothing much, but it was at least a salary, and it was usually paid in cash so nothing was 'lost' through taxes, as Shota put it.

The hotel and restaurant business was booming in Batumi in the years following the revolution. Or at least attempts were being made to create a boom. These were financially supported by the government, which wanted Batumi to once again become a tourist hotspot on the Black Sea coast (Frederiksen 2012a). Of all business sectors in Georgia, this was the one most severely marked by informal economies. A 2008 UNDP survey revealed that the contribution of nonobserved activities (or the shadow economy) in the restaurant and bar sector was a staggering 87 per cent (Christie 2008, 9). Such numbers correspond well with the perception of businessmen among many locals in Batumi. As one young man in Batumi, who was himself a thief, told me, 'If you are a businessman and successful, you are surely corrupt' (see also Frederiksen 2012b, 172ff.). The difference between people such as Mr Ruslan and Levan was that Levan had always openly been a criminal, engaged in informal economic activity and opposed to the political sphere. Conversely, Mr Ruslan was not openly engaged in the informal economy and he was not opposed to the political sphere, but rather was seen as being connected to it. Still, the safety or help they in their different times provided did not differ as such.

Ambiguous Informality and Spectres of Illegality

What is interesting in Levan's story is not so much what he had once been but rather what he had come to be. Indeed it would seem, as also argued by Gavin Slade (2012a, 2012b), that the power and influence of the mafia in Georgia was exhausted in the wake of the revolution and the anticorruption and anticrime reforms following it. However, in terms of informal networking and illegality, this only forms one part of the picture. Stories of illicit business and political deals, and their impact on informal economies, continued to flourish both in Batumi and in Georgia at large.[3] Whether they were truthful or not is difficult to say. Some most likely were. What *can* be said for certain is that such stories were widespread.

While the mafia, as mentioned, was a highly visible and often quite public feature of daily life in the Ajara region in western Georgia during the 1990s, in the relatively speaking more secure period of my fieldwork in 2008–09 it had been rendered more opaque. Said differently, from having been an obvious part of life in Ajara it had gained the character of something spectral – something indeterminate yet present.[4] Informality and illegality had become surrounded by questions of unease, murkiness and disquiet, but also questions of obviousness and being taken-for-granted – the latter in the sense that most people readily acknowledged such phenomena to be there, the former in the sense that determining exactly who was there, who and who did what, etc. was opaque. In that sense the division between 'the real' and 'the conceptual' mafia depicted by Verdery in relation to Romania in the 1990s is not a division applicable to Batumi in the late 2000s – the boundary between the two having been blurred.

What is important to note is that the reform-based attack on the mafia in Georgia following the revolution in 2003 was also, albeit perhaps in an unintended manner, an attack on a particular way of doing business – that is, doing business informally. This, however, was a way of doing business that had not been spawned by the mafia, but which actually preceded it – it had been a foundational, everyday aspect of economic life in Georgia during the late Soviet period. This was a time in which up to 30 per cent of all economic activity in the country was informal or 'hidden' (Mars and Altman 2008, 58). Writing about the same period, Stephen Jones similarly notes that while 'the private realm of memories and informal agreements was considered trustworthy and believable, the public realm of Soviet propaganda, laws, and political campaigns was not' (2013, 11). Indeed, it is naive both to think that informal practices in the economic sphere did not exist before the collapse of the Soviet Union and likewise to think that these hidden economies have not survived under new names and disguises up to the present day (Mars and Altman 2008, 68).[5] It is beyond my aim here to establish whether or not the business of a man such as Mr Ruslan was illicit or criminal or not. The point is that he was seen as working through the same principles as Levan (and those like him) did a decade earlier, and as Soviet managers did before him.

Viewed from this perspective, Levan and his kind became scapegoats for a principle that could only be eradicated figuratively. Hence, as noted by Lili di Puppo (2012), the process of reforms against crime and corruption that were undertaken in Georgia after 2003 can be viewed as a symbolic narrative depicting form rather than content. In Georgia politics itself is widely seen as not being possible if not for personal networks and informality, and despite the political reforms undertaken during the presidency of Mikheil Saakashvili, a 2008 World Values Survey found that confidence in parliament, government, the civil service, the police and the justice system had actually fallen since the revolution (CRRC 2012). Another report, from the Terrorism, Transnational Crime and Corruption Center (TraCCC), showed that only 0.2 per cent of the population believed no one to be corrupt (Jokhadze 2006). Similarly, in interviews with locals from Batumi it was often noted that it was impossible to be a politician and not be corrupt. This was not necessarily a denigration of politics but rather a matter-of-fact statement of how things worked. Talk about politics often included statements that politicians always sought to 'milk the system', 'eat grants' or 'fill their own pockets' before they did anything else.[6] This adds an ironic facet to the governmental reforms against corruption and informal economies, as these reforms, in this sense, were a fight against the very basis on which politics was seen to rest.

Hence, what we are dealing with is not only the government looking (through Western glasses) at parts of the population as being engaged in informal-cum-illegal practices. Within civil society boundaries were also drawn. The young men gathering in Levan's house recognised that their activities were not necessarily fully legitimate, but in their eyes they could still be justified and legitimised as being either a form of 'honest banditry' or a form of informal practice taking place everywhere in society. And the activities were, from their point of view, certainly no more illicit than the practices of the government. Whereas they saw their own informal practices as ways to secure and survive everyday life, politicians, they stated, were much greedier. Ledeneva's depiction of informal practices as an ambiguous aspect of everyday life that can be condoned and condemned by the same people is thus revealing in relation to the case of Georgia: while informality of one's own practices was not seen as problematic as such, the informality of *others'* often was. For Levan and the young men in Batumi, the informal practices underlying politics and business were seen as verging on illegality, and, conversely, for the government so were the informal practices of people such as Levan. At the same time all parties claimed their own practices to be transparent: politicians because of reforms implementing (and even building) transparency, and Levan in the sense that his activities had always been precisely that – open, clear cut and transparent. Transparency, it would seem, was everywhere and nowhere to be found.

The Last Honest Bandit, or, Transparency as a Grey Zone

Shortly after my last meeting with Levan in 2009 he moved to Ukraine to live with his daughter. He died there a year later. As one of the last classic 'honest bandits' in Georgia, his exit in a sense marked the success of the political reforms against organised crime introduced after the revolution – there was no longer room for him in the country. However, the sphere of the informal economy in which people such as Levan had thrived did not simply disappear with him. Rather, it had taken on a different and perhaps even more indeterminate character in terms of the possibility of determining both where it was located and whether aspects of it were illegal or not. To be sure, incidents of actual crime (such as assault, armed robbery, burglary or theft) decreased significantly after the introduction of the new reforms (Slade 2012b, 48), yet talk of corruption and accusations of informality and illegal measures did not seem to follow suit. As one of my local friends noted while we were discussing the building of new glass-facaded police stations, 'the more transparent things become here, the more difficult it becomes to see through anything'. In his opinion the imported reforms did not simply change local circumstances, but were conversely changed by them. Although he applauded political attempts to eradicate organised crime, these had not predicted a change in, and perseverance of, informal practices. In fact, under the guise of transparency, informal deals had become easier to make because they were now more difficult to expose – if everything is transparent, where can one even look? In a paradoxical manner transparency comes to stand forth as a grey zone in this context. Despite being a political device to create clarity, in Georgia it created just as much obscurity (see also Ballestero 2012, 60) – or said differently, transparency became part of the grey zone of legality and illegality that it was supposed to have changed. The honest bandits of the

1990s were a problematic feature of socioeconomic life in Georgia, but they were also easy scapegoats in a defunct society, a society for which they were not necessarily the only ones to blame. As shown, the existence of informal practices and activities cannot be explained only with reference to the post-Soviet period, as such practices existed both before and during the Soviet Union itself. As a consequence, making the honest bandits 'disappear' through reforms did not simultaneously make all the practices they had undertaken disappear as well. There were still people who were in need of a favour in order to obtain a job, or a tender, or a licence. While transparency might have created clarity in the sense that such favours could no longer be provided by bandits or members of the *vory-v-zakone*, it simultaneously created a corresponding zone of grey within which it was difficult, if not impossible, to determine who was now doing the same thing in their place.

Notes

1 All names in this chapter have been altered to ensure anonymity. Quotes from interlocutors throughout the text have been translated from Georgian to English by the author.
2 See Frederiksen (2012a, 2013).
3 Not just in colloquial terms but also in the media. See for instance Simonishvili (2010).
4 See Frederiksen (2013), chapter 3, for a longer account.
5 In 2005 a report found the informal economy to account for up to 40 per cent of the total output (Beridze 2005).
6 Indeed, as one of my interlocutors stated, the only reason why he had voted for Saakashvili, despite disliking him and his politics, was because he knew that 'his pockets are already full; if someone new enters our parliament a lot of tax money will be spent filling a new pocket'.

References

Ballestero, A. 2012. 'Transparency in triads'. *Political and Legal Anthropology Review* 35(2): 160–66.
Basilaia, E. 2006. 'Another "serious error": Special operations lead to more and more deaths'. *Georgian Messenger*, 5 July.
Benda-Beckman, F. von, K. von Benda-Beckman and J. Eckert (eds). 2009. *Rules of Law and Laws of Ruling: On the Governance of Law*. Burlington, VT: Ashgate.
Beridze, T. 2005. 'Measuring Georgia's non-observed economy'. *Problems of Economic Transition* 48(4): 43.
Borenstein, E. 2007. *Overkill: Sex and Violence in Contemporary Russian Popular Culture*. Ithaca, NY and London: Cornell University Press.
Caucasus Research Resource Center (CRRC). 2012. *Corruption in Georgia*. Caucasus Research Resource Center.

Christie, E. 2008. *The Non-observed Economy in Georgia: Economic Analysis and Recommendations*. New York: United Nations Development Programme.

Coombe, R. J. 1997. 'The demonic place of the "not there": Trademark rumors in the postindustrial imagery'. In A. Gupta and J. Ferguson (eds), *Culture, Power, Place: Explorations in Critical Anthropology*, 249–74. Durham, NC: Duke University Press.

Di Puppo, L. 2012. 'The Role of Narratives in Georgia's Anti-corruption Reforms'. Conference paper. Available at: http://www.miamioh.edu/cas/_files/documents/havighurst/2012/dipuppo,pdf (accessed 16 November 2014).

Dudwick, N. 2003. 'No guests at our table: Social fragmentation in Georgia'. In N. Dudwick, E. Gomart and A. Marc (eds), *When Things Fall Apart: Qualitative Studies of Poverty in the Former Soviet Union*, 213–58. Washington DC: World Bank.

Dunn, E. C. and M. D. Frederiksen. 2014 'Introduction: Ethnographies of absence in Georgia'. *Slavic Review* 73(2): 241–45.

Frederiksen, M. D. 2012a. 'Insecurity and suspicion in the wake of urban development projects in Batumi, Adjara'. *Caucasus Analytical Digest* 38: 8–11.

_____. 2012b. 'Good hearts or big bellies: *Dzmak'atcoba* and images of masculinity in the Republic of Georgia'. In V. Amit and N. Dyck (eds), *Young Men in Uncertain Times*, 165–87. New York: Berghahn Books.

_____. 2013. *Young Men, Time and Boredom in the Republic of Georgia*. Philadelphia: Temple University Press.

_____. 2014. 'The would-be state: Reforms, NGOs and absent presents in post-revolutionary Georgia'. *Slavic Review* 73(2): 307–21.

Hetherington, K. 2012. 'Agency, scale, and the ethnography of transparency'. *Political and Legal Anthropology Review* 35(2): 242–47.

Humphrey, C. 2002. *The Unmaking of Soviet Life: Everyday Economies after Socialism*. Ithaca, NY and London: Cornell University Press.

Jokhadze, N. 2006. 'Corruption in Illegal Construction in Urban Territories'. Online report. Available at: http://traccc.gmu.edu/pdfs/publications/Georgia_Publications/Jokhadze_Report_eng.pdf (accessed 18 March 2012).

Jones, S. F. 2013. *Georgia: A Political History since Independence*. London and New York: I.B. Tauris.

Larson, J. L. 2008. 'Ambiguous transparency: Resumé fetishism in a Slovak workshop'. *Ethnos* 73(2): 189–216.

Ledeneva, A. V. 2006. *How Russia Really Works: The Informal Practices that Shaped Post-Soviet Politics and Business*. Ithaca, NY and London: Cornell University Press.

Mars, G. and Y. Altman. 1983. 'The cultural basis of Soviet Georgia's second economy'. *Soviet Studies* 35(4): 546–60.

_____. 2008. 'Managing in Soviet Georgia: An extreme example in comparative management'. *European Journal of International Management* 2(1): 56–70.

Ries, N. 2002. '"Honest bandits" and "warped people": Russian narratives about money, corruption and moral decay'. In C. Greenhouse, E. Mertz and K. B. Warren (eds), *Ethnography in Unstable Places: Everyday Lives in Contexts of Dramatic Political Change*, 276–316. Durham, NC and London: Duke University Press.

Shelley, L., E. R. Scott and A. Latta (eds). 2007. *Organized Crime and Corruption in Georgia*. New York: Routledge.

Simonishvili, J. 2010. 'Mafia "tourism in Adjara"'. *Geonews*, 14 October.

Slade, G. 2006. 'Georgia's poisoned soil'. *Georgian Messenger*, 13 June.

_____. 2012a. 'No country for made men: The decline of the mafia in Post-Soviet Georgia'. *Law and Society Review* 46(3): 623–49.

_____. 2012b. 'Georgia's war on crime: Creating security in a post-revolutionary context'. *European Security* 21(1): 37–56.

_____. 2013. *Reorganizing Crime: Mafia and Anti-mafia in Post-Soviet Georgia.* Oxford: Oxford University Press.

Taussig, M. 1980. *The Devil and Commodity Fetishism in South America.* Chapel Hill: University of North Carolina Press.

Verdery, K. 1996. *What Was Socialism, and What Comes Next?* Princeton: Princeton University Press.

Wedel, J. R. 2003. 'Mafia without malfeasance, clans without crime: The criminality conundrum in post-communist Europe'. In P. C. Parnell and S. C. Kane (eds), *Crime's Power: Anthropologists and the Ethnography of Crime*, 221–45. New York and Basingstoke: Palgrave Macmillan.

West, H. G. and T. Sanders. 2003. 'Introduction: Power revealed and concealed in the new world order'. In H. G. West and T. Sanders (eds), *Transparency and Conspiracy: Ethnographies of Suspicion in the New World Order*, 1–38. Durham, NC and London: Duke University Press.

Part IV

BROADER PERSPECTIVES

Chapter 11

MAKING GREY ZONES AT THE EUROPEAN PERIPHERIES

Sarah Green

Introduction

Grey zones are ambiguous places, a spatial and conceptual expression of obscurity. The aspect that I will explore in this chapter is the relation between such a condition of ambiguity and the different types of work that borders do, particularly along the eastern peripheries of Europe.[1] Formally, a key point of making marks on maps (and sometimes on the ground) and calling them borders is to remove ambiguity: to clearly establish, on paper at least, where one thing ends and another begins. In that sense borders are classification systems, as I have argued elsewhere (Green 2012): they order the world according to a particular epistemological logic, one that sets the rules for establishing the difference between 'here' and 'somewhere else'. Marking borders on maps and in places is intended to deny greyness, to assert that there is no room for doubt about the difference between here and somewhere else. Of course, such assertions have variable levels of success, and they always exist in the company of other opinions, both about where exactly to locate the mark that will be called a border and about the logic, usually accompanied by a moral justification, used to assert that the border belongs here, rather than there.[2] Moreover, many borders are crosscut by, or overlap, other borders that have been marked using different logics.

The fact that the current geographical locations of many borders are regularly contested, and that they exist in the company of other border regimes, are the key elements that tend to generate a sense of greyness. I will be arguing that it might be helpful to think of this process as involving three dimensions, rather than two: border regimes existing in layers that sometimes overlap, sometimes interact and sometimes slide past each other. Thinking of the process in these terms raises the obvious possibility that, in conditions where two different border regimes overlap, two different places will coexist within the same geographical space. I will provide one example of this from the Aegean region later on, in which a state border regime (involving Greece and Turkey) overlaps with the border regime of the EU and, in at least some respects, the two run in parallel, not interfering with each other a great deal.

This layering aspect of border regimes is one element of the way grey zones are made in the contemporary moment, at least around the European peripheries: greyness is generated by contesting the proper location of borders, or by the coexistence of overlapping, parallel or mutually contradictory border regimes. But there is another element as well, and it follows on from the notion that borders are a form of classification system that result from a certain epistemological logic: i.e., that some epistemologies valorise the idea of ambiguity in itself and deliberately generate it. In such cases grey zones are the logical, or ideological, outcomes of particular epistemological projects, rather than being generated accidentally, informally or illegally.

Here, the shift from the Cold War era in Europe, which strongly asserted an unambiguous alignment of mutually opposed political-economic, ideological and geographical borders in the European region, to the 'multiple posts' era (postsocialist, postplural, postmodern, poststructural), in which endless differences exist, but none of them appear to make any difference, is an example of changes in epistemological forms of making grey zones. I will suggest that this second form makes the potential for politics quite narrow, by rendering the difference between here and elsewhere of little, if any, account. From this vantage point it does not really matter where the borders are located, for all sides are simultaneously endlessly different and endlessly the same.

This point about the logical implications of some forms of 'post' ideology has been made before, of course, notably by Doreen Massey (2005) and David Graeber (2001). Massey, in commenting on certain types of postmodern analyses of economic globalisation, suggests that:

> If this is the imagination which is to replace modernism's temporal alignment of regions, then it is a move straight through from a billiard-ball world of essentialised places to a claustrophobic holism in which everything everywhere is already connected to everywhere else. And once again it leaves no opening for an active politics. (Massey 2005, 77)

My aim here is to explore two aspects of this assertion. First, to consider how the kind of holism Massey refers to might work in terms of border regimes – whose explicit purpose, after all, is to clarify and classify, to break things into parts, rather than to blend everything together into a seamless whole. And second, to show, through an exploration of the Imia/Kardak dispute and some small ethnographic examples from the Aegean and the Greek–Albanian border region, that the coexistence and overlapping of different border regimes will probably always undermine any regime whose logic is to render differences of no account. This is not the same as saying that social, political and economic inequalities inform the implementation of just about all border regimes, and that such inequalities end up causing conflicts and border disputes (although they do). Instead, I am focusing on the regular coexistence of different epistemological regimes that inform the creation of borders in the first place. This coexistence exposes the inadequacy, and incapacity, of any one such regime to encompass and define all that there is without let or hindrance, as it were. Inevitably, the outcome is the simultaneous making of grey zones *and* the making of differences (between epistemologies) that make a difference (Bateson 1972, 453). At least for the regions that I discuss in this chapter, no border regime exists alone, which means that their current forms are always the outcome of attempted assertions that can only ever be partially successful.[3]

Greek–Albanian Balkan Epistemologies

My interest in the implications of grey zones began in the early years of what came to be called the postsocialist period in Europe in the early 1990s, with research on the ambiguities of the Greek–Albanian border (Green 2005). My work at that time concerned the political implications of an inability to distinguish one thing clearly from another in any long-term or fixed way. Part of that work tried to understand why the Balkans had the reputation of being dangerously chaotic. During the 1990s when I was doing that research, there was a strong story circulating in the media, after conflicts began in former Yugoslavia, that suggested that the Balkans constituted an endless proliferation of chaotic disputes between peoples about the proper location of borders that both created world wars and defied any logic. As Bakić-Hayden famously noted, this apparently inherently chaotic and potentially violent situation in the Balkans was also often understood to repeat itself at every level in the Balkan region, like a Russian doll – from the most intimate and detailed parts of people's everyday lives right up to state politics, a partial replication of the same thing would occur: a constant tendency to fragment into ever smaller parts, recombine and then fragment again (Bakić-Hayden 1995).

As a result of that research, I argued that the appearance of chaos was due to a clash of knowledge systems: that the logic behind the idea of nation-states, which informed contemporary border regimes in the area, conflicted with the ideology that organised the relationship between people and territory in the way that the Ottomans had done, before nation-states were introduced to this region. The Ottomans organised things on the assumption that people regularly travelled and moved, so for the Ottomans there was no fixed relationship between location and identity. Identity was tied to other things: to religion in a legal, political and ideological sense; and to kinship, to the network of family relationships created through alliances (marriages) that made persons part of one people rather than another. Identity was not directly related to territory under the Ottomans. I suggested that the clash between the logic that informs a nation-state way of thinking and organising location and movement, and an Ottoman way of thinking about and organising these things, led to a sense that what was going on in the Balkans was incomprehensible, chaotic, monstrous.

I also suggested that the conflicts which occurred with depressing regularity in the Balkan region were not the outcome of some inherent characteristic of the Balkan landscape, nor some kind of cultural characteristic of its peoples. Instead, it was the outcome of a structural problem: if you try to shift between an administrative system that, for over four hundred years, organised different groups of people so that they were territorially thoroughly mixed together, into an administrative system in which they are supposed to be neatly separated out, so that only one kind of people (the nationals) belong to each territory (the nation), then it is inevitable that there will be a mess in trying to sort out which people belong to which territory. It resulted, unsurprisingly, in multiple overlapping claims to the same territory. The creation of proliferating and overlapping 'grey zones' was, I suggested in that work, a structural (and of course ideologically inflected) matter. It was through that research that I began to understand the importance of divergent epistemological logics that inform the marking of differences between here and somewhere else.

Aegean Disambiguation

The Greek–Albanian border research concerned places becoming too mixed up together, generating too much connection and overlap. In contrast, the Aegean Sea is a very different kind of political location: it is one in which a great deal of political effort has been expended to ensure that the difference between the two sides is unambiguously clear, to the extent of being iconic (Green 2010; Hirschon 2003b). In the 1920s, following a particularly violent conflict between the Greek and Turkish armies regarding the Aegean, a compulsory exchange of populations was enforced by the League of Nations between the two sides: all Muslims who were Greek nationals were moved to Turkey, and all Orthodox Christians who were Turkish nationals were moved to Greece (Hirschon 2003a). This was intended to stop the repeated conflicts between the two sides that had followed the collapse of the Ottoman Empire, and to stabilise the new, national borders between them.

Ever since that period there have been regular disputes between Greek and Turkish governments about the precise location of the border in the Aegean. Partly, this was because the Aegean was the location of the final war that led to the establishment of the Republic of Turkey and the final location of Greece's current borders, which both countries have used as symbolic capital to build their particular accounts of their nations (Milton 2009; Aktar 2003; Keyder 2003). However, the disputes have also been fostered by the difficulties of establishing exactly where one country begins and the other ends in a sea that is full of a scatter of islands and through a definition of borders that starts from a premise of territory as land rather than sea or air. Most of the disputes between Greece and Turkey in terms of the Aegean in recent decades have concerned air space or a sea boundary (Acer 2003; Heraclides 2010). For example, the Greek government has suggested it has the right, under the United Nations Convention on the Law of the Sea, to claim 12 nautical miles of sea that stretches off any Greek territory, including its islands. As almost all the islands in the Aegean belong to Greece, this would effectively mean that in order to pass through the Aegean, Turkish ships would have to sail through Greek waters (Pratt and Schofield 1996, 62). The Turkish government has stated that if Greece tries to enforce such an interpretation of the law, it will in turn interpret that as a hostile act (*casus belli*).

Imia/Kardak Dispute: Meaningful and Meaningless Grey Zones

It was in this context that a dispute between the Greek and Turkish governments about two uninhabited Aegean islets occurred. The bare facts of the case are as follows.[4] On 26 December 1995 the captain of a Turkish cargo ship ran aground on one of these two islets, or rocks, which are named Imia in Greece and Kardak in Turkey. When the Greek coastguard offered assistance, the Turkish captain refused, on the grounds that the rocks were in Turkish, not Greek, territory. The Greek and Turkish embassies exchanged notes about the event, disagreeing on the matter of in whose territory the rocks were located. In late January 1996 the Greek media reported the story as an explicit Turkish attempt to annex Greek territory. People from the local island of Kalymnos, five miles away from the rocks, sailed out and planted a Greek flag on one of them. A group of Turkish journalists from the national daily newspaper *Hürriyet* then went out and replaced the Greek flag with a Turkish one.[5] Quite quickly both the Greek and Turkish military and the Greek and Turkish prime ministers became involved, as did an envoy sent from Bill Clinton, the then president of the USA.

At the height of the dispute representatives from the Turkish side suggested that the Imia/Kardak rocks were just two of many other islets and small islands in the Aegean that together constituted 'grey zones' (*gri bölgeler*). The grounds were that these rocky outcrops were not explicitly named in any treaties, so which state could claim them was an open question, a grey area. The Greek government instantly and consistently rejected this argument, saying the concept of grey zones was entirely invented by the Turkish authorities as a ploy to create a sense of uncertainty about what was, in fact, clearly within the boundaries of Greek territory.

So that was one border regime at work. The greyness asserted here was operating, for both sides in the dispute, entirely within the logic of national/state borders. The disagreement did not concern the form of the border or the rationale for its existence. Instead, there were competing interpretations of the meaning of the words that governed the precise location of the border in practice.

Yet at the same time as this argument about the two islets was going on, an EU-initiated agreement was signed in Barcelona that would highly improve contact and communication between the Turkish and Greek sides, and its implementation progressed without being affected at all by Imia/Kardak dispute. This was the Barcelona Process, and both Turkey and Greece were among the 29 Mediterranean and adjacent countries that signed up to it.[6] The agreement established procedures for encouraging greater political, economic and social cooperation between all the Mediterranean countries. This agreement fairly instantly led to much more relaxed regulations governing both trade and travel across the Aegean. So whatever the political tensions that might have existed between Greece and Turkey in terms of the Imia/Kardak dispute, agreements organised by the EU that covered cross-border relations – which encompassed, and went well beyond, the Aegean region – continued without being affected. In other words, at the same moment relations between Turkey and Greece both worsened and improved.

This is one rather simple example of two overlapping border regimes at work. In this case, the implications of one of them did not directly affect the workings of the other. Of course, the Imia/Kardak islets were not highly significant, except in the symbolic terms of asserting the right to maintain the integrity of national/state territory. So in practice, there was no chance at all that the Barcelona Process, which had been years in the making and involved 27 countries other than Greece and Turkey, would be negatively affected by a local argument about two rocks. Yet that is precisely the point: the logic informing the border agreement between the 29 states as enshrined in the Barcelona Process was quite different from the logic informing the calling out of the Greek and Turkish navies to the Imia/Kardak islets in the Aegean Sea. Not only were the issues involved in each case entirely different, the sense of proportion in each was entirely different as well. The Barcelona Process was one of a series of projects undertaken by the EU that was aimed at generating relations, rather than separations, between the countries on the EU's peripheries and their immediate neighbours. The culmination of that approach is the European Neighbourhood Policy, which aims to draw neighbouring countries into specific types of relations with the EU area (Cardwell 2011).[7] It is worth noting here that Turkey cannot gain the status of being a 'European Neighbour', as that status is only given to countries that are clearly outside the EU; as Turkey has been a candidate for accession to the EU since 1987 (longer than any other country), it does not qualify. This is another form of grey zone, generated by what was intended to be a temporary status for any country wishing to become an EU member but which has lasted for more than two decades now in the case of Turkey.

In general the EU's approach towards border regimes could be called an exercise in contemporary *bricolage*: it constitutes a multiplicity of diverse interests and groupings, overlapping and criss-crossing with others.[8] As there is no overarching power that can entirely control or align the different interests and ideologies among the countries within the European region, the maps of the different border regimes that involve the EU's activities sketch out a convoluted example of the outcomes of numerous compromises between overlapping and cross-cutting interests and powers: there is no *single* border regime here. What is more, there is no sense of a settled border regime either: the next compromise always appears to be on the way. The need for a three-dimensional layered image, rather than the more familiar two-dimensional map with lines on it, becomes rather obvious here. And it also raises some questions about what the meaning of border regimes might be: If they are both multiple and always subject to yet another adjustment as another compromise is reached, does the conceptual point of borders as a means of denying greyness actually begin to become its opposite – a means of establishing greyness?

Borderless Borders

This brings me on to the ongoing debate about the effects of neoliberal political and economic conditions on border regimes. The most familiar story about the period since the end of the Cold War in Europe, and most particularly since the rise of the EU, is that it is marked by neoliberal political and economic dynamics, informed by an ideology that simultaneously celebrates all kinds of differences while insisting that differences make no difference anymore: the transgression of boundaries – the creation of mixtures, blends and combinations without any regard for the strict separation between one thing and another – is a key trope of neoliberal ideology. It is this characteristic of neoliberal ideals that has caused David Graeber, among others, to compare neoliberalism to postmodern and poststructural thought, arguing that such 'post' theories actually have the effect of justifying neoliberal ideology (Graeber 2001, x–xi). Graeber argues that the postmodern perspective, in which reality is a collection of disparate fragments that do not come together into any coherent whole but in which endless, fluid and hybrid recombinations are constantly possible, is closely related to a neoliberal account of the world, in which life is entirely multiple, flexible and has no beginning, middle or end. For Graeber, the assertion of an absence of any universal values in the 'post' era, whether by postmodern thinkers, or promoters of neoliberalism, is a lie. Instead, he suggests, this is 'the era of the triumph of the World Market – one in which the most gigantic, totalizing, and all-encompassingly universal system of evaluation known to human history came to be imposed on almost everything' (Graeber 2001, 89). And he adds, most damningly: 'Behind the imagery of most postmodernism is really nothing but the ideology of the market' (ibid.).

As will be clear from my comments so far on the coexistence of differing epistemologies in the European peripheries, my thoughts differ from Graeber's comments about the all-encompassing character of world markets: no epistemology, however powerful, exists alone in the world. However, on the issue of how neoliberal ideals generate a sense that all differences can be celebrated, while at the same time, that no differences actually matter, I can see his point. If neoliberal ideology and the economic structures built in its image promote simultaneous transgression of previous boundaries and new interconnections between everything, then arguably the result is meaningless distinctions, distinctions with no values attached – or in other words, grey.

Some suggest that during the Cold War the ideals of socialism created a different kind of grey: a lack of difference asserted through socialism's egalitarian ideals, through the concept of removing all differences that might lead to inequalities. In contrast, neoliberal approaches appear to be creating grey through an assertion of endless difference: the promotion of limitless possibilities of combining and recombining things without any values being attached to any of these recombined results.

Many years ago, Marilyn Strathern implied something of the same idea in her book *After Nature* (1992). In that book Strathern described an ideological shift from the concept of a 'plural society' to one of a 'postplural society'. In a plural society, Strathern argues, the world is classified into distinctive, different domains, in which meaning is created through the combination of ways in which the different domains come into relation with one another. One example she uses is the concept of persons. In a plural society persons are assumed to have preexisting identities into which they are born: these identities are part biological (genetic) and part social – derived from kinship and the social position in which a person's kin exist in a wider social world. In this situation each of the parts that make up a person, the biological and the social, are quite distinct and separate domains. In contrast, within a postplural concept of persons these domains do not remain separate. Instead people are increasingly regarded as an 'assemblage of parts perceived as substitutable or replaceable for one another' (Strathern 1992, 183). In other words, and again borrowing from Bateson, the post-plural society generates differences that make no difference.

The plural society to post-plural society analogy could be applied to the changes that have occurred within the European region's border regimes in the shift from the Cold War period to the post–Cold War period. During the Cold War period, East and West defined themselves through their contrasts and relations with one another. In recent years an increasing number of social and cultural studies have shown how this worked in practice, and Alexei Yurchak's study *Everything Was Forever, Until It Was No More* (2006) is a good example. But in the post–Cold War period, many suggest, since the Wall came down, both literally and metaphorically, everything is simultaneously different and the same on all sides, fragmented and recombined endlessly according to market logic, containing no hard edges, beginnings, middle or ends. There is no Iron Curtain to act as a measuring stick to distinguish one set of clear values from another set of clear values: instead, it has been replaced by that multi-overlapping Venn diagram set of EU borders.

In the prologue to *After Nature* Strathern explicitly relates this shift – from the ideals of a plural world to those of a post-plural world – to a shift towards a political economy in which the concept of freedom is equated with the concept of free choice: choice with no values and no relations attached. Many people nowadays call that concept a neoliberal perspective. In Strathern's view the ideal of free choice, of the ultimate value being the ability to choose, is a value that removes the value of anything else. As she puts it in the prologue:

> Such free-ranging access, such apparent freedom of choice, in the end turns the sense of plurality into an artifact of access or choice itself. An approximation to the insight, then, of what it might be like to belong to a culture whose next imaginative leap is to think of itself as having nothing to construct. (Strathern 1992, 7)

In other words, if you have to choose between differences that have no value except the value of the ability to choose between them, then you are choosing between differences that make no difference. The concept of a totally interconnected world whose interconnections are driven by these kinds of neoliberal or post-plural principles (call them whatever you like) implies the existence of a world in which all differences simply are; they make no difference.

As compelling as this idea might be, I want to suggest that the Imia/Kardak dispute and the EU's Barcelona Process simultaneously existing in the Aegean region demonstrates how a clear shift between one regime and another does not often occur in practice. The EU's multiple border regimes coexist with the national/state border regimes that led to the Imia/Kardak dispute. In themselves I have suggested that EU border regimes are the ongoing and always-imperfect outcomes of endless compromises and negotiations, so although the ideals that the EU promotes may often encourage what many see as neoliberal outcomes, the results are never entirely successful reflections of such attempts. The grey zones within the EU's border regimes are generated by this constant need to compromise, and when this is combined with the continued existence of other border regimes – and in the case of the Aegean, rather strongly expressed nation/state regimes – then the overlapping existence of parallel border regimes that do not always directly affect one another becomes obvious, as does the inability of the EU's border regimes to encompass all spatial expressions of difference.

In short, there are different ways of making sense of the meaning of 'here' as opposed to 'elsewhere', and these methods often coexist in the same space. This simple condition – the coexistence of different border regimes, each of which uses a different logic to establish the meaning of places – inevitably makes grey zones, ambiguities and uncertainties at the interface between border regimes. This not only questions the capacity of any one regime to encompass all that there is; it also questions the implication that there are no differences that make a difference in a neoliberal world: in fact, the world appears to be ever more full of stark differences.

Now, one could suggest, and indeed many have, that neoliberal ideals represent the antithesis of a global approach: nothing universally exists, everything is in the constant flux of being reconstituted anew, a little like the constant restructuring of EU border structures. Yet in order for that principle to work in logical terms, no differences can have a fixed value anymore: all differences are contingent, dependent upon circumstances. This is importantly different from the concept of cultural relativism: having no basis for any value (other than choice) is different from the coexistence of diverse values. And this is where the implicit universal claim of neoliberal logic comes in that narrows the possibility of politics: within that logic, differences simply exist.

Doreen Massey rather famously defined politics as contingency: if the outcome of something is open, if it is not possible to predict with certainty what will happen next, then the outcome is negotiable, it is open to political activity that could push the outcome in one direction rather than another (Massey 2005, 12–13). If you have a situation in which all outcomes will be the same, to the extent that no outcomes result in any difference that makes any difference, then politics disappears: the world is both one and many simultaneously. What I am suggesting is that border regimes contain differences that matter in spite of, or perhaps even because of, any rhetoric which might suggest otherwise, and that the EU's endlessly complicated and compromised border regimes, combined with the ones that mark the difference between one nation and another, make grey zones of uncertainty about the ability of any one of them to encompass all that there is. And that uncertainty makes the possibility of politics much *more* likely, not less so.

In sum, what I have been trying to look at here is an example of coexisting border regimes that run in parallel rather than clashing with one another, but whose coexistence nevertheless makes the world a more contingent place than it would otherwise be. I have also suggested that far from being an enormous hegemonic power that is destined to overwhelm any state that belongs to it, the EU, in border terms at least, has proven itself to be the outcome of constant and never-ending compromises between incompatible interests and positions, and that actually, given the alternatives, as border regimes go, that's not so bad.

Notes

1   Much of the background work for this article was carried out through the European Cooperation in Science and Technology (COST) research network EastBordNet, and I gratefully acknowledge the support provided by COST over a period of four years (see www.eastbordnet.org for further details). I was prompted to explore the Imia/Kardak dispute in particular by Emmanuel Brunet-Jailly and Martin van der Velde, who invited me to write an encyclopaedia entry on the topic (Green forthcoming). I am also grateful to Ida Harboe Knudsen and Martin Demant Frederiksen, the organisers of the conference 'Exploring the Grey Zones', for encouraging me to work on the concept of grey zones, and to the Universities of Oslo, Manchester and Eastern Finland for giving me the opportunity to think further about these issues and for the feedback given in presentations of parts of this chapter.

2   At the time of writing, the president of Russia, Vladimir Putin, had recently arranged for the formerly Ukrainian Crimean Peninsula to become a part of Russia, having hastily organised a referendum through the Crimean regional parliament about whether the people would rather belong to Russia or Ukraine. Putin announced the annexation

of Crimea by the Russian Federation on 18 March 2014. http://www.theguardian. com/world/2014/mar/18/putin-confirms-annexation-crimea-ukrainian-soldier-casualty (accessed 27 March 2014).

3 A slightly different but closely related point is made by Strathern in *Partial Connections* (1991), in which she considers the levels of comparability and compatibility of different ways of generating knowledge across disciplinary regimes, as well as across contexts. What she concludes is that connections between these differences are always partial, and there is never a way to generate some form of overarching epistemology that can encompass all of them.

4 I discuss this case in detail in a forthcoming encyclopaedia entry (Green forthcoming).

5 Pictures can still be found on the internet. See, for example, http://www. hurriyetdailynews.com/Default.aspx?pageID=238&nid=40732 (accessed 7 November 2014).

6 A useful account of this process can be found in Scott (2006).

7 See also Kølvraa (2012) for a detailed and up-to-date discussion of the EU's European Neighbourhood Policy.

8 Further details of quite how intricate this *bricolage* has become can be found in Del Sarto (2010) and Green (2013)

References

Acer, Y. 2003. *The Aegean maritime Disputes and International Law*. Aldershot: Ashgate.

Aktar, A. 2003. 'Homogenising the nation, Turkifying the economy: The Turkish experience of population exchange reconsidered'. In R. Hirschon (ed.), *Crossing the Aegean: An Appraisal of the 1923 Compulsory Population Exchange between Greece and Turkey*, 79–96. New York and Oxford: Berghahn Books.

Bakić-Hayden, M. 1995. 'Nesting Orientalisms: The case of former Yugoslavia'. *Slavic Review* 54(4): 917–31.

Bateson, G. 1972. *Steps to an Ecology of Mind*. Chicago and London: University of Chicago Press.

Cardwell, P. J. 2011. 'EuroMed, European Neighbourhood Policy and the union for the Mediterranean: Overlapping Policy frames in the EU's governance of the Mediterranean'. *Journal of Common Market Studies* 49(2): 219–41.

Del Sarto, R. A. 2010. 'Borderlands: The Middle East and north Africa as the EU's southern buffer zone'. In D. Bechev and K. Nicolaidis (eds), *Mediterranean Frontiers: Borders, Conflict and Memory in a Transnational World*, 149–65. London: I.B. Tauris.

Graeber, D. 2001. *Toward an Anthropological Theory of Value: The False Coin of Our Own Dreams*. New York and Basingstoke: Palgrave Macmillan.

Green, S. F. 2005. *Notes from the Balkans: Locating Marginality and Ambiguity on the Greek–Albanian Border*. Princeton: Princeton University Press.

_____. 2010. 'Performing border in the Aegean: On relocating political, economic and social relations'. *Journal of Cultural Economy* 3(2): 261–78.

_____. 2012. 'A sense of border'. In T. M. Wilson and H. Donnan (eds), *A Companion to Border Studies*, 573–92. Oxford: Wiley-Blackwell.

_____. 2013. 'Borders and the relocation of Europe'. *Annual Review of Anthropology* 42: 345–61.

_____. Forthcoming. 'Imia/Kardak – Greece, Turkey'. In E. Brunet-Jailly (ed.), *Border Disputes: A Global Encyclopedia*. Santa Barbara, CA: ABO-CLIO.

Heraclides, A. 2010. *The Greek–Turkish Conflict in the Aegean: Imagined Enemies*. Basingstoke and New York: Palgrave Macmillan.

Hirschon, R (ed.). 2003a. *Crossing the Aegean: An Appraisal of the 1923 Compulsory Population Exchange between Greece and Turkey*. New York and Oxford: Berghahn Books.

_____. 2003b. '"Unmixing peoples" in the Aegean region'. In R. Hirschon (ed.), *Crossing the Aegean: An Appraisal of the 1923 Compulsory Population Exchange between Greece and Turkey*, 3–12. New York and Oxford: Berghahn Books.

Keyder, C. 2003. 'The consequences of the exchange of populations for Turkey'. In R. Hirschon (ed.), *Crossing the Aegean: An Appraisal of the 1923 Compulsory Population Exchange between Greece and Turkey*, 39–52. New York and Oxford: Berghahn Books.

Kølvraa, C. 2012. *Imagining Europe as a Global Player: Imagining Europe as a Global Player*. Brussels: Peter Lang.

Massey, D. B. 2005. *For Space*. London: Sage.

Milton, G. 2009. *Paradise Lost: Smyrna 1922 – The Destruction of Islam's City of Tolerance*. London: Sceptre.

Pratt, M. and C. Schofield. 1996. 'The Imia/Kardak rocks dispute in the Aegean Sea'. *IBRU Boundary and Security Bulletin* Spring: 62–9.

Scott, J. W. 2006. 'Wider Europe: Geopolitics of inclusion and exclusion at the EU's new external boundaries'. In J. W. Scott (ed.), *EU Enlargement, Region Building and Shifting Borders of Inclusion and Exclusion*, 17–34. Aldershot and Burlington, VT: Ashgate.

Strathern, M. 1991. *Partial Connections*. Savage, MD: Rowman & Littlefield.

_____. 1992. *After Nature: English Kinship in the Late Twentieth Century*. Cambridge: Cambridge University Press.

Yurchak, A. 2006. *Everything Was Forever, Until It Was No More: The Last Soviet Generation*. Princeton and Oxford: Princeton University Press

Chapter 12

CODA: REFLECTIONS ON GREY THEORY AND GREY ZONES

Nils Bubandt

Introduction

Grey is good to think with, as this edited volume demonstrates in wonderful detail. The phrase that something is 'good to think' comes, of course, from the reflections of Claude Lévi-Strauss on the value of animals for human thought (1963, 89). Given the structuralist ambition for rationalist clarity that drove this phrase, it is perhaps ironic that the value of greyness for contemporary thought, as this volume also demonstrates, has largely been to undermine the 'black-and-white' analysis that has become structuralism's main legacy in anthropology (if not necessarily its only one: there are also many 'grey' ways of reading Lévi-Strauss). Grey is resolutely poststructuralist, it would seem. In their introduction to this anthology, Martin Demant Frederiksen and Ida Harboe Knudsen usefully reference Primo Levi (quoted in Auyero 2007, 32) to suggest such a poststructuralist thrust to the colour grey. A grey zone is ambivalent throughout.

> a zone of ambiguity that severely challenges pervasive polarities such as we/they, friend/enemy and good/evil – what Levi refers to as the 'Manichean tendency, which shuns half-tints and complexities [...] prone to reduce the river of human occurrences to conflicts, and the conflicts to duels – we and they'.

This is an intriguing proposition: Greyness is opposed to opposition, dichotomies and clarity, while it highlights ambiguity, ambivalence, absence, complexity, doubt, excess and paradox. These latter concepts are all highly valorised in contemporary social and anthropological theory. Flick through any recent issue of an anthropological journal and you are likely to find a domination of analyses whose figuration is that of ambivalence, multiplicity, absence or another of the terms above, authorised by references to Agamben's *homo sacer* (1998), Deleuze and Guattari's notion of the rhizomic (2013), Derrida's concept of *différance* (2001), Badiou's concept of the event (2013), Haraway's cyborg (1991) or some other term that denotes a reality in conflict with itself, an ambivalence of identity, or the subversion of an imagined order. Paradox is the theoretical order of the day, one might say, and its colour is grey. As such, this volume is not merely about Eastern Europe; it is the sign of as well as an implicit manifesto for a certain analytical poetics and theoretical politics of anthropology today. Contemporary anthropology is grey.

I do not want to be misunderstood here: I am a grey anthropologist, too. I want to analyse the world in terms of doubt and ambivalence as much as the next anthropological fellow (Bubandt 2012, 2014b). I am therefore also convinced by the overall premise of this volume as it identifies grey zones in all aspects of life in Eastern Europe. Indeed, the contributions to this volume demonstrate forcefully that greyness is a useful analytical tool to understand most dimensions of contemporary life: identity can be grey, when for example outside representations contradict it (Cash, this volume) or when one inhabits a dual identity (Halilovic-Pastuovic); nation-states can be grey, both at the level of official politics (Green) and informal practices (Joyce); politics itself can be grey, both in its revolutionary (Gotfredsen) and legal (Frederiksen) incarnations; and, finally, the economy can be grey, for instance when labour is lost (Šliavaitė) or hard to find (Harboe Knudsen).

I use 'grey analysis' of a very similar kind to understand the contemporary world in Indonesia all the time, and find that greyness diffuses into most aspects of life there, too. Perhaps there are good reasons for this. Indonesia and Eastern Europe share a similar political history: both have an authoritarian past and have experienced an exuberant turn to democracy that quickly evaporated into disappointment, conflict and accusations of corruption. The authoritarianisms of these two regions are however also very different, and Indonesia reminds us that greyness thrives as much in the afterlife of right-wing regimes as on the historical coattail of socialist authoritarianism. The greyness of Indonesia's democracy – a democracy that alternates between being tepid and at boiling point – also supports the suggestion of this volume that the grey aspects of a nation's life are nurtured as much by its democratic present as by its authoritarian past. Grey may in fact be the universal colour of the contemporary moment.

But even though I employ grey theory, I am also troubled by the contemporary fascination with the multiple shades of grey in anthropology and philosophical theory (in their introduction Frederiksen and Harboe

Knudsen point to the striking homology between the popularity of grey literary eroticism and the academic attraction to grey). My ambivalence about greyness as a theoretical concept is as follows. I would like the anthropological application of grey theory – to understand Southeast Asia, Eastern Europe or the contemporary moment – to come out a little more, to declare its true colour. I would like anthropological grey theory not just to be satisfied to point to the absence, ambivalence and paradox of things, but to be more specific about its method (How does one know greyness?), to be more precise in its language (If greyness can be many things, what can it not be?), and to understand 'absence', 'ambivalence' and 'paradox' in a specific analytical context that is bigger than area studies and smaller than 'the human condition'. My ambivalent loyalty to grey theory (itself as sign of greyness, I suppose) will structure the contribution that follows by describing four grey examples from Indonesia under the sign of a series of critical questions to grey theory.

Is Grey an Experience or a Condition?

Grey scene 1: Indonesian trust 2009

Seventy-four per cent of Indonesians in the 2009 Global Corruption Barometer published by Transparency International stated that they found the current efforts of their government in curbing corruption to be effective. This level of trust in their government's anticorruption efforts was higher than in any other country. Only 24 per cent of citizens in the EU and 27 per cent of citizens in the US shared this optimism in their government's corruption-eradication efforts (Transparency International 2009, 30). The same survey, however, shows that 47 per cent of Indonesian respondents believed that the parliament and legislature were the most corrupt sectors in the country. This suspicion of institutionalised government corruption was higher than in any other country included in the survey (Transparency International 2009, 30). The grey paradox is this: On a global scale, Indonesians trust (more than the citizens of any other country) the effectiveness of their own parliament to curb corruption, a parliament that Indonesians (more than citizens in any other country) simultaneously regard as corrupt!

For me this paradox is a fascinating sign of greyness. It points to a fundamental ambivalence about a political system that Indonesians trust and regard as corrupt at the same time. Although it is not the place here to analyse this ambivalence in detail, it grows, in my view, from the confluence of an authoritarian past, a certain ontology of power and the contradictions of democracy itself, a confluence that has interested me for some time (Bubandt 2014a). The account above, however, raises a question: namely, of whether this greyness is an experience or a condition. Is it Indonesian democracy or people's experience of it that is ambivalent, or grey? This is unclear from my account above. The Transparency International report claims to reflect stakeholder perceptions of corruption, but it not obvious whether the people who answered the questionnaire were aware of this contradiction. The contradiction is also not highlighted in the report itself, nor has it to my knowledge been discussed in Indonesia. It arose because I pulled the two statistics out and put them alongside each other to provide an illustrative example of a contradiction at the heart of Indonesian democracy, a contradiction that other academics have also noticed (Aspinall 2010; Horowitz 2013). I have been struck many times by a certain 'grey ambivalence' in the representations of politics among people I know in Indonesia. But whether they experience this ambivalence themselves, I do not know. Attributing this, my analytical greyness, to Indonesian citizens on this basis would therefore be problematic. The paradox is, so far, mine, not theirs. I do not think I am alone in sliding imperceptibly between assertions about conditions and assertions about informant experiences when it comes to grey ambivalences such as this. The contributions to this volume demonstrate that greyness is both a condition and an experience in Eastern Europe. My concern is that, in the tumbles of grey analysis, the analytical shift from one to the other is obscured. So, to use my own case above as an example, is it legitimate to move from my analytical assertions about a certain paradox in Indonesian democracy to a claim about an Indonesian ambivalent experience of it? In other words, is ambivalence an Indonesian experience or my analytical assertion about Indonesian democracy? As the next section will demonstrate, one possible way to connect analytical assertions about conditions to the level of experience could be to find ambivalence represented in language.

Is Grey an Informant Category?

Grey scene 2: Bank Indonesia, 2000
In late 2000 Sjahril Sabirin, then governor of Bank Indonesia, was accused of involvement in a money forgery racket. Some 2.2 million US dollars' worth of 50,000 rupiah bills had allegedly been printed on government-issue paper and given duplicate serial numbers by national bank employees (BBC News 2000). However, as happens so often in Indonesia, the case was dropped before it made it to court. Sabirin was in 2002 sentenced to three years in prison for his part in a different corruption scandal.

Multiple kinds of grey powers struggle for domination in this extraordinary incident. The money had been printed, allegedly, at the behest of Tyasno Sudarto, the head of the Indonesian military intelligence service (Badan Intelijen Negara, or BIA), to finance pro-Indonesian paramilitary operations in East Timor in 1999 as East Timor prepared to vote for independence from Indonesia (Kingsbury 2003; *Tempo* 2001). The forgery racket only came to light when a leader of the militia decided to put the money into his own bank account and the bank refused the counterfeit money (Aspinall and Van Klinken 2011, 3). It took corruption to reveal forgery, just as it took one bank to reveal the forgery of another. The fake and the authentic blur when the head of the national bank is accused of involvement in making counterfeit money. But before certainty can shed light on this kind of greyness and the person be brought before a judge, a second kind of grey intervenes, namely the grey dimensions of the law that operate before and in front of the legal institutions: the kind of mechanisms and corridor deals that prevent instances such as this one from ever becoming legal cases in the first place. Two low-level military officers were the only people ever convicted in the case.

In English the two convicted men would probably be described as 'scapegoats'. In Indonesia they would just as likely be called 'jockeys' (*joki*): people who are paid off to take the blame or serve the sentences of others, to act as stand-ins for others in exams or driving licence tests, or to sit in the passenger seats of cars to allow them to use specially reserved congestion lanes in Indonesia's larger cities. The word *joki* expresses, one might say, an experience of political 'murkiness' (Bubandt 2008; Spyer 2006), a grey awareness of the way legality and illegality, power and pretence, and authenticity and forgery are each others' conditions of possibility. A second word for this murkiness is *aspal*. The concept of *aspal* mixes the word for 'original' (*asli*) with the word for 'fake' (*palsu*) to make a composite word that means not only 'tarmac' or 'bitumen', but also refers to the inherent falsity of authenticity. *Aspal* may in this second and metaphorical sense perhaps be translated as 'authentic-fake'. The counterfeit bank notes made on government-issue paper by bank employees or the fake travel papers issued by migration authorities to otherwise illegal migrants are *aspal* (Ford and Lyons 2011), an (il)legal tender issued by an (il)legal power.

Aspal might be the closest to an Indonesian word for what in this volume is called 'grey'. But what kind of informant category is it? Do *aspal* and 'grey' cover the same thing? Grey theory needs to have, it seems to me, both a strongly particularist and an explicitly comparative ambition if it wants to explore greyness as an anthropological reference to lived experience, rather than as just an analytical and implicitly universal concept. This means exploring not only the variety of reasons why it is produced as a condition, but also the variety of ways in which it is experienced.

Aspal marks, I suggest, a recognisable but also uniquely Indonesian experience of greyness. I have tried elsewhere to explore this experience through the notion of trust (Bubandt forthcoming). I argue that the political life of trust in Indonesia highlights how ideas of authenticity that are often taken to be universal to and uniformly present in modern life are in fact peculiar to Euro-American modernity (and possibly only a certain perception of this version of modernity). If the dilemma of power on the North Atlantic Rim is how one can trust those in power who claim themselves to be authentic but who one suspects are not, the dilemma of power in Indonesia is that one accepts as given a political power whose authority exists along with its fundamental inauthenticity. The next section will illustrate this.

Is the Past Grey? Is the Future?

Grey scene 3: The Beautiful Indonesia Miniature Theme Park (Taman Mini)
Built in the early 1970s, Taman Mini is a 174 ha theme park in southern Jakarta. The park is the brainchild of Ibu Thien, the wife of President Suharto, the authoritarian ruler of Indonesia during its New Order period (1965–98). Ibu Thien, who allegedly conceived the idea of the park after a trip to Disneyland, intended it to celebrate the Indonesian nation, to make it visible to its citizens. The park is an eclectic collection of kitsch and reconstructed copies of ethnic architecture and attire from around the archipelago, each of its 27 pavilions representing the cultures of the 27 provinces that until 1999 made up the nation (Acciaioli 1985). In a perceptive analysis of the park, John Pemberton argues that no pretence to authenticity motivates it. The pavilions are not meant to represent a preexisting provincial culture as much as to conjure it into being through power. In the same way, artefacts in the museum are not original pieces and no pretension to original authenticity is made. In fact, the opposite claim is made: the pieces are authentic *because* they are new. As the Indonesian first lady declared in the 1970s: 'We may call it a museum now because someday everything in it will be antique' (Pemberton 1994, 256).

Authenticity, in other words, is an effect of political power, not the other way around. Taman Mini is a museum with a particular conception of temporality and power; it is, as Pemberton calls it, 'somewhere beyond the postmodern' (1994, 256). The theme park collapses past and future into one political present that bestows authenticity all by itself. Authenticity does not come from history but in spite of it. Historical authenticity is an effect of power (of course, the irony of this is, as I have suggested above about *aspal*, that this power is itself inherently inauthentic).

The Indonesian play with the temporality of power is decidedly grey. On the one hand, power may hold the promise of revealing the new as a better and more original and authentic version of the old. A strongly millenarian tonality to Indonesian politics lies buried here, as is evidenced in the enthusiasm that has accompanied every shift of power since Indonesian independence in 1945 (see for instance Anderson 1990; Berger 1997; Dahm 1969). On the other hand, since power itself is always potentially inauthentic, its promise of moving 'back to the future' also has a dark, violent and dystopian side (Heryanto 2006; Schrauwers 2003; Siegel 2006). Accordingly, people in Indonesia want to trust political power, being also convinced of its fundamental inauthenticity. It is this paradox, I believe, that the statistics discussed in grey scene one express, a paradox that haunts Indonesian democracy as much as it did the New Order (Bubandt 2014a). Indonesia's democratic future is in that sense as grey as its authoritarian past.

This example reminds us that grey does not have a linear temporality, a grey nonlinearity that is also evident in Eastern Europe. Frederiksen and Harboe Knudsen in their introduction point to the fallacy of much of the early political science literature on the transition in Eastern Europe that painted grey as the colour of socialism while democracy shimmered on a brightly coloured horizon. As it turned out, postsocialist democracy in Eastern Europe (and democracy elsewhere) held many kinds of grey (Gaonkar 2007). Grey may sometimes be presented as the colour of the past. But to capture the many kinds of grey – present and future – in Indonesia, Eastern Europe and the rest of the world, new kinds of 'post-post-transition theories' are called for (Buyandelgeriyn 2008).

Can Grey Be Contained in a Zone?

Grey scene 4: My Indonesian sister

'Who are you going to vote for?', I asked one of my adopted sisters in Indonesia just before the 2004 general election. Her crisp reply was: 'For whoever wins!'

A decidedly grey answer, to be sure. But I am unsure whether her answer is testimony to an authoritarian mentality, built up during three decades of carefully orchestrated elections during the New Order, or whether it is an expression of democracy fatigue and signals the kind of disenchantment with democracy that one can find on a global scale in the contemporary world (Diamond 2008). Although the cause is probably a mix of the two, I am inclined to favour the latter out of a discomfort with attempts to territorialise greyness, to assign greyness to a region. Perhaps the notion of 'zones' does exactly that? A zone, after all, refers to 'any continuous tract or area, usually circular, which differs in some respect or is distinguished for some purpose, from adjoining tracts or areas' (*Webster's Dictionary* 1994, 1662). There are time zones, temperate zones and parking zones. Can greyness be assigned to a zone in this sharply bounded, logical and administrative fashion? Does the notion of zones in short reintroduce the very kind of boundary logic against which grey theory rebels in the first place? And do zones suggest a kind of territorial exceptionalism that will fail to capture the global production of greyness in the contemporary world?

Take state illegality or the business of counterfeiting and forgery for instance. Both exist throughout the world. Neither Indonesia nor Eastern Europe are alone in being home to these phenomena. Nor are postauthoritarian countries the only ones affected by it. A frequent tendency has been to see state failure as a problem of the Global South and those parts of the globe that used to be the Third World, as a kind of 'flawed imitation of a mature Western form' (Hansen and Stepputat 2001, 6). But this fails to see how 'parapolitics' in the Global South or in the postcolonies is part of a global assemblage of power that also includes the West itself (Wilson 2009). The production of fake products, certificates and money, as John and Jean Comaroff have suggested, is a global industry that appears to have become an increasingly important aspect of the production systems in what used to be the Third World because of a reorganisation of global production itself (Comaroff and Comaroff 2006). Similarly, the paradoxes of democracy in Indonesia – for example, its complicity with and reproduction through corruption and patrimonialism – are closely linked and homologous to the paradoxes of global democracy (Bubandt 2014a). The challenge of studying greyness as a condition and experience in the contemporary world, whether one finds 'zones' to be a useful concept or not, is to remain open to both its situated peculiarities and its global links.

Is Grey Theory Colour Blind?

My last and admittedly undigested set of reflections about grey theory and grey zones concerns colour itself. 'The first thing to realize about the study of colour in our time', writes Charles Riley, 'is its uncanny ability to evade all attempts to codify it systematically. The sheer multiplicity of color codes attests to the profound subjectivity of the color sense and its resistance to categorical thought' (Riley 1996, 1).

Two things stand out for me in this quote. Firstly, grey is not alone in resisting dichotomies and categorical thought. All colours resist, it would seem, categorical thinking. Grey does not have a monopoly on ambivalence after all. What does this do to grey theory? Perhaps there are many other political ethnographies of colourful ambivalence out there waiting to be written after we have exhausted grey theory. Secondly, colour is both a perceptual and a classificatory phenomenon, and the two are partly at odds.

Colour theory is one thing and colour experience another, as Maurice Merleau-Ponty has already pointed out (Merleau-Ponty 1962). Might the objectivity of colour theory blind us at times? In their introduction to this volume, Frederiksen and Harboe Knudsen rightly point out that it would be wrong to see grey merely as a mix between black and white. Rather, grey can more rightly be seen as a mix of all colours: 'Although grey is an achromatic colour – that is, a colour without colour – it is also a blend of all colours, a mix of white (created by blending all colours in the light spectrum) and black (created by a mixing all pigments).' This fascinating possibility points to the kind of multicoloured analysis I also imagined above. And yet this is a possibility derived from classical Newtonian colour theory, in which colours are the products of mixing and fragmenting the primary colours. What if grey as a political condition and experience was not produced by the mixing of black and white (or other colours)? What if the inverse was the case: if black-and-white classifications and dichotomies in political life arose out of grey conditions? Experiences of ambivalence, after all, often trigger black-and-white ideas, as conflict theory and theories of modernity highlight. An intriguing possibility raised by the contributions to this volume is the following: that the experiential problem may not be ambiguity at all, but how one constructs and maintains moral order, territorial distinction and recognised certainty (and visibility) out of, within and through ambiguity. Grey may, in other words, sometimes experientially be the primary colour, with black and white its unstable and ambiguous derivatives. Is it in this light also useful to hold on to some black-and-white theory?

References

Acciaioli, G. 1985. 'Culture as art: From practice to spectacle in Indonesia'. *Canberra Anthropology* 8(1–2): 148–72.

Agamben, G. 1998. *Homo Sacer: Sovereign Power and Bare Life*. Stanford: Stanford University Press.

Anderson, B. 1990. 'The idea of power in Javanese culture'. In B. Anderson (ed.), *Language and Power: Exploring Political Culture in Indonesia*, 17–77. Ithaca, NY: Cornell University Press.

Aspinall, E. 2010. 'The irony of success'. *Journal of Democracy* 21(2): 20–34.

Aspinall, E. and G. van Klinken (eds). 2011. *The State and Illegality in Indonesia*. Leiden: KITLV Press.

Auyero, J. 2007. *Routine Politics and Violence in Argentina: The Gray Zone of State Power*. Cambridge: Cambridge University Press.

Badiou, A. 2013. *Being and Event*. London: Bloomsbury.

BBC News. 2000. 'Indonesia bank chief in forgery row'. 8 December. Available at: http://news.bbc.co.uk/2/hi/business/1060962.stm (accessed 10 October 2014).

Berger, M. 1997. 'Old state and new empire in Indonesia: Debating the rise and decline of Suharto's new order'. *Third World Quarterly* 18(2): 321–61.

Bubandt, N. 2008. 'Rumors, pamphlets, and the politics of paranoia in Indonesia'. *Journal of Asian Studies* 67(3): 789–817.

_____. 2012. 'Shadows of secularism: Money politics, spirit politics and the law in an Indonesian election'. In N. Bubandt and M. van Beek (eds), *Varieties of Secularism: Anthropological Explorations of Religion, Politics and the Spiritual in Asia*, 183–207. London: Routledge.

_____. 2014a. *Democracy, Corruption and the Politics of Spirits in Contemporary Indonesia*. London: Routledge.

_____. 2014b. *The Empty Seashell: Witchcraft and Doubt on an Indonesian Island*. Ithaca, NY: Cornell University Press.

_____. Forthcoming. 'Trust in an age of inauthenticity: Power and Indonesian modernity'. In S. Liisberg, E. O. Pedersen and A. L. Dalsgård (eds), *Anthropology and Philosophy: Dialogues on Trust and Hope*. New York: Berghahn Books.

Buyandelgeriyn, M. 2008. 'Post-post-transition theories: Walking multiple paths'. *Annual Review of Anthropology* 37: 235–50.

Comaroff, J. and J. Comaroff. 2006. 'Law and disorder in the postcolony: An introduction'. In J. Comaroff and J. Comaroff (eds), *Law and Disorder in the Postcolony*, 1–56. Chicago: University of Chicago Press.

Dahm, B. 1969. *Sukarno and the Struggle for Indonesian Independence*. Ithaca, NY: Cornell University Press.

Deleuze, G. and F. Guattari. 2013. *Anti-Oedipus*. London: Bloomsbury.

Derrida, J. 2001. *Writing and Difference*. London: Routledge.

Diamond, L. 2008. 'The democratic rollback: The resurgence of the predatory state'. *Foreign Affairs* 87(2): 36–48.

Ford, M. and L. Lyons. 2011. 'Travelling the *aspal* route: grey labour migration through an Indonesian border town'. In E. Aspinall and G. van Klinken (eds), *State and Illegality in Indonesia*, 107–22. Leiden: KITLV Press.

Gaonkar, D. P. 2007. 'On cultures of democracy'. *Public Culture* 19(1): 1–22.

Hansen, T. B. and F. Stepputat. 2001. 'Introduction: States of imagination'. In T. B. Hansen and F. Stepputat (eds), *States of Imagination: Ethnographic Explorations of the Postcolonial State*, 1–38. Durham, NC: Duke University Press.

Haraway, D. 1991. *Simians, Cyborgs, and Women: The Reinvention of Nature*. London: Free Association Books.

Heryanto, A. 2006. *State Terrorism and Political Identity in Indonesia: Fatally Belonging*. Abingdon and New York: Routledge.

Horowitz, D. 2013. *Constitutional Change and Democracy in Indonesia*. Cambridge: Cambridge University Press.

Kingsbury, D. 2003. *Power Politics and the Indonesian Military*. London: Routledge.

Lévi-Strauss, C. 1963. *Totemism*. Boston: Beacon Press.

Merleau-Ponty, M. 1962. *Phenomenology of Perception*. London: Routledge.

Pemberton, J. 1994. 'Recollections from "beautiful Indonesia" (somewhere beyond the postmodern)'. *Public Culture* 6(2): 241–62.

Riley, C. A. 1996. *Color Codes: Modern Theories of Color in Philosophy, Painting and Architecture, Literature, Music, and Psychology*. Lebanon, NH: University Press of New England.

Schrauwers, A. 2003. 'Through a glass darkly: Charity, Conspiracy, and power in New Order Indonesia'. In H. G. West and T. Sanders (eds), *Transparency and Conspiracy: Ethnographies in the New World Order*, 125–47. Durham, NC: Duke University Press.

Siegel, J. 2006. *Naming the Witch*. Stanford: Stanford University Press.

Spyer, P. 2006. 'Some notes on disorder in the Indonesian postcolony'. In J. Comaroff and J. Comaroff (eds), *Law and Disorder in the Postcolony*, 188–218. Chicago: University of Chicago Press.

Tempo. 2001. 'Smiling all the way to the bank'. *Tempo* 44, 10–16 July.

Transparency International. 2009. *Global Corruption Barometer 2009*. Berlin: Transparency International.

Webster's Encyclopedic Unabridged Dictionary of the English Language. 1994. New York: Gramercy Books.

Wilson, E. (ed.). 2009. *Government of the Shadows: Parapolitics and Criminal Sovereignty*. London: Pluto Press.

LIST OF CONTRIBUTORS

Čarna Brković is a social anthropologist exploring politics of survival and wellbeing, public spheres, state, nationalism, and clientelism in former Yugoslav countries. After obtaining a PhD (University of Manchester, 2012), she has held Postdoctoral Fellowships at the CEU Institute for Advanced Study (2013/14) and at New Europe College, Institute for Advanced Studies (2014/2015). She is co-editor of *Negotiating Social Relations in Bosnia and Herzegovina* (Ashgate, forthcoming), as well as of *Anthropology Matters* journal.

Nils Bubandt is Professor of Anthropology in the Department of Culture and Society at Aarhus University, Denmark. He has conducted fieldwork in Indonesia since 1991 and has published on a variety of topics related to political and ontological grey zones. Recent publications include *Democracy, Corruption and the Politics of Spirits in Contemporary Indonesia* (Routledge, 2014), *The Empty Seashell: Witchcraft and Doubt on an Indonesian Island* (Cornell University Press, 2014), and (with Rane Willerslev): 'The dark side of empathy: Mimesis, deception, and the magic of alterity', *Comparative Studies in Society and History* (2015).

Jennifer R. Cash is an Associate of the Max Planck Institute for Social Anthropology. Her research covers the themes of identity, cultural politics, hospitality, and the interrelations between economy and ritual life. She is the author of *Villages on Stage: Folklore and Nationalism in the Republic of Moldova.*

Martin Demant Frederiksen holds a doctorate in anthropology and is Assistant Professor in the Department of Cross-Cultural and Regional Studies, University of Copenhagen, Denmark. Since 2005 he has conducted long-term fieldwork studies in the Republic of Georgia and published on issues such as urban planning, hope, youth, crime, temporality and ethnographic writing. His current research concerns the role of meaninglessness in social life. He is author of *Young Men, Time, and Boredom in the Republic of Georgia* (Temple University Press, 2013) and co-editor of the *Slavic Review* theme-issue 'Ethnographies of absence in contemporary Georgia' (2014).

Katrine Bendtsen Gotfredsen is Lecturer in Caucasus Studies at the Department of Language and Linguistics, Malmö University. She has done extensive ethnographic fieldwork in the Republic of Georgia and her research focuses in particular on subjects such as political transformation and uncertainty, religion, history, identity and morality, and political forms and practices. Other works include her PhD dissertation entitled 'Evasive politics: Paradoxes of history, nation and everyday communication in the Republic of Georgia' (2013), and the journal article 'Void pasts and marginal presents: On nostalgia and obsolete futures in the Republic of Georgia' (*Slavic Review*, 2014)

Sarah Green is Professor of Social and Cultural Anthropology at the University of Helsinki. She specializes on issues of location and borders, which provide a means to analyze how people classify the world, their location in it as well as the location of others. She is interested in the political, social, economic, epistemological and historical dynamics involved in that process of defining the difference between here and somewhere else. She is author of *Notes from the Balkans* (2005), *Urban Amazons* (1997), and joint author of *Borderwork* (2013) with Lena Malm (photography; additional contributions by Robin Harper and Markus Drake).

Maja Halilovic-Pastuovic teaches forced migration, ethnic cleansing and post-refuge transnationalism in Department of Sociology, University of Dublin, Trinity College, Ireland. A graduate of Trinity College, her PhD focused on ethno-racial state of post-Dayton Bosnia and policies and politics of the Dayton Agreement. Her current expertise and interests include: sociology of race, ethnicity and conflict; post-refugee transnationalism; racial states; biopolitics, regimes of governmentality and constitutional racism. At present her research focuses on segregated education in post-Dayton Bosnia.

Aimee Joyce is currently a Lecturer in the Department of Anthropology at Goldsmiths, University of London. Her undergraduate degree was at Trinity College, University of Dublin, and she completed her PhD at Goldsmiths, based on fieldwork conducted on the Polish/Belarusian border. Her work focused on regionalism, border studies, theories of place and particularly religious plurality and material religion. She is currently interested in the anthropology of religion, regionalism and migration, and borders.

Ida Harboe Knudsen is external Lecturer at the Institute of Culture and Society, Aarhus University, Denmark. She wrote her PhD on the topic of changes for small farmers in light of the EU accession at the Max Planck Institute for Social Anthropology in Germany. She published the book *New Lithuania in Old Hands: Effects and Outcomes of EUropeanization in Lithuania* (2012) with Anthem Press. Her latest project, financed by the Danish Independent Research Council, has targeted invisible citizens and informal working strategies. She has published on the topics of agriculture, the EU, the market and consumption, and shadow economies.

Frances Pine is a Reader of Anthropology at Goldsmiths, University of London. Before that she taught at Cambridge, and was a Research Associate at the Max Planck Institute for Social Anthropology. She has been conducting research in Poland since the late 1970s, and is the author of many articles on economy, kinship and gender, and memory. She is co-editor of *Surviving Post-Socialism*, *On the Margins of Religion, Memory, Politics and Religion: The Past Meets the Present in Europe*, and *Global Connections and Emerging Inequalities in Europe: Poverty and Transnational Migration*, among other volumes.

Kristina Šliavaitė is a Research Fellow at the Institute for Ethnic Studies at the Lithuanian Social Research Centre in Vilnius. She is also a Lecturer in social anthropology at the Department of Sociology at Vytautas Magnus University, Kaunas, Lithuania. Her PhD in social anthropology was granted at the University of Lund (Sweden) in 2005 and focused on how the Russian-speaking community in Visaginas perceived the dissolution of the Soviet Union and the closure of the nuclear power plant Ignalina. Current research interests are issues of ethnicity and social inclusion, and intercultural approaches in education.

INDEX

www.ingramcontent.com/pod-product-compliance
Lightning Source LLC
Chambersburg PA
CBHW022357280326
41935CB00007B/222